The Mystery of God

COLUMBIA SERIES IN REFORMED THEOLOGY

The Columbia Series in Reformed Theology represents a joint commitment of Columbia Theological Seminary and Westminster John Knox Press to provide theological resources for the church today.

The Reformed tradition has always sought to discern what the living God revealed in scripture is saying and doing in every new time and situation. Volumes in this series examine significant individuals, events, and issues in the development of this tradition and explore their implications for contemporary Christian faith and life.

This series is addressed to scholars, pastors, and laypersons. The Editorial Board hopes that these volumes will contribute to the continuing reformation of the church.

COLUMBIA SERIES IN REFORMED THEOLOGY

The Mystery of God

Karl Barth and the Postmodern Foundations of Theology

WILLIAM STACY JOHNSON

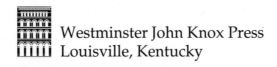 Westminster John Knox Press
Louisville, Kentucky

Grateful acknowledgment is made to T. & T. Clark Ltd., Edinburgh, for permission to reproduce material from Karl Barth, *Church Dogmatics*, vols. I–IV, edited by G. W. Bromiley and T. F. Torrance; published by T. & T. Clark 1936–75.

Book and cover design by Drew Stevens

First edition

Published by Westminster John Knox Press
Louisville, Kentucky

This book is printed on acid-free paper that meets the American National Standards Institute Z39.48 standard. ⊚

PRINTED IN THE UNITED STATES OF AMERICA

97 98 99 00 01 02 03 04 05 06 — 10 9 8 7 6 5 4 3 2 1

Library of Congress Cataloging-in-Publication Data

Johnson, William Stacy.
    The mystery of God : Karl Barth and the postmodern foundations of
theology / William Stacy Johnson.
        p.   cm. — (Columbia series in Reformed theology)
    Includes bibliographical references.
    ISBN 0-664-22094-0 (alk. paper)
    1. Barth, Karl, 1886–1968.   I. Title.   II. Series.
BX4827.B3J64   1997
230'.044'092—dc21   96-40011

*For Virginia
and Bill Samuels*

CONTENTS

ACKNOWLEDGMENTS

I have many to thank for helping to bring this book into being. I am especially grateful to three former teachers whose influence is visible throughout these pages, and who have remained continuing conversation partners since my student days in the Committee on the Study of Religion at Harvard University. Richard R. Niebuhr supervised my 1992 dissertation on Barth and the question of theocentric theology in which the present volume had its beginnings. For his friendship and for his example of deep and thoughtful reflection on classical theological texts I am forever indebted. Gordon D. Kaufman has profoundly influenced my thinking about the mystery of God and the postmodern foundations of theology, and he bears significant responsibility for prodding me to see new things in the theology of Barth. Ronald F. Thiemann has nurtured me in all my scholarly endeavors. His concern for the public dimensions of theology reinforces my belief that theologians influenced by Barth need not fall into a narrow and parochial neo-orthodoxy.

Others at Harvard who influenced me during the formative stages of this project include John Carman, Arthur Dyck, Diana Eck, Elisabeth Schüssler Fiorenza, Francis Schüssler Fiorenza, William Graham, Margaret Miles, Ralph Potter, Hilary Putnam, Tu-Wei Ming, and Preston Williams.

Two of the scholars most responsible for the recent revival of interest in Karl Barth, George Hunsinger and Bruce L. McCormack, are friends from whom I have learned much about Barth over the past several years. Both were good enough to read early portions of the manuscript and to offer insightful criticism. A preliminary version of chapter 6 was presented to the Karl Barth Society of North America at the November 1993 meeting in Washington, D.C. The conversation there was quite stimulating, and I benefited especially from dialogue with Walt Lowe. The final manuscript was much improved due to suggestions from James J. Buckley.

Shirley Guthrie and George Stroup of the Editorial Board of the Columbia Series in Reformed Theology have been most patient and supportive as I have readied the manuscript for publication. Also the editorial staff of Westminster John Knox Press has been of considerable assistance.

My colleagues at Austin Presbyterian Theological Seminary, Lewis R.

Donnelson, Scott Black Johnston, Terry C. Muck, Stephen Breck Reid, and Cynthia L. Rigby, have read and offered helpful comments on portions of the manuscript. The Academic Dean, Robert M. Shelton, and the President, Jack L. Stotts, have done much to promote my teaching and research.

An Andrew W. Mellon fellowship at Harvard helped to fund some of the early research on this volume.

I first learned to appreciate Karl Barth years ago at Davidson College in a course with the late Elmer G. Homrighausen, a friend of Barth and former Dean of Princeton Theological Seminary, and also to criticize him at Davidson while working with the philosopher Earl MacCormac. That appreciation and criticism of Barth continued during my days at Union Theological Seminary in Richmond, especially during many hours of conversation with John H. Leith, whose lifelong commitment to the study of theology in both the academy and the church stands as a remarkable achievement.

As always, I owe a special debt to my family, Liz and Carson and Paige, who are a constant source of thankfulness and joy. Finally, for all their support over the years, I want to thank my mother, Virginia Samuels and stepfather, Bill Samuels, to whom this book is dedicated.

W.S.J.

Austin, Texas
May 1996

INTRODUCTION

Upsetting the Balance

> [I]n dogmatics . . . there are no comprehensive views, no final conclusions, no permanent results. There is only the investigation and teaching which take place in the very act of dogmatic work and which . . . at every point must continually begin again at the beginning.
>
> Karl Barth, *CD*, I/2, 868 (rev.)[1]

This book is an exercise in rethinking the theology of Karl Barth. Like the music of Wolfgang Amadeus Mozart whom he so much admired, Barth's theology is a composition in which melody and reverberant countermelody run in ceaseless competition. Highly complex and rich in nuance, Barth's theological opus defies the easy summaries to which it has too often been subjected.

Upon first encountering Barth's magisterial *Church Dogmatics*, the most audible strain is, of course, the sonorous harmony of his so-called "christocentrism." This is the side that stresses the positive content of divine revelation, the side that accentuates God's gracious determination to be "for" and "with" human beings in Jesus Christ by the power of the Spirit. The humanity of Jesus Christ, Barth announced, is the earthly sacrament of the living God. No reading of Barth can ignore this clear enunciation of the priority of God's grace in Jesus Christ.

Nevertheless, there is also a countermelody at work, a tone more sober and restrained, a tone that stands in equiprimordial balance to the other. Sometimes dissonant and submerged beneath the rest of the composition, while at other times featured more prominently, this other sound represents the "theocentric" facet of Barth's score.[2] It is the side that incessantly underscores the hiddenness and mystery of God. Like the sound of persistent drumming, this more ominous, tympanitic dimension insists that the God who is revealed in Jesus Christ remains, nonetheless, an utterly unfathomable mystery.

In 1922 Barth stated the theologian's predicament concerning these two sides of the mystery of God with aphoristic clarity:

> As theologians we ought to speak of God. We are, however, human beings and as such cannot speak of God. We ought to recognize both our obligation and our inability—and precisely in that recognition, give God the glory. This is our affliction (*Bedrängnis*). Everything else is mere child's play."[3]

The English edition translates *Bedrängnis* as "perplexity"; but the German word conveys a more problematic sense of conflict. This conflict, or

1

"affliction," is occasioned by the collision of these positive and negative elements, neither one of which can prosper by itself. If one tries to say something positive about God, one inevitably speaks falsely. And yet to speak only negatively, or to remain in apophatic silence, also brings its own degree of falsification.

Barth's theology is entangled in the classic gap of Western Christianity between a God who is inconceivable but who also subsists in a gracious relationship with human beings. To negotiate this gap, Barth sought to achieve in his own theology what he once attributed to the music of Mozart, namely, "a glorious upsetting of the balance."[4] Like the music of Mozart, theology is in a ceaseless interplay between the "no" and the "yes," between a God who is made known in Jesus Christ but who remains profoundly unknown in the impenetrable depths of mystery. Both sides of this interplay are necessary. Without the appeal to mystery, theology would devolve into nothing more than an ideological support for the biases of one's own community. By the same token, without some positive, christological content, the appeal to mystery would evaporate into the silent pondering of the void. Both "christocentric" point—with its stress on mystery as *grace*—and "theocentric" counterpoint—with its emphasis on grace as *mystery*—are necessary to make the music of Christian theology resound for what it is. Moreover, Barth also included "pneumatocentric" embellishments, though often these references to the Spirit arise in rather roundabout ways. At all events, his goal was to hold these various themes together as diverse sides of a trinitarian whole, a dynamic structure that forever exceeds the sum of its parts.

The significance for constructive theology of Barth's theocentric countermelody has not been adequately appreciated. If God is ultimate mystery, then theology remains but a fragile and provisional venture. No claims to infallible or self-evident certainty can prevail, and no theologian can seek to have the final word against the intractableness of this mystery. Never can a theologian rest comfortably with simply reiterating insights drawn from the past, as though the goal were to restore them to some pristine state. Instead, the theologian must continually resolve to wipe the slate clean and be willing, regarding each theological topic, to "begin again at the beginning."

The conviction guiding this study is that we now need to "begin again at the beginning" in our reading of Karl Barth. Too many have misinterpreted Barth's insistence that theology be tied to the "Word of God" as the rigid reassertion of an outmoded theological tradition from the past. Having heard the maestro's first emphatic notes of one-sided Christian confession, many have simply quit listening, anticipating that the rest of the score would be riddled with the parochial clichés of a narrow "neoorthodoxy."[5] But for those who choose to keep listening there are unexpected tonalities to be discovered. The last thing Barth wished to do, it will soon become clear, was to repristinate a bygone orthodoxy. Barth's focus on divine mystery calls into question any theology that tries to prop itself up according to ready-made foundations somehow "given" in advance and presumed to be self-evident or beyond revision. In the face of divine mystery, theology remains a thoroughly fallible enterprise, a ceaseless activity with neither resting place nor any fixed point of unerring certainty.

In perhaps his best short definition of theology, Barth declared, "Theology means rational wrestling with mystery" (*CD* I/1, 368, rev.). Focusing on the theme of mystery not only uncovers neglected dimensions in Barth's theology, but it may help to reconfigure contemporary discussions surrounding the "foundations" of theology in a "postmodern" age.

Regarding "foundations," Barth's theology invites us to a "nonfoundationalist" mode of theological inquiry.[6] Nonfoundationalism as I am using the term has more to do with a style or method of thinking than with a particular content that must be believed. In general, nonfoundationalist approaches share a common goal of putting aside all appeals to presumed self-evident, non-inferential, or incorrigible grounds for their intellectual claims. They reject the idea that among all their many beliefs there is a single irrefutable "foundation" that must be protected from critical scrutiny and upon which all other claims are grounded. Nonfoundationalists are willing to subject all their beliefs to criticism and reconstruction. This does *not* mean that nonfoundationalists in every case simply disavow belief, or that they are forced somehow to hold in abeyance everything their tradition teaches. As Francis Schüssler Fiorenza has put it, to pursue a nonfoundationalist strategy is to realize that one's approach to intellectual questions "is rational not because it has a foundation, but because it is a self-correcting enterprise that examines all claims, all relevant background theories—even though not all at once."[7] To subject one's concepts and background beliefs to critical scrutiny, that is to say, does not require that one abandon them altogether.

Lest it be thought the contemporary term "nonfoundational" is either misplaced or anachronistic in reference to Barth, one should note that long before the issue of whether "to have or not to have foundations" became intellectually fashionable, Karl Barth erupted on the European scene with his claim that there can be no "ground" or "givenness" (*Fundament, Gegeben*) to theological reflection. To be sure, Barth did retain foundationalist assumptions about some matters, as, for example, his typically Kantian assumptions about the universal components of human psychology. Nevertheless, when it came to *God*, things were different. The truth about God does not exist as a "truth among other truths" waiting to be verified according to the supposedly self-evident canons of modern rationality. Rather, as he put it in *The Epistle to the Romans*, the truth about God "sets a question mark against all truths."[8] It places us before an incomparable mystery in the face of which all our designs are forever brought up short.

What we need to do, then, is consider how in Barth's hands the uniqueness of God led to a uniquely *theological* brand of nonfoundationalist thinking. One implication of Barth's nonfoundationalism is that theology must be neither one-dimensional nor two-dimensional but multidimensional.[9] It will not do to reduce God to a single dimension of reality that is beyond critical inquiry. Not even the biblical story itself can function as a proxy for the living God. There is more to theology than plumbing the "cultural-linguistic system" of the Christian West.[10] If theology is not one-dimensional, neither is its subject matter adequately treated in the ever-popular, two-dimensional theologies of "correlation." In these theologies, the transcendental and universal features of human existence are correlated with the eternal content of faith (Karl Rahner); or a series of culturally derived "questions" is correlated with a set of theologically conceived "answers" already known in advance (Paul Tillich); or, in a somewhat more revisionist mode (the early David Tracy), the cultural "situation" (including its *own* answers) is correlated with the Christian "message" (including its *own* questions).[11] The problem here is that the theologian treats his or her sources as objective "givens" to be manipulated at arm's length. But do we already know in advance what it means to be Christian? Or can we reduce culture to a single *Zeitgeist* or worldview that then dictates how one must revise inherited tradition?

This leads us to the idea that Barth's writings point toward a "postmodern" theological possibility, one that is genuinely constructive and multidimensional in its implications. Just as a resolutely "modern" thinker such as Hegel helped pave the way for contemporary "postmodern" reformulations of the past, so also Karl Barth—clearly an heir to the "modern" theological legacy that began with Schleiermacher—has much to contribute to today's "postmodern" theological reflection.

The term "postmodern" should be employed cautiously as a way of indicating a diverse range of sustained and serious challenges posed against the "foundations" of knowing in the modern world. Whereas modernity sought to attain rational certainty according to a single "center" of knowledge, postmodernity doubts whether there can be any access to a monolithically-conceived "center" and seeks instead to advance plural and contextual ways of knowing.

Some are justifiably suspicious of postmodernity, believing that it signals, at best, a sort of perpetual adolescence that refuses to take responsibility for its ideas and actions, or at worst, a radical form of nihilism that questions the meaning of all inherited verities.[12] For example, according to Jean-François Lyotard, the dominant feature of the "postmodern" is what he calls an "incredulity toward metanarratives (*grands récits*)." On this view, postmodernity represents a protest against every abstract, comprehensive, universally-applicable, and legitimating "story"—whether Christian, Marxist, or otherwise—by which people have sought to understand life in its "totality."[13]

But there is another side of postmodern thought as well. This is the side that is driven by a profoundly moral concern. It points out the contradictions and hypocrisies in dominant cultural assumptions, and does so not to revel in the inconsistencies but to use them as leverage to call people to account for their own highest and best ideals. It is this side of contemporary postmodernity that I think would have fascinated Karl Barth. For Barth was forever intent on calling into question a self-satisfied and complacent bourgeois Christianity. If God is ultimate mystery—never a "caged bird" but always a "bird in flight"—and if reflection about God must always "begin again at the beginning," then Barthian theology is best conceived not as a repristination of past orthodoxy but as an ongoing response to divine mystery.[14]

To further this postmodern reassessment, Part 1, "Decentering Theology," argues that for Barth God is decentering mystery. It explores the inaccessibility Barth perceived at the core of theology, an inaccessibility "like the opening in the center of a wheel[15] (CD, I/2, 867). This "open" center referred to the dynamic encounter between God and humanity, as mediated through Christ by the power of the Holy Spirit. On the one hand, Barth advances a powerfully confessional way of identifying this "center"—it is Christ-centered and trinitarian. On the other hand, this same "center," in both its divine and human aspects, bears a certain indeterminate, unsettling, and disruptive significance. It is, paradoxically, never simply "given" to our own manipulation or control. To borrow the language of the postmodern philosopher Jacques Derrida, the center can never be conceived as a simple "presence." Apart from grace, according to Barth, we do not know what we are saying when we say, "God," nor what we mean when we say, "human being." Mystery, I will argue, was at the core of the early Barth's "Quest for the God of Theology" (chapter 1).[16]

The character of God as decentering mystery leads to a related conviction about the character of theology itself. In the mature Barth's "Quest for a Theology of God" (chapter 2), theology must be more than the one-dimensional descriptive enterprise of exegeting the Bible or the tradition as a foundational "given." If God is impenetrable mystery, then the supposed "givens" of theology are continually called into question by the very nature of their unique theme. Some may assume that revelation in Jesus Christ functions, in fact, as the "given" in Barth's theology. To the contrary, neither "revelation" nor "Jesus Christ" are self-evident to theological analysis. We have them only as concepts or "signs" that can do no more than "point" to the God who is ultimate mystery. As indicators of mystery, they must become the subjects of continual inquiry and constructive revisioning. To be sure, Barth believed our claims may "become" true as a matter of grace, but he never arrived at a foolproof way of discovering when this "becoming" has actually occurred in human experience. The fallibility of our situation is unrelenting.

Part 2, "The Mystery of God: Creator, Reconciler, Redeemer," offers a reading of Barth on the mystery of God. Chapter 3 considers Barth's nonfoundationalist understanding of divine mystery as triune. "Triunity" marks the particular way that divine mystery is configured in Christian confession. For Barth, divine mystery confronts human beings in a threefold way as *act*. The singularity of divine action comes to fruition in three ways or "modes" of being (*Seinsweisen*): creation, reconciliation, and redemption. God's every action is the act of the primordial God, in solidarity with human beings in Jesus Christ, by the power of the Spirit. God confronts human beings not as three "nouns" but, so to speak, as a single verb modified by three adverbial phrases.

Accordingly, chapters four through six trace the meaning of the triune event as a single dynamic act of creation, reconciliation, and redemption. In Jesus Christ, by the power of the Spirit, God is "for" us (chapter 4), God is "with" us (chapter 5), and God is at work "in" and "among" us (chapter 6). This threefold story moves along an axis from protology to eschatology, from "creation" at its point of beginning to "redemption" at its denouement.[17] Between these two horizons, "reconciliation" stands at the "center," as a mediating moment between the other two (see figure I.1). To substantiate this Part 2 looks at what I call the "triadic" pattern that runs throughout Barth's mature theology.

This triadic (as opposed to linear) pattern opens up a fresh perspective on the complexity of Barth's trinitarian theology. By "triadic" I mean a pattern in which there are three points of reference: a beginning point, an ending point, and a midpoint suspended between them. The beginning point is always primordial, lying behind the present moment. The ending point is always eschatological, lying on the distant horizon. The midpoint signifies the present moment, an instant marked by God's ongoing work of reconciliation.

In one respect, this triadic pattern reflects the traditional Christian story of unity, alienation, and restoration. But there is also a difference. For Barth the points of origin and destination remain draped in mystery, representing a distant horizon and not something readily given or present at hand. His is not Hegel's closed triad (what William James derided as a "block universe") in which the eschaton has already been clearly perceived by the philosopher-theologian. Barth's triad, as we shall see, is open-ended. The present moment remains indeterminate as long as divine and human action remain set against one another. The present moment is

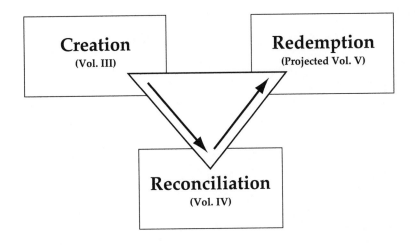

FIGURE I.1

one of ethical crisis, a midpoint that is, so to speak, stretched out between a no longer accessible *archē* and a not yet visible *telos*.

This triadic pattern applies not only to Barth's treatment of creation, reconciliation, and redemption, but also to his treatment of other concepts *within* the broader framework, such as the divine perfections and justification, vocation, and sanctification.

These triadic arrangements in the *Church Dogmatics* are not merely of aesthetic interest, for once the triadic pattern is fully recognized, it yields a more open-ended understanding of how Barth viewed the Holy Spirit and Christian experience, an area of his theology that Barth left incomplete and that interpreters have often alleged to be fatally flawed. Within Barth's triadic arrangement of divine-human reconciliation in volume IV of the *CD*, the divine work of the Spirit and the human witness of Christian vocation form a tensive, intervening moment stretched out between justification as primordial event and sanctification as eschatological goal (see figure I.2).

On this view, the Christian life can never be considered a "given," but only a continual "task" on the horizon out in front of us. From the standpoint of constructive postmodern theology, this open-ended understanding of the Holy Spirit and Christian experience, rather than marking a weakness in Barth (as is often alleged), may actually constitute an area of great strength.

Part 3, "The Mystery of the Other," underscores the character of theology as an open-ended task guided by an ethics of otherness. Ethics, as

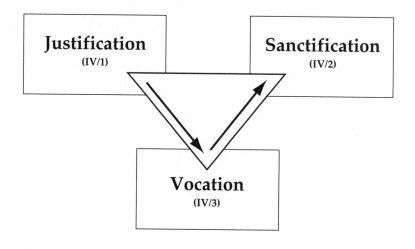

FIGURE I.2

demonstrated in chapter 7, forms the summit of each of the volumes of the *CD*, and for a special reason. Even though Barth's own preferred vineyard was that of conceptual, doctrinal analysis, the broad trajectory of his thought suggests that ethics becomes the primary sphere in which his theology should be validated. We must think of all the many pages of doctrinal analysis that make up the *CD* as a prelude to ethics. Charles Sanders Peirce said that our beliefs project rules for action.[18] In a similar way, the doctrinal concepts over which Barth took such painstaking care are meant to function as "rules" that set forth presuppositions to action.

For Christians two of the mandated actions are baptism and the Lord's Supper, actions which, Barth argues, are not "sacraments" at all in the traditional sense but ethical responses to God's primary sacramental action in Jesus Christ through the "baptism of the Holy Spirit." All those interpreters—and there are many of them—who assume that Barth's treatment of the sacraments marks an ill-fitting deviation from the rest of his theology need to think again. To reject Barth on this point may be to have misunderstood him on all the other points. His teaching on baptism in the final fragment of the *CD* is but the consistent outworking of a theology that is reticent to speak of a "real presence" of God in earthly media. If we wish to locate divine presence within human experience, for Barth we must look to the realm of ethical action.

Formally, Barth links ethics to a doctrine of divine command; materially, however, his understanding of ethics is remarkably open-ended. He speaks of ethics as a multidimensional inquiry that opens the door to wis-

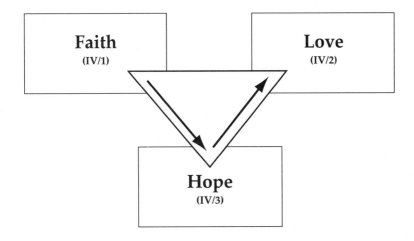

FIGURE I.3

dom from non-Christian sources of truth. Indeed, Barth declared an openness, in principle, to a diversity of theological sources, both Christian and non-Christian, so long as the Christian theologian takes her initial bearings from the way God is identified in Jesus Christ by the power of the Spirit. It is as though what Barth takes away with the one hand he then gives back with the other.

This open-ended way of conceiving and doing theology, mind you, is more of a possibility to which Barth's theology points than a reality he himself achieved. Barth himself did little to bring nontheological sources explicitly into his work, and even less to show us how the practical and ethical contextualization of theology ought to be pursued. But the fact remains that these are tasks to which his own reflections explicitly invite us.

Chapter 8 returns to the "triadic" pattern to show how the virtue of "hope" forms the central feature of the Christian life (see figure I.3). The Christian life begins in faith, moves toward love, and is configured in the here and now by a hopeful openness to the other.

The concluding chapter sums up some of the implications of reading Barth in the postmodern era. Some may object that the way of interpreting Barth being proposed here focuses more on what Barth *should* have said than on what he actually did say. Such an objector will have come close to the aspiration toward which this study pushes. It seeks to uncover a *possibility* to which Barth's theology, perhaps despite some of its own countervailing intentions, points us—a possibility that may open up new avenues of fidelity to the God who is ultimate mystery.

PART ONE

DECENTERING THEOLOGY

[T]he center . . . cannot be articulated or expressed by any word or voice of angels, and certainly not of human beings. . . .

Karl Barth, *CD*, IV/3.1, 122

1

IN QUEST OF THE
GOD OF THEOLOGY

> The true dialectician knows that the center is imperceptible and incomprehensible and will thus permit himself to give as little direct information about it as possible. . . .
> Karl Barth, "The Word of God as the Task of Theology"[1]

It is commonplace to interpret Barth as a "christocentric" theologian. Yet this simple designation does not end the matter. One cannot focus on Jesus Christ in himself, according to Barth, without understanding his life as caught up in a more dynamic trinitarian movement of God's Word and Spirit. As Barth put it in his first lectures in theology at Göttingen, "impermissible . . . is the . . . so-called christocentric way, in which Jesus is directly and nondialectically made into an entity that is God in itself."[2] With this in mind it might be tempting to make God rather than Jesus the center of theology. But if the "center" cannot be equated with Jesus of Nazareth, neither is the "center" flat-footedly identified with God considered apart from human beings.

Rather, the "center" of theology for Barth is more broadly the divine-human *relationship* focused in Jesus Christ by the power of the Holy Spirit. For this reason, Barth sometimes spoke of his theology as "theanthropocentric." His focal point, to this extent, strikes a formal parallel to that of Friedrich Schleiermacher, for whom, as well, the object of theology is never God in the abstract. For Schleiermacher and for Barth, theology is "centered" in the relationship between God and humanity, a relationship already "given" in an experience of God which he labeled the "feeling of absolute dependence."[3] On this point, however, Barth and Schleiermacher differed rather significantly. For one of Barth's bedrock goals was to call into question the "givenness" of that divine-human relationship as a matter of immediate human experience. From a human point of view, the relationship is not a "given" (*Geben*) but a problem and an ongoing task (*Aufgabe*). The answer to this problem is made visible in Jesus Christ; the realization of this task is effectuated by the power of the Holy Spirit. But from the standpoint of present experience, these things do not constitute a "given."

So then, how should one refer to this divine-human center? Can it be referred to at all in any straightforward way? Throughout his career Barth spoke of this elusive "center" using the metaphor of a "wheel" with an open space at its core. The first significant usage occurred in *The Epistle to the Romans*, that remarkable manifesto that transformed Barth from an obscure pastor amid the rural hills of Switzerland into Europe's most celebrated twentieth-century theologian. The center of theology, said Barth, is the subject of unrelieved questioning. The ongoing questions being raised by theology anticipate an answer that lies hidden and unobtainable, like the empty hole in the middle of a "wagon wheel."

> May the perimeter of that *hole* in the center of the wagon wheel, of which Lao-Tzu was already aware, be marked off [by questions] right pointedly. For the answer is the thing which forms the content of that circle, the meaning of which is circumscribed by questions which never for a moment cease to be questions.[4]

This cryptic image suggests that theology finds its orientation in a "center" that, although vitally real, remains beyond accessibility. It is a "center" completely encircled by questions (the "spokes") which never cease to be posed as questions. The necessity for theological inquiry, that is, never ends. From a human point of view, God—and relationship with God—are as impossible to possess as the empty center of this continually rotating wheel.

To put it plainly, in order to "center" on God one must effect a "decentering" of theology. This is the insight that lies at the heart of Karl Barth's theological quest. Nor can it be otherwise, if God is truly to be judged a mystery. To "center" upon God is to converge upon the untamed and the uncoercible. It is to focus upon that which calls us fundamentally into question, upon that which brings about a shaking of the foundations, an overturning of all that was previously considered stable and secure. The mystery of God, far from safeguarding (*Sicherung*) theology, precipitates an act of endangerment (*Entsicherung*), like removing the safety from a loaded gun (*KD*, I/1, 171, *CD*, 164–65).

The term "decentering" has become widespread in recent nonfoundationalist and postmodernist literature. As a "decentered" existence, postmodern life is said to proceed without a resting place and in the absence of fixed norms. Whereas modernity, through the hubris of dismissing the centrality of God, attempted to secure the centrality of human beings, postmodernity has discovered that a single-minded focus on human beings is not enough. Tempted toward despair, the postmodern mind-set has sometimes chosen to jettison belief in any "center" or "essence" altogether. Rather than pursuing a centered existence, postmodern life finds itself laced with disruptions and perpetually off balance. It is able to orient itself only within "centerless webs of meaning" (Quine), or from the "unceasing play of texts" (Derrida). Neither the autonomous self of the Enlightenment nor the sacrosanct confines of a particular cultural-linguistic tradition seem to provide any reliable point of orientation.

The theology of Karl Barth injects a similar decentering into Christian theology. It does so, however, not from blank skepticism but from its own uniquely confessional commitments. Barth's decentering flows not from denatured disbelief but from the full-bodied conviction that God, the center of theology, is beyond human fathoming and ought to be beyond the self-interested manipulation of religion. To reflect upon God is to consider that which calls all of life radically into question.

Some theologians wish to turn centering upon God into a straightforward exercise, as though one were somehow able to read "God" or "Christian faith" off of the data present in the mundane world. This was the mistake Barth discerned in a certain aspect of Schleiermacher's work, an aspect he believed came to fruition in the early twentieth-century "historicism" of Ernst Troeltsch. Although Barth held Schleiermacher in the highest regard and continued to engage his writings throughout his life, from his earliest days as a student he followed the lead of his teacher Wilhelm Herrmann in rejecting Troeltsch.[5]

That Barth departed from the trajectory of liberal theology that runs from Schleiermacher to Ritschl to Troeltsch is not anything new. But it is instructive to consider the postmodern theological implications opened up by this rejection. Understanding why Barth rejected Troeltsch will carry us a good distance in understanding what I am calling Barth's "decentered" and "nonfoundationalist" perspective.[6]

Brian Gerrish has summarized nicely Schleiermacher's understanding of the theological task: "As a historical-empirical discipline, dogmatics does not have to establish its object of inquiry; it takes it as given (a *datum*) and seeks only to explicate its content."[7] Schleiermacher envisaged theology as a positive science divided into philosophical, historical, and practical components. Dogmatics proper he conceived as falling under historical theology. As such, dogmatics provided the historical foundation of practical theology and the historical verification of philosophical theology.[8]

Building upon Schleiermacher's emphasis on the historically empirical, Ernst Troeltsch sought in his turn to evaluate Christianity as an objective phenomenon to be gleaned solely from its ascertainable development out of the past. This in itself was a subtle departure from Schleiermacher and an implicit calling into question of the latter's understanding of revelation, for in Schleiermacher's view revelation has such an original and originating character that it "cannot itself . . . be explained by the historical context which precedes it."[9] Be that as it may, by starting from the idea of theology as a historical discipline, Troeltsch's intention was to relate the results of historical inquiry to "the whole life experience of our race" in order thereby to construct a new synthesis oriented to the exigent needs of his own generation.[10]

The fundamental energy that fueled Troeltsch's work was the task of making religion compatible with the modern scientific worldview (*Weltanschauung*).[11] This zeal to synthesize Christianity with a modern "worldview" was something Barth considered especially pernicious. To accomplish his goal Troeltsch developed a global theory of religion, a philosophy of history, and an idealist religious metaphysics.[12] First, according to his theory of religion, each religious tradition has its own naive loyalties and distinctive integrity which push it towards historical goals unique to it alone, goals that could never be predicted in advance.[13] In each new epoch a tradition achieves a "contemporary cultural synthesis" which preserves but also reformulates elements of the past in light of present-day interests and needs.[14]

Second, Troeltsch's philosophy of history dictates that data be assessed according to criteria of "criticism," "analogy," and "correlation."[15] Data alleged to be gathered by any other procedure are beyond historical knowing. *Criticism* means that the historicity of any purported fact is amenable to nothing more than a probability judgment. Probability judgments depend, furthermore, upon *analogies* drawn from our own customary experience. Since things occur in roughly the same manner throughout the ages, analogy alone is able to provide a benchmark for assessing probability. This principle of analogy operates to level all historical phenomena to one and the same plane; appeals to the unusual, the miraculous, or the supernatural are thereby ruled out of bounds as unscientific. Compare this, say, with the scientific approach of someone like William James, for whom the unusual and extraordinary in religious experience may in fact constitute the best evidence from which to learn.[16] Troeltsch's rather restrictive rule of analogy, in turn, makes way for a principle of *correlation* signifying that every historical event occurs in a specific context but that diverse contexts must also cohere with one another in a mutuality of global interaction.[17]

Criticism, analogy, and correlation combine to eliminate both conservative appeals to events deemed to be supernatural as well as liberal resorts to the alleged immediacy of past events, as, for example, Wilhelm Herrmann's putative experience of the "inner life" of Jesus.[18] Rather than trying to locate some ahistorical "essence of Christianity," one must look to the whole continuum of Christian history in order to comprehend Christian identity.[19] In this way, Troeltsch's historicism removed all bastions for protecting religious dogma, subjecting every aspect of religion to the cold light of critical historical scrutiny.

Troeltsch's philosophy of history is a precursor to the "postmodern" to the extent that it envisions nothing more than a relativistic, multiperspectival, and polycontextual web of experience.[20] Yet there was another aspect of Troeltsch's program which many postmodernists would reject, and this aspect, significantly, was also at the heart of Barth's rejection of Troeltsch. For in the end, Barth perceived Troeltsch's approach to religion as serving only to buttress the sociopolitical consensus of a conservative, middle-class life style.

This leads us to the third aspect of Troeltsch's intellectual program, his idealism. If one side of Troeltsch's position pressed toward a radically historical approach to religion, there was another, residual side to his thought that never distanced itself from the naive view of religious experience found in the predecessors whom he otherwise criticized, namely Ritschl, Harnack, and Herrmann.[21] Having mounted a demolition operation against the whole contemporary theological playing field, Troeltsch continued to invoke an idealistic and transcendental religious metaphysics, a feature that caused Troeltsch to draw back from the radically relativist implications of his overall position in a most striking manner.[22]

Troeltsch, in the end, could not be wholly satisfied with a purely empirical approach to the study of religion.[23] According to Troeltsch the contingent and variable aspects of religious history also point to an "unconditioned" and "rationally necessary" element in religion that grounds its condition of possibility. This transcendental element is apprehended in an inward intuition of being grasped by the absolute spirit.[24] Remarkably, Troeltsch departed from his own historicist predilections by appealing to an inward realm thought to be protected from historical relativity: "Our engagedness [Zugewandtheit] with the majesty of God has nothing to do with history. God is *immediately present*, and in the movements of our feelings rests a permanent self-relation to him."[25]

This last point made the mistake, as Barth would have it, of transmuting the mystery of God into a human given. In the process it posed a dual problem. On the one hand, Troeltsch's pretension to arm's length objectivity vis à vis inherited tradition worked to shove faith imperiously to the side. On the other hand, when he did invoke faith, arguably in violation of his own historicist assumptions, he treated it as though it were something self-evident and "given" (*gegeben*) rather than the exacting and "problematic" (*aufgegeben*) matter Barth knew it to be. Troeltsch's work thus posed what Barth considered a "fundamental distraction" (*gründliche Zerstreutheit*) from theology's true goal.[26] God is not accessible through the ferreting out of tradition alone, nor is God "given" to the immediacy of religious experience. To think of God as a possession in either one of these ways ultimately serves only to prop up the current cultural synthesis of the day. By simply sustaining the status quo, this historicist approach offered no lever for cultural criticism, no way the God of the objective study of history could call humanity itself fundamentally into question (*CD*, I/2, 786). In the end, the manner in which Troeltsch's theology supported the bourgeois status quo could not sway the young Barth who was also, during the years he encountered Troeltsch, a budding socialist.[27]

Barth's theological and ethical concerns, in other words, were more revolutionary in character than those of Troeltsch. The goal of theology was not to baptize the "given" but to seek that which was not-yet-given, the world as it *ought* to be.[28] Accepting the givenness of a particular experience or a particular tradition did not permit the sort of critique that Barth wished to level against a world of fragmentation and sin. For it was this very connection, this presumed "givenness" between God and humanity, which the mature Barth would so vigorously oppose.

It was to be Barth's own mentor, and, incidently, Troeltsch's primary rival, Wilhelm Herrmann, who helped Barth forge the alternative path that pointed him in a nonfoundationalist direction. I have already alluded to Herrmann's naive appeals to religious experience, which Barth agreed with Troeltsch in refusing to follow. Instead, Barth drew from the more thoroughgoingly critical side of Herrmann's teaching. "A wind of freedom blew through [Herrmann's] auditorium. . . . We listened gleefully as traditionalism on the right, rationalism on the left, mysticism in the rear were thrown to the scrap heap, and then finally 'positive' along with 'liberal dogmatics' were hurled into that same grave."[29] This ground-clearing left no secure firmament upon which to stand:

> Herrmann told us specifically of all the things on which religion is *not* grounded. He opened up a wide and empty chasm before which most of his contemporaries felt obligated to shake their heads and draw back. Who could bear to gaze with him into this abyss? No! How many were willing, after throwing off all safety devices, to hurl themselves right down into that abyss?[30]

It was precisely this sort of "ground-clearing" in which Barth found himself increasingly engaged as his discomfiture with "modern" theology, in both its Troeltschian and Herrmannian forms, grew.[31]

My point here is not to pursue a study into the origins of Barth's thought but to give some context for Barth's pursuit of an alternative approach to theology.[32] Could Barth's annoyance with the modern also precipitate the beginnings of a postmodern way in theology? In *Romans* Barth would call this sort of demolition exercise he learned from Herrmann an *Aufräumungsarbeit*, "a ground-clearing that clears a place in this present reality for that which is beyond it."[33] Thus there is a deconstructive moment in theology that must precede any legitimate reconstructive maneuver. The mature Barth, as we shall see, was one who did not shrink from taking the plunge into the abandonment, into the openness of a theology from which all the props had been kicked away. The problem with Herrmann was that he had failed to follow his own clearest lead. Instead of eliminating *every* human starting point from which to speak of God, Herrmann proceeded to "fill in the hole," to build a theological firmament grounded in a putatively immediate experience of the "inner life" of Jesus. Barth queries:

> What if, in [Herrmann's] last attempt to fill in, by means of "individual experience," the yawning chasm of religion's inability to be grounded (*Unbegründbarkeit*), it *too* [i.e., individual experience] should be surren-

dered in the knowledge that truly no one can assert a claim to *this*, the great *autopistis*, which can only be an *indicator* (*Hinweis*) pointing to that which is actually its own self-grounded foundation (*in sich selbst begründeten Grund*), which is now actually in no sense "object," but is unsurpassably subject? If [it is] not [grounded] in humanity, and hence also not in its experience and even less in its thought, then would that the datum with which theology (*Dogmatik*) had to begin were *God* afresh in [God's] Word. . . . [34]

To begin afresh with the mystery of God's "Word" did not imply a retreat to some precritical or premodern fortress but a new excursion into the postcritical and the postmodern.

It was this need for ground-clearing in the face of mystery that led Barth to speak of an "openness" at the very center of theology. One must make way for this "open space" by oneself being open and receptive in faith to the "new thing" God is doing in humanity's midst. For if faith "wishes to be anything other than an open space (*Hohlraum*)," said Barth in *Romans*, it is sheer "unbelief."[35]

This curious metaphor of an open center represented Barth's way of wrestling with the perennial gap modern theology has posited between a God conceived as inconceivable difference, on the one hand, but acknowledged as standing in gracious relationship with the world and human beings as their Creator and Redeemer, on the other. Ronald Thiemann has stated the dilemma quite well:

> If we bring God into a context dominated by our categories and concepts, we treat [God] as if [God] were simply another object among the many objects we know through rational schematization. If we set God outside that framework and allow [God] to create [God's] own conditions and content of knowledge, then we cannot say how it is that *we* know [God]. The former option denies [God's] divinity; the latter denies us our humanity.[36]

I suggest we call this the "diastatic" dilemma. A "diastasis" is a separation that also at the same time involves a falling into place, as with a bone that is separated but without fracture.[37] This dilemma in reference to God is "diastatic" because it prompts us to think of God as occupying a place betwixt and between our own reality and God's reality, a "place" that is "no place." The problem is this: how are humanity and divinity to be considered in the same breath, without either reducing God to a foundation in human experience or rendering God absent from the human horizon altogether?

The most common theological strategy for overcoming this impasse has been to locate some sacrosanct "point of contact" (*Anknüpfungspunkt*) between divinity and humanity.[38] In this way, one area of divine-human encounter is carved out in which the diastasis is simply removed. Like the heel of Achilles, the "point of contact" is the one region that supposedly does not get dipped into the River Styx of the diastatic problem. Yet like Achilles's heel, Barth considered placing faith in a "point of contact" to be the downfall of modern theology. For it removed the element of God as mystery. Or, in contemporary terminology, it established an illegitimate "foundation."

The positing of a "point of contact" was the problem Barth perceived at the heart of so-called "natural theology." Thus, when Emil Brunner attempted to revive natural theology in the 1930s he was greeted with the full brunt of Barth's thundering "No!"[39] Already Barth had rejected natural theology implicitly in *Romans*, and he did so explicitly not long afterwards in his 1924 Göttingen lectures on theology.[40] Barth rejected natural theology because it seeks to speak about God from information derived strictly from the order of being itself and without some specific revelatory event from God. In terms of the diastatic dilemma, it reduces God to a "foundation" accessible in the mundane order of things.

Barth thought of God as *other* than being.[41] The mystery of God cannot be reduced to the being of the world as it is. One must quickly add, however, that neither is God in simple opposition to the world of being, for that too would perpetuate the diastatic predicament. When Barth spoke of God in *Romans* as the *"ganz anders,"* he was not speaking about a God that is "wholly other," in the sense of a spatially-defined distance from the world and humanity. Such a conception would inappropriately separate God from creaturely reality. God as *ganz anders* is not a "wholly other" but a "completely different" God—a God whose life and character are enacted within the drama of human history, but on a different moral plane. The righteousness of God is of a different caliber than the unrighteousness of mere mortals. With this in mind, the only way to overcome the diastatic dilemma is through a new moral situation made possible by God.

This conviction that God is other than being is evidenced in a recurring trope that runs throughout the Romans commentary as well as the *Church Dogmatics:* "God would not be God if. . . . " For example, "God would not be God," if straightforwardly available in mere human traditions. "God would not be God," if God were a datum of ordinary human experience. "God would not be God," if wholly comprehensible in human thought. The same reasoning extended to other concepts logically related to God. "Grace would not be grace if. . . . " "The gospel would not be the gospel if. . . . " It embraced concepts such as "image of God," "creation," "Son of God," and "Spirit of God" as well—none of these, according to Barth, can be said to constitute a theological "given." Both God and the things of God are mediated only in an indirect way. For there always remains an irreducible openness at the center of the wagon wheel.

In speaking of God in this way, Barth was attempting to overcome what Eberhard Jüngel has called the "metaphysical concept of God." According to Jüngel, God in Western theology "had to be thought as one who is absolutely present."[42] By this logic of "presence" one makes the audacious attempt to say "Lo, here," or "Lo, there," in reference to God (cf. Luke 17:21). The "presence" and the "absence" of God, by this brand of logic, are said to be diametrically opposed. But Jüngel argues we must attempt to reconceive the mystery of God. There is no absence without the residue of God's presence, and there is no presence but that which bears the mark of God's inescapable hiddenness.[43] We must move beyond stark oppositions and dualities in conceiving God by embracing a more holistic notion of God as mystery.

Something very much like this critique of pure "presence" was visible in Barth's *Epistle to the Romans*. We are aided in rereading *Romans* along these lines by the recent analysis of Walter Lowe, *Theology and Difference: The Wound of Reason* (1993).[44] Lowe believes we can better understand Barth's intention in *Romans* by taking note of two of the concerns of the contemporary French deconstructionist Jacques Derrida, himself a noteworthy critic of pure "presence." Two of Derrida's concerns, as Lowe notes, are a critique of pure "presence" and a calling into question of "binary oppositions." I shall return to both of these in due course.

Let me hasten to say, the point of enlisting Derrida as a conversation partner is not to imply that we should judge Barth's work by whether it would gain the approval of postmodern philosophers generally or Derridean deconstructionists in particular. Barth's work should be judged, at least in the first instance, by the criterion it set for itself, namely, whether it remains true to its divine subject matter. Even less is the purpose of discussing Barth and Derrida together to intimate that Barth was already saying in his own way what Derrida would say more definitively later on.[45] Rather, the reason for the comparison is heuristic: it may be that certain dimensions of Barth's theology become more understandable in the light cast by some of Derrida's concerns. As a way of leading up to Lowe's comparison of Barth and Derrida, I shall briefly sketch some pertinent aspects of Derrida's thought, supplementing Lowe's insights with a few of my own.

Derrida's work is an inquiry guided by the phenomenon of "difference" or "otherness." Derrida uses a technical term, *différance*, which is meant to insinuate both otherness (*différence*) and postponement (*différer*).[46] "*Différance*" is a term of art meaning to "differ" as well as to "defer"—both implications are there at once. On the one hand, there is an ineluctable unlikeness and dissimilitude that attends all efforts to make language refer to an object. Everything is caught up in "difference." On the other hand, our very efforts to speak this unlikeness are ceaselessly "deferred."

Many of Derrida's reflections on *différance* are raised as a way of questioning the philosophy of language known as "structuralism."[47] Derrida accuses structuralism of positing a straightforward correspondence between language and its referent, or between the "sign" and the thing "signified."[48] Now because of what he calls the indeterminate play of *différance* (difference-deferment) in language, Derrida considers such a correspondence highly questionable. The meaning of all our "signs" or "signifiers" is never as clear-cut as is usually assumed. To establish the definition of even a single "signifier" from a dictionary, after all, requires reference to another "signifier," and to another in unending succession. One never arrives at a final "signified" in itself. Instead, it is signifiers, so to speak, all the way down.

Consequently, there is an instability and open-endedness at work in all our language. Reality is never directly present to the mind, nor does meaning take up permanent residence in any vocabulary. Words must be written "under erasure," meaning that one crosses them out as soon as one writes them, for while they are indispensable for communication, they are nonetheless inadequate in their attempts to refer. All straightforward attempts at reference are defied by the ceaseless play of difference-deferment.

As Lowe notes, Derrida sees a persistent competition in Western metaphysics between two misguided strategies for eliminating this ambiguity and instability. One is a one-dimensional monism that hungers for immediate "presence," the other a two-dimensional dualism that thinks in categories of "binary opposition."[49]

The first strategy, the yearning for the singularity of a "presence," reflects the desire for a "center" that is absolute. "Presence" is a technical term, as Lowe observes, for "any reality which is taken to be autonomous and self-sufficient, and which is regarded as being at some point accessible in a direct and unmediated way." The Western intellectual tradition has proposed a number of candidates that supposedly mediate such "presence." These include the empiricist's search after "sense data," or the idealist's quest for the "self."[50] Signifiers such as these are thought to refer to something "signified," that is, to something determinate and readily accessible.

The "signifier" par excellence, of course, is the idea of "God," together with such related categories as "Logos," "Reason," and "Truth." These concepts refer to an ultimate "transcendental" signified, an absolute "presence" that provides an accessible foundation for all other knowledge. This foundationalist strategy is what Derrida calls "logocentrism." "Logocentrism" is the presumption of having attained the "center" by dint of reason. "Logocentrism" posits a fixed and essential order of meaning that exists *outside of* or *apart from* the structure of language. But how can we have access to any such order of meaning apart from our own structure of language? The claim of logocentrism, which Derrida denies, is that there is some foundational category that can serve as the determinate and accessible "core" that mediates "presence."

To sum up, the positing of "presence" is Derrida's name for the monistic way of seeking to eliminate difference-deferment. It is "monistic" because it embarks upon this quest for certainty under the aegis of unity and sameness. The chief quality of a "presence," whatever form it may take, is its character as standing in self-evident unity with the ultimate, a bedrock "foundation" that makes sense of everything else.

Now Derrida's challenge, to repeat, is to "problematize" whether we ever have any unmitigated access to such a "presence." Is there any particular moment, any "now" in which such access is given? Is not each "now" but a vanishing point that disappears into the "no longer" of the past and whose meaning is still not fully ascertainable until the "not yet" of the future? In a similar way Barth contends that one's encounter with revelation is always either "not yet" or "no longer" the Word of God.

Derrida's "deconstruction" is a method of pointing out the gaps, the aporias, the contradictions that attend our knowing, and especially our language. We must agree with the critics of deconstruction that "to pronounce something 'problematical' is not a conclusion nor is it an intellectual achievement; when we do so, all we have done is point the way to a need for much more thought and analysis of the issues involved."[51] Still, there is a great deal more going on in Derrida's reflections than naked skepticism. Care should be taken lest we commit the error of assuming that Derrida is simply the enemy of "presence." He is often misread as pursuing a campaign to do away with all reference to the foundational and the present. To the contrary, he is convinced that no such elimination is possible. Deconstruction has no choice but to use the language it inherits, even if it seeks to problematize the presuppositions of that language. The reflections of deconstruction, one might say, are parasitic on the foundational yearning for "presence" being adduced in whatever text happens to be under consideration. In one sense, we human beings cannot avoid speaking of these hoped-for verities. It is not that we must refrain from talking about the truly true and the really real. The question is whether our typical ways of talking about these things make any sense. And the purpose in raising this question is to prevent the hubris of thinking we have already arrived at a point of presence that is unsurpassable.

In an early essay, Derrida spoke, somewhat tongue in cheek, of two different ways of interpreting how we ought to interpret. One way seeks to escape the play of difference and to decipher "truth" and "presence" in some definite way. The other way revels in the play itself and has no interest in locating a point of "presence" that is final. Many simply misread Derrida as having already made his own choice against the existence of truth and in favor of a permanent unknowing. But he remarks, "I do not believe that today there is any question of *choosing*—in the first place because here . . . the category of choice seems particularly trivial; and in the second, because we must first try to conceive of the common ground, and the *différance* of this irreducible difference."[52] In other words, this "irreducible difference" involves a ceaseless interplay between presence and absence, between the yes and the no. Both sides of the interplay are necessary. Perhaps the two options themselves—the one more negative and the other more positive—in their perpetual give and take, point to further options arising within the interstices that fall between them.

Where does this leave us regarding Barth and the "center" of theology? Although there persists a human longing for the "center," are we ever able, strictly speaking, to *refer* to it directly? And if we cannot, is this inability of itself necessarily to be considered as a loss? Might it not be in its own way a gain? Asks Derrida,

> Can one not affirm the nonreferral to the center, rather than bemoan the absence of the center? Why would one mourn for the center? Is not the center, the absence of play and difference, another name for death?[53]

This reference to death in connection with the "center" is ironic. For in monotheistic religious traditions death is not at all a pure negation but, in fact, the gateway into the presence of God.[54]

When Derrida writes about religion, it is often to uncover the perplexities and anguish that attend religious obligation. Where is the "center" as we ferret out our conflicting obligations? Yet, ironically, these perplexities only become visible in the first place because of light cast by the perception of that obligatory "center" itself.

Astute interpreters of Derrida, such as Lowe, are therefore quick to see a profoundly moral impulse at work throughout his writings. There is an "ought" that drives his reflections. To this extent, Lowe has located Derrida within a certain peculiar strain of the Kantian tradition with its concern for the categorical imperative. We shall uncover a similar concern of Karl Barth in chapter seven on the ethics of otherness.

Before returning to Barth, let us briefly consider the second, dualistic strategy Derrida identifies for avoiding true difference. This is the penchant in Western thought for binary opposition. By transforming the ambiguity of difference-deferment into rigid opposition, dualism assigns a priority to the one in order to override the other by disgracing or demonizing it. Oppositions such as transcendence/immanence or truth/falsehood, which typify so much of our thinking, lead to distortions in which one member of the pair is implicitly labelled "good" and the other "bad." For example, males may grant pride of place to the universality of a supposed objective form of "reason," a form which they then identify with themselves. Simultaneously, they may denigrate the vagaries of "feeling" and the vulnerability of the "body," as well as the nurturing and care for the body which they relegate to the female. Thus is perpetuated the oppressiveness in which people who are labelled as different from "us" are disparaged by being defined in reference to the subordinate or "inferior" side of a dyad.

Derrida's project of deconstruction is, in significant part, a challenge to these hierarchical oppositions. He contends that there is an "undecidability" at the base of all language, or an ongoing play of "difference" that renders any quest for certainty problematic.

At first glance one might think that Karl Barth's theology offers a prime example of the very foundationalist "logocentrism" that Derrida so roundly rejects. Does not Barth consider the divine "Logos" or "Word" to be the present possession of a privileged community, the church? And is it not given with unrestrained clarity in the texts of scripture? Not so, insists Lowe.

Looking back at Barth from the vantage point provided by Derrida, what Lowe notices in *The Epistle to the Romans* is a struggle to portray God as one who calls all things radically into question and an insistence that our present historical reality is one of fundamental ambiguity. Moreover, Barth was struggling to develop a new vocabulary to speak of divinity. God is made known in a *revealing* that constitutes neither a fixed "presence" nor, by the same token, a simple "absence." Lowe observes that some of Barth's most familiar images for the divine-human encounter are properly geometrical and not, strictly speaking, spatial. Barth says God is to humanity as a line that is tangential to a circle. Or again, the divine-human encounter is like the intersection of two planes. With this use of geometric language, it is, once again, the diastatic dilemma that Barth is trying to negotiate. Rather than a straightforward centering on what is either known or unknown about God, Barth's "emphasis falls . . . upon the intersection of the two. And what happens at that intersection is not mere bafflement, but an occurrence which Barth seeks to depict in carefully balanced terms."[55]

Who God is presses for recognition in human existence, but this divine revealing "is not self-evident," or in Derridean terms, it is not a "presence."[56] Neither is it correct to say that God is simply an "absence," for Barth never places God in a stark, dualistic opposition to human beings. As noted earlier, God should be thought of not as the "wholly other" but as the "completely different" God. This suggested reinterpretation is supported by Barth's allusion to Kierkegaard in the preface of *Romans*. If there was any method to his madness in *Romans*, Barth said, it consisted in what he had learned from Kierkegaard about the "unbounded qualitative difference" between God and humanity. The term "difference" here, as Lowe suggests, does not signal a divine-human opposition, as the phrase "wholly other" is sometimes interpreted, but a crisis that is moral in nature. The crisis, in other words, is qualitative and not merely spatial. The crisis is that the relationship between humanity and God, a relationship that "demands and wants to be known," has become fractured due to sin.[57]

In support of this "qualitative" rendition of divine-human difference, I would add to Lowe's analysis of *Romans* other texts as well. Listen to what Barth said just two years after *Romans* in his first lecture on theology:

> In revelation God is always, not quantitatively (for gigantic or infinite does not make God), but qualitatively different from us, not spatially, but occupying a totally different place according to the mode of space.[58]

This crisis in the divine-human relationship is provoked because of humanity's utter failure to enact on the moral plane God's qualitatively different possibility. The gospel of God calls into question the world as it is and points to a new world as it ought to be. The gospel, as Barth says in *Romans*, is not "one truth among others" that needs to be set in dualistic contrast to the world, but the gospel is the truth that "places all truths in question." "Through the dissolution [*Aufhebung*] and reestablishment [*Begründung*] of all givens [*Gegebenen*]," the gospel "is the victory which overcomes the world."[59]

It is often said that in *Romans* Barth rediscovered the "deity" of God. With his departure from liberalism, he had embarked on a new quest for the God of theology. Such a quest must be an ongoing venture in which one can do no more than make one's humble gestures toward God, hoping for God to be at work within the ongoing dialectic of one's reflections. There is no recipe for certainty in the theology Barth forged in *Romans*. The goal of theology is—somehow—that "God be recognized as God. . . . " And this occurs only "where human beings dare . . . to hurl themselves into the wind and to love the unfathomable God."[60]

In the early Barth one is confronted by the thrill of someone who has rediscovered the mystery and deity of God. On the one hand, this is a far cry from Derrida's preoccupation with writing, language, and the aporias of the Western intellectual tradition. On the other hand, the very thought of "God" led Barth into a similar sort of problematizing. Most of the writings of this formative period addressed the question of how it is possible to overcome the diastatic dilemma and to be true to this God who is never simply theology's "given."[61]

The clearest insight into Barth's handling of diastasis and of opposing what Derrida calls "binary opposition" is gained from his 1929 Dortmund lectures on "Fate and Idea in Theology."[62] Published just a year before his important seminar on Anselm and two years before the first part-volume of the *Church Dogmatics*, they offer Barth's earliest explicit rejection of the Roman Catholic concept of an "analogy of being" (*analogia entis*) between God and humanity.[63] More importantly, they demonstrate theology's inability to be grounded—either in the "given" or in the "non-given." These lectures are an indispensable resource for understanding Barth's mature theology.

Barth used the terms "Fate" or "Destiny" (*Schicksal*) and "Idea" (*Idee*) to signal the twin horizons of all intellectual endeavor, the "double determination" of every "act of thinking" (*Denkakt*) and every "act of living" (*Lebensakt*). We have no choice but to live out our "ideas" and to think through our "destinies." The dichotomy set by "fate" and "idea," maintained Barth, is the same one at work in the pairings, "reality and truth," "nature and spirit," "the particular and the general," "the given and the not-given," "the objective and the non-objective," "the conditioned and the unconditioned," "being and thinking," "heteronomy and autonomy," or "experience and reason." Too often, these concepts have been reified and turned into systems, the clashing "isms" of "Realism and Nominalism" or "Romanticism and Idealism."[64]

Each side of these various dyads reflects an aspect of life that is inescapable for theology. "Realism" is necessary because faith looks to the reality of God as God's gift of grace. "Idealism" is necessary because, as Anselm put it, faith must seek understanding; it must try to render a portrait of God couched in human concepts and images.

Barth began with a consideration of realism, observing that a certain degree of realism is inescapable in theology. The statement "God is" represents a typically realistic utterance. God is true actuality (*Wirklichkeit*), and so must become the "object" of theology, even if we must place the word "object," so to speak, in quotation marks. Theological "realists," says Barth, seek God in the "givenness" of experience or of reality "as it is." They seek to base their knowing and doing before God on what postmodern thinkers would call a "foundation" in reality, or on what Barth himself termed a "basic orientation that does not permit itself to be further grounded."[65] Realists seek this foundation either in the objective realms of nature and history, or in the subjective sphere of human experience.

One quickly gathers that Barth will not settle for a straightforward realism when one notices the historical examples he adduces. Rather than ascribing theological realism to the Protestant reformers, as one might expect, Barth announces that the two exponents of realism par excellence were Thomas Aquinas and Friedrich Schleiermacher, two theologians who, as is well-known, catch more than their share of criticism from Barth throughout his writings. Through the *analogia entis*, Thomas Aquinas focused on both the subjective and the objective givenness of God. Schleiermacher, for his part, also stressed both the subjective and objective poles, but he gave the emphasis to a subjective givenness focused in the "feeling of absolute dependence."

One must aspire to speak of the "real," said Barth, if theology wishes to avoid "mystical silence."[66] To remain silent about God is no less to dishonor God than to speak about God falsely. Hence one must put aside silence and speak, believing that God in Jesus Christ has already spoken. Nevertheless, theological realism runs the risk of exhausting God within the vagaries of humanity's own empirical "destiny" or "fate." Rather than celebrating the immediate "givenness" (*Gegebensein*) of God—whether in experience, in history, or anywhere else—Barth argued that a theologian must look to God's "self-givenness" (*Sichselbergeben*) in revelation. This is an unfolding reality, one that cannot be "reified," or turned into a "thing" (*res*). The reality of God cannot be statically and objectively described.

While theology must share many of the *intentions* of a theological or philosophical realism, it must also carry serious reservations. Even if one were to assume that the Word of God "takes place in the same general framework" as that in which philosophical realism operates, one still cannot equate God's "Word" with that framework without remainder (*ohne weiteres*).[67] In "Fate and Idea" this "without remainder" specifies Barth's reservations both about Thomas's *analogia entis* and about Schleiermacher's "feeling of absolute dependence." But it extends to any effort to turn God into a "given." If one were to adopt a straightforward realism in theology, Barth asks, then why not dispense with the concept "God" altogether and opt instead for another term such as "nature"? Although a certain degree of realism is theologically necessary, when carried to the extreme it reduces everything to a simple naturalism.

If Barth attested the necessity of realism, he nevertheless quickly turned the tables to observe that idealism too is indispensable to theological reflection, even for theological reflection cast in a predominantly realist mode. This is so, since every theological realism depends on the inherently dialectical character of "analogy" for all its statements about God.[68] Revelation itself is "a revealing and not a state of being revealed (*Offenbarung und nicht eine Offenbarheit ist*)."[69] The problem is that a straightforward theological realism includes "no underside of the apprehension and unsettledness before the non-givenness of this God."[70] To put it another way, for Barth the divine non-givenness itself is part of the very "reality" with which theology must contend.

In distinction from the realist, then, the "idealist" is attracted to a mode of critical reflection in theology. The philosophical exponents of "idealism" were figures such as Kant, Hegel, and the neo-Kantians Hermann Cohen and Paul Natorp, the latter two having been teachers both of Karl Barth and his brother Heinrich. For idealists the "given" or the "real" is known only through the grid of one's own knowing activity. Idealism operates at a level one step removed from the straightforward "reality" of realism, focusing on self-reflection, the non-given, and spirit over nature.

Idealism offers a critique both of reality itself—the world as it is—and of the "realism" that seeks to explain that reality. As opposed to resting on the "givenness" of experience, idealism accents the "non-given." The "idealist"—or today we might say the "constructivist"—viewpoint poses fundamental questions about that which the realist simply takes as self-evident. It raises these questions not to negate reality but to reconsider it from a different angle.

Following idealism, theology cannot rest content to focus on the givens of a particular tradition, or experience, or way of life, but must also inquire into whether these things are also true. It strives to uncover that which is the noetic and ontological "presupposition" of the supposedly self-evident and objective. The idealistic critique of "reality" stands as a reminder that all human conceptualization of God is inadequate.

Lest we assume it to be sheer skepticism that motivates the idealist, Barth counters that the unsettling concept of God itself has provided the impetus for critical-idealist thinking from Plato, to Descartes, to Kant. Moreover, the extent of Barth's sympathies with idealism (or constructivism) should become clear once we read the list of its great exemplars among the theologians. Augustine, Luther, Zwingli, and Calvin—these are theological "idealism's" most outstanding advocates.[71] Moreover, as Zwingli and Calvin emphasized, in relative dissent from Luther, God must never be confused with the other objects of revelatory experience.[72]

Barth acknowledges that the radical nature of idealism, with its emphasis upon the non-given, leads to greater risks than realism. This is so because the intellectual stakes are higher: human reflection has now pushed to a deeper level. Though it respects the element of mystery in theology, the risk posed by an idealistic or constructivist theology is that it will degenerate into "ideology," the tendentious linking of God to one's own culturally conditioned aspirations.[73]

To guard against this, idealism must affirm God's own initiative, transcendence, and priority in graciously making known who God is. Theology must maintain its own integrity and not become entangled in any particular political agenda, or with this or that party line. Whereas theological realism threatens to commingle its approach to God with the natural sciences, theological idealism becomes confused with the social sciences and humanities.[74] Theology in this mode is tempted to equate itself with some hidden agenda and thereby degenerate into a utilitarian religion.

Might there be any way to combine or synthesize these two poles into a greater whole? Would such a thing even be desirable? *Not* from Barth's perspective. Barth's point in "Fate and Idea," in formal parallel to the later claim of Derrida, was that the interplay between the given and the non-given is ceaseless. There can be no synthesis, no convergence upon a point of ultimate "presence." To pursue some grand synthesis of realism and idealism in the manner of Hegel would build upon an arbitrary and mundane "foundation" and not upon "the manna" which is the Word of God.[75] The best a theologian can do is to keep the two sides of realism and idealism (or constructivism) in a ceaseless interplay. By keeping the two sides in play, theology always enjoys a built-in corrective to the dangers of either side. Together each side finds itself driven to attend to the concerns of the other. To interrupt this dynamic prematurely would be illegitimate, and to seek to move beyond it is not a possibility that belongs to human beings. On their own, human beings have no way to escape pursuing *either* a realistic or idealistic path.

In short, theology is permanently decentered. As Derrida would have it, human beings are caught in the bind of binary alternatives. Or as Barth himself would put it, apart from grace either "our thinking can be realistic or idealistic but it cannot be Christian" (I/1, 175). For our thinking ever to become "Christian" requires the intervening grace of God.

2

IN QUEST OF A
THEOLOGY OF GOD

God may speak to us through Russian Communism, a flute concerto,
a blossoming shrub, or a dead dog.

Karl Barth, CD, I/1, 55

In his early writings Barth was struggling to understand how theology
could remain true to the mystery of who God is. How can the unfathomable God become the subject of human reflection and the object of human
action? Grappling with this question led him radically to rethink the theoretical underpinnings of nineteenth century liberal theology. It would not
do, Barth decided, to reduce God to any humanly-conceived "foundation,"
whether in reason or experience, in tradition or text.

The same nonfoundationalist and dialectical style of thinking was
carried forward into the *Church Dogmatics*. If the early Barth was redis-
covering the "God of theology," the burden of the mature Barth was to
formulate a suitable "theology of God." In so doing, he still had to negotiate the problem posed by the diastatic dilemma. This is the dilemma of
how to conceive a relationship between humanity and divinity without
either reducing God to a human foundation or rendering God beyond human experience altogether.

According to the method forged in the *CD*, there can be no systematization of the mystery of God's Word and no reducing theology to a single
"fundamental principle." Instead theology must remain open in all directions, "like the opening in the center of a wheel" (I/2, 867). Here the same
wagon wheel metaphor first encountered in *Romans* recurs in a pivotal
section of the *CD* on theological method (I/2, §24). But this time the wheel
of theology boasts another uncommon characteristic. In depicting this
wheel, says Barth, one must "refrain from drawing a second circle around
the whole." In other words, not only does this wheel possess an open center but it is in the peculiar condition of lacking a "rim." Barth will use this
unusual image of a rimless wheel to make two seemingly un-Barthian
points: first, to insist on the open-ended character of Christian theology;
and, second, to place the "center" of his theology in a relationship, albeit
an ambiguous one, to testimony drawn from the whole range of Christian
tradition and even from non-Christian sources.

The open-endedness of theology is suggested by the wheel's first feature, the one already encountered in *Romans*, namely its "open center." In
the *CD* the metaphor becomes a way to speak about a nonsystematic and
nonfoundational approach to theological method. Such is the only approach possible, for "this center is not something which is under our control, but something which exercises control over us" (I/2, 866).

"Open-ended" does not mean that the center of Christian theology is opaque or absolutely indescribable. In comparison to *Romans*, the "center" in the *CD* is identified in a much more straightforward manner. In the *CD* as in *Romans*, the "center" of organization is none other than the divine-human relationship. In the *CD* this relationship is more specifically designated as the work of God the "Reconciler," and knowledge of this relationship is more clearly focused in a well-developed concept of the "Word of God." The Word of God is even said to form the "center and foundation of dogmatics and of Church proclamation" (I/2, 869).

Still, the "Word of God" is not the sort of "foundation" that can provide the self-evident building block for a rational system. Rather, the "Word of God" is a dynamic and even a precarious concept (I/1, §4; I/2, §22). In the first place, the Word of God is mediated in human proclamation. In this God assumes a remarkable risk: committing the unimpeachable "Word" to the care of witnesses who are themselves thoroughly impeachable. Second, the Word of God is attested in written form in scripture. Yet scripture is never the Word of God per se, but it can only bear witness to that Word. Third and above all, the Word of God is the revealed Word in Jesus Christ. But this revealing is a dynamic event that is made available only in the mode of a "coming presence" (I/2, 95).

Thus we are speaking of a "center and foundation" that is not anywhere "given" to our disposal. Indeed, Barth can speak quite provocatively of Christian theology as a "foundationally nonfoundational" (*grundsätzlich Ungrundsätzliche*) affair. This means that theology takes its cue from no totalistic, all-embracing points of view (*Totalansichten*) and must seek "no final summations, conclusions, or results." Speaking from no "assured platform," and with no premature fix on what might comprise the "essence of Christianity," unending investigation must be its sole work; "openness to receive new truth" its sole technique; and the measure of its adeptness is the extent to which it can learn to "continually begin again at the beginning" (*KD*, I/2, 971, *CD*, 868).

This self-styled nonfoundational approach involves an interminable oscillation between "center" and "periphery":

> The foundational lack of foundations [*grundsätzlich Ungrundsätzliche*] in theological method is clear from the fact that [theology] does not proceed from the center but rather from the periphery (or metaphor apart, from the self-positing and self-authenticating Word of God)." (*KD* I/2, 971)

What does it mean to say that faithfulness to the "Word of God" requires the theologian to speak without foundations from the periphery?

This mention of the "periphery" leads us to the wheel's second feature, its peculiar lack of a "rim." To follow Barth's meaning, we must understand that his wagon wheel, in fact, has two "peripheries." The first is the "inner" periphery that surrounds the open center of the wheel itself. This is the "periphery" referred to in the block quotation above. It is from the "inner" periphery that the wheel's "spokes" jut out towards the second and outer periphery. This second periphery is the outer penumbra that ordinarily would form the wagon wheel's "rim." But remember, this is a wheel that has no rim. What is the point of a wagon wheel with an open center and a rimless periphery?

Barth declared in his *Protestant Theology in the Nineteenth Century* that in order to take up a genuinely "theocentric" stance (the terminology is Barth's), one must position oneself, as did the Protestant reformers, not at the "center" itself but at the *Nebenzentrum*. The *Nebenzentrum* means the region that is "next to" (*neben*) the center.[1] This is so, because the "center" itself is never directly accessible. In the terminology used by the *CD* this *Nebenzentrum* would be the "inner" periphery, the first of the two circles that make a wheel what it is. The first circle is the inner ring that immediately surrounds the open place at the wheel's "center." It is the "inner" band from which the "spokes" radiate outward towards the periphery.

In contrast to the theoretically indefinite number of "spokes" or questions jutting out from that "*Nebenzentrum*" in *Romans*, now in the *CD* we encounter "a definite number of lines which in dogmatics are to be drawn to a certain distance in all directions" (I/2, 868, rev.). Rather than trace out some "total number of theoretically possible lines," there are now just four "spokes" in particular that beg to be addressed. These just happen to be the four loci around which the *CD* itself is organized: "God" (volume II), "Creation" (volume III), "Reconciliation" (the never-completed volume IV), and "Redemption" (the never-written volume V).

Having thus limited the scope of the "questions" to be addressed, Barth is striving to make the *CD* more doctrinally focused than was *Romans*. And this doctrinal focus shall mark one of the major features of his theological method. Indeed, much of the *CD* is taken up with what Hans Frei has called the conceptual redescription of Christian doctrine.[2] But must there not be more to theology than this?

The answer is "yes," if we pay attention to some of the peculiar implications of this open-centered, rimless wagon wheel. The open-endedness represented by the wheel in the *CD* is just as unrelenting as in *Romans*. In the *CD* as in *Romans*, the theologian has no direct access to the mystery of the "center" itself. No theologian can venture closer to the "center" than this "inner periphery" that surrounds it (I/2, 868). Barth's point is that the theologian has no access to nor can stand within the open center itself but can only begin from that which falls all around the center. For Barth this "inner periphery" is the ongoing discourse of the believing community.

But this raises a question. Why does Barth start with the confessional discourse of the church and not from some other point? Are ecclesial resources the only ones permissible to the Christian? The answer, no doubt surprising to many, is a resounding "no." As we shall see, Barth does not limit himself, at least not in principle, solely to Christian sources. But before addressing that issue, let us consider what function the traditional "Creed" of the confessing community—this "inner periphery"— plays in Barth's overall approach. We may best do this by pointing out a few of the features of his 1931 book on Anselm of Canterbury.

Barth's reading of Anselm fits directly into the line of analysis we have been tracing. According to Barth, Anselm studies the orthodox faith not to appropriate it as a foundationalist "given" but to pursue a particular "way" or "path" of theological thinking characterized by free reflection. Anselm's mode of inquiry is so free, in fact, that it even abandons supporting citations and quotations.[3] It is, after all, the very quotations themselves, the statements drawn from the historic Creed, which need to be considered, reconsidered, sifted, and understood. Not even the scriptures themselves function for Anselm as an absolutely conclusive foundation for theology, for "nothing can be achieved by an appeal to the authority of Holy Scripture."[4]

The overarching rubric in Anselm's theology like that of Augustine, of course, was, "I believe in order to understand": *Credo ut intelligam*. Or, put slightly differently, faith seeks intelligibility (*fides quaerens intellectum*), meaning that Anselm's theology starts from "belief" and journeys towards consummate "vision." The "knowledge" it seeks lies suspended like a looming "gap" between "faith" at the beginning of one's theological pilgrimage and the consummation of beatific "vision" at its eschatological end; or, as Barth puts it, between a person's subjective "credo" and the objective "Credo" of the historic church towards which he or she strives. Thus historic faith includes both the past faith of the church and the living community's own appropriation of that faith today as it moves into the future.

This subjective appropriation of the faith is a continuing venture, a task (*Aufgabe*), as Barth puts it, and never a given (*Gegeben*). This is because the affirmations expressed in the Creed (*ratio fidei*) do not stand in a simple one-for-one correspondence with the unreachable veracity of the gospel truth itself (*ratio veritatis*). As Bruce McCormack argues, Barth himself wished to draw an even sharper distinction than Anselm between the truth of the Creed and God's own Truth. Thus the theology articulated in the Anselm book, no less than that of *Romans*, "remains . . . incomplete and broken, in constant need of correction."[5]

Keeping in mind the previous discussions about the problem of the "given" in theology, listen to what Barth found most admirable about Anselm's work in this passage drawn from the opening pages of the *Church Dogmatics:*

[Anselm's] aim in *intellectus fidei* [the understanding the faith] is not a repetition of the *legere* [survey] of belief, but an actual *intus legere* [inquiry into] the scriptures and dogmas *apart from any foundation* [*Begründung*] . . . in their authoritative givenness [*Gegebensein*]. (*KD*, I/1, 15, *CD*, 16, emphasis supplied)

Following Anselm, Barth took his bearings from the ancient Christian Creed, but he employed the Creed not simply to repeat it but to test it. As he put it in the *CD*, the theological task is to subject the Creed to an ongoing "self-test" (*Selbstprüfung*). The appropriate question is "how far" and "to what extent" is the historic utterance of the Credo true (I/1, §1). One proceeds by rethinking the thoughts of the Christian centuries, but not without a certain critical reserve. Theology cannot be *theo*logy without also being a critique of theo*logy*.

Arguably, then, the Anselm book did not eliminate, as some readings would have it, but actually intensified the question mark which hangs over all theological endeavor. In all theology, "the [way] of divine simplicity and the way of the most incredible deception have always run parallel, separated only by the merest hair's breadth. It can never be at all evident in any statement of any theologian whether it stands on this or that side of the boundary."[6] Or as he put it later in the *CD*, the orthodox tradition provides "fluid material for further work" (I/2, 773). Theology must always offer thoughts that are new, or else it will be nothing more than an elementary historical report (I/2, 779). Theology forever remains a fallible, unfinished, and constructive task and not simply the reassertion of a single cultural-linguistic system. As Barth summed it up in the *CD*, "[Theology] ought not become merely a report on various doctrines of the fathers, nor have as its goal, not even as a subordinate goal, the repristination of such doctrines" (*KD*, I/2, 936–37).[7]

This freedom to plumb the "how far" and the "to what extent" of the Creed, a freedom Barth was convinced he detected in Anselm, is all well and good. Nevertheless, does not "free theological reflection" require that the Creed itself be brought into a more serious and critical conversation with other perspectives than Barth himself ever attempted?

The relationship between theology and other disciplines, philosophy in particular, has posed a perennial question for modern religious thought. Since Barth held a fairly optimistic view about the ultimate unity and mutual coinherence of all truth, he asserted (no doubt naively) that all human discourse aspires to truth. Still, he was well aware, despite this optimism, of the massive disparity between the unity which ought to be and the current situation of intellectual fragmentation and disagreement which is.

In the opening sections of the *Church Dogmatics*, Barth spoke to this disparity between the ideal and the actual that afflicts the search for truth. Although not all human speech can claim to be talk about God, it "indeed could and ought to be." Since every reality and every truth proceeds from God, "there can and should be no profane speech at all, but only, in the final reality, talk about God" (I/1, 47). In theory, theology as a separate intellectual discipline is altogether unnecessary, since its task could just as well be performed by philosophy, anthropology, psychology, or a host of other disciplines, if only they would rise to the occasion. It is not that theology must reject these disciplines; rather, these disciplines have rejected their true calling, which is theology. Thus, the necessity of theology as a discrete discipline comes about only as an "emergency" measure. It is a "stop-gap in a disordered cosmos," a crisis occasioned by the failure of other disciplines to set themselves to the task (I/1, 10).

As he stated in a 1960 essay dedicated to his philosopher brother, Heinrich Barth, the division of truth into theological and philosophical insights is but an abstraction.[8] The opposition between the disciplines arises concretely only in the interested, committed stance of actual human beings. The theologian and the philosopher each proceeds on the presupposition that he or she confronts the "one, single, and whole truth," thus assuring both a confrontation and a cooperation in the pursuit of their mutual agendas. Each approaches his or her task in a thoroughly fallible manner, hence guaranteeing that neither shall have the last word. Pursuing their separate priorities, the theologian begins with the primacy of the Creator and moves to the creation, while the philosopher tries to move in reverse order, beginning with creation. Nevertheless, Barth left open the prospect that a "Christian" philosophy was a *possible* avenue of genuinely theological inquiry. Whether philosophy, or for that matter theology itself, could qualify as "Christian," would depend on the presuppositions and intent of the project in question.

If a "Christian" philosophy represents a possible goal, mused Barth in the *CD*, it is still as yet a goal unattained (I/1, 5f.). After all, who is in a position to claim the "Christian" character of his or her work? (I/1, xii–xiii). As he had put it in *Romans*, "there are no Christians: there is only the eternal opportunity of *becoming* Christians—an opportunity at once accessible and inaccessible to all human beings."[9] Rather than claiming for himself the imprimatur of the word "Christian," he would settle for the more modest designation of a "church" theology, a *Church Dogmatics*, a theology confessed within this particular worshiping, believing community but professed before all the world. In a set of 1962 lectures delivered to American audiences in Princeton and Chicago, Barth advised a cautious usage even of the word "church," since it is often taken as a synonym for "Christianity," which as a human cultural-linguistic endeavor is as subject to corruption as any other religion.[10] (Cf. I/2, §17.) God's truth does not belong to the Christian religion; nor is Christianity somehow superior to all other religions (I/2, 298).

If this is true, then why is Barth so reticent to incorporate the data of philosophy, anthropology, psychology, or for that matter, other religions, into his own theological reflections? If theology itself is as thoroughly problematic as Barth contends, then arguably there is no justification for limiting the various voices to which one will listen. Respect for the mystery of God would seem to demand nothing less than a multidimensional approach to the theological task. And yet Barth is usually credited with constricting the focus of theology rather than opening it up. We must ask, then, whether there are resources in Barth that point to an alternative that is multidimensional in its reach.

A most noteworthy example of Barth's pursuing a more multidimensional approach occurs in his theological ethics, a subject to be discussed in chapter six. But there are others as well. In his survey of *Protestant Theology in the Nineteenth Century,* for example, Barth professed a desire to attend to "all the voices of the past," and not merely the ones which have stood in official favor. This is necessary, he said, because one cannot anticipate in advance which voices will speak to the genuinely "theological" elements in human endeavor.[11] Theological understanding ought to be an ongoing and shared endeavor in which no one ever "gets it right" but in which all participants share a sense of being "on the way."[12] A theological hermeneutic must proceed as though it were solving an equation to which no one already holds the solution beforehand. It is an equation in which God is the unknown "x" to which each age gives its provisional solution. Each voice must be understood sympathetically in its own terms, for each individual shares this "x" as a common factor, and each can contribute to solving the equation.[13]

To be sure, this way of solving the equation still works within the Christian cultural-linguistic system. But it does not presume in advance to define that system as something "given." Barth seems to presume, instead, that each different perspective provides its own unique angle into theological truth. This potential veracity is attributed even to those perspectives from which one might least anticipate agreement. Thus, in his *Protestant Theology* Barth lent a more sympathetic ear to such radical critics of traditional theology as Rousseau, Kant, Hegel, and Feuerbach, than he did to a mainstream theologian such as Albrecht Ritschl, whom he treated merely as an afterthought.[14]

In a similar way, though still limited to the confines of the Christian religion, Barth seems to advocate drawing the "truth" about God in Jesus Christ from a composite of perspectives from many participants. Theology is the work of the whole church; indeed, "the whole church must seriously want a serious theology if it is to have a serious theology" (I/1, 77). Theological work takes time, since human beings do not know God "at a stroke" or "once and for all." Instead the identity of God is only recognized through the gradual processes of time (II/1, 61). As we shall see in more detail in chapter five, such knowledge revolves around the thoroughly human figure of Jesus Christ as the sacramental "sign" and "center" of God's reality.

This stated intention of viewing Christian truth from the angles of the many voices, both pro and con, that happen to be speaking about it bears a formal similarity to the even more wide-ranging procedure of Hegel in his philosophy of religion.[15] For Hegel the history of all the religions (and not just Christianity) is a story of struggle for consummate knowledge of God. Each of the non-Christian religions is a so-called "determinate" (*bestimmte*) religion, that is, a particular manifestation of "Spirit" under the exigencies of particular historical contexts. Each determinate religion portrays God and the divine-human relationship in ways that are true but only partially so. Each different portrayal must be sifted by the philosopher-theologian for the element of truth it contains. The information collected in this way is then sublated (*aufgehoben*) into a developing vision of the whole. This holistic conclusion reaches its culmination in the "consummate" (*vollendete*) religion, which Hegel (all too triumphantly) equates with Christianity. At one level Barth is even more radical than Hegel, insisting that Christianity, too, belongs to the throroughly relativized and determinate religions of the world. Christianity, too, must be completed from beyond itself.

Like Hegel, Barth believes that knowledge of God is an ongoing process that requires a "composite" drawn from a wide array of perspectives. This is made clear in a section in *CD* II/1 entitled, "The Fulfillment of the Knowledge of God" (II/1, §25). There Barth declared that knowledge of God is something that must be actively brought to fruition. Or, to put it in Hegel's language, knowledge of God must become "consummate." And this happens in a process that is stretched out over time. Barth's understanding of how this trek toward consummate knowledge is accomplished is quite radical. God must be known in the "entirety," he says, or not at all. Knowledge of God that is only "partial" cannot qualify as knowledge of God (II/1, 51).

This last point, that God must be known in the "entirety," seems on its face to contradict his assertion that knowledge of God occurs in a ongoing process. It is also not clear, at first glance, how it squares with his constant conviction about human fallibility. How can God, who is ultimate mystery, be known in a way that is both partial and complete at the same time? In saying that God must be known in the entirety, Barth is not in any way aiming to lessen his insistence on divine mystery or on human fallibility. This knowledge of God is always a mediated and never a direct knowledge. It comes only through the mediation of certain "signs" which bear the character of "sacrament." By "sacrament" Barth means "the self-witness of God, the representation of [God's] truth" (II/1, 52). There is a broad, sacramental character to the reality of God's revelation, but "sacrament" here has largely to do with "sign" and "symbol" and little to do with the theology of real "presence." Barth considered the "sign" or "sacrament" of God par excellence to be the humanity of Jesus Christ. Jesus' humanity is "the basic reality and substance of the sacramental reality of revelation" (II/1, 53). The humanity of Jesus Christ is at the "center" of God's sacramental disclosure of God's identity in the world.

A crucial point is that this sacramental reality of revelation is not static but dynamic. As the preeminent attestation of God's grace, the humanity of Jesus is "a beginning of which there are continuations." Jesus' humanity, his achievement of becoming truly human, is not the only sacrament; but "the humanity of Jesus is as such the *first* sacrament." There is a "sacramental continuity" that "stretches backwards into the existence of the people Israel . . . and forwards into the existence of the apostolate and the Church founded on the apostolate" (II/1, 54, emphasis added). It requires the sacramental reality of the "whole," in other words, and not just a presence at the "center" to display the reality of who God is.

To anticipate the subject of the next chapter, this sacramental way in which God is known has a trinitarian shape. First, in correspondence to who God is primordially as the Creator, God "unveils" God's identity by becoming "veiled" in the sacramental humanity of Jesus (II/1, 53–57). This divine manifestation of "unveiling" is such that God still remains draped in mystery. God is revealed in Jesus Christ—this much is clear. But one must still inquire into the meaning and significance of Jesus' life. It is possible to know of Jesus Christ, the true "sign," but still fail to recognize God, who is the "sign-giver." "A complete non-recognition of the Lord who has instituted and used this medium is possible." The sacramental medium of Jesus' humanity "is not in itself and as such identical either with revelation or with the real knowledge of God. It serves it . . . But it can also not serve it; it can even hinder and prevent it" (II/1, 55). The primordial Creator God, that is, remains hidden even in the act of revealing.

Second, in keeping with the fact that God is the Reconciler, this knowing of God occurs in a genuine encounter. There is a reconciliation between God and humanity that is still being accomplished in the person and work of Jesus Christ. It happens through an encounter in which one knows God by name, but by the unique name according to which God continues to proclaim God's freedom: "I am that I am, I will be who I will be" (Exod. 3:14) (II/1, 57–61).

Third, and indicative of the redemptive work of the Spirit, knowledge of God occurs not in some otherworldly region but squarely within the bounds of human time. Because we are temporal beings, we are never in a position to know God "at a stroke." Rather, we know God "in a cognition that progresses" in time. We know God, moreover, through a re-cognition that "constantly begins afresh." It happens through a "series of attestations" which "anticipate and indicate one another, condition and are conditioned by one another." We know God through a series of individual perceptions that always need to be repeated (*wiederholungsbedürftig*). For no single perspective is ever sufficient to capture the mystery of God. All the various perceptions of God must combine to form a composite recognition of who God is (*KD*, II/1, 66–67, *CD*, 61–62). And this composite recognition comes to fruition (*Vollzug*) not through a zeroing in on the "center," but rather "it happens in the whole circumference of this center, in the whole circumference of sacramental reality" (II/1, 61).

This reference to a holistic and sacramental circumference of meaning that surrounds what is there at the "center" brings our attention back to the peculiar "outer periphery" of Barth's wagon wheel. And it also brings us to a mode of inquiry that can potentially call the Christian cultural-linguistic system itself into question.

Recall that the penumbra of this wheel, as Barth said in *CD*, I/2, cannot be enclosed. The wagon wheel of theology has no "rim" (I/2, 689). To delimit the wheel's "rim" would be to follow the Hegelian presumption of "presenting the whole as a whole." The "whole" cannot be circumscribed prematurely but must remain open in deference to the openness that characterizes the "center" itself. This is because "the Word of God . . . does actually speak in all directions, and . . . like the periphery of a circle, something is said in all directions." The "outer rim" must remain indeterminate and, as un-Barthian as it may sound, it even includes voices from *outside* the believing community as well as those from within.

According to this comment, there is a diversity of perspectives needed to see God "whole." This rather cryptically expressed need for a diversity of perceptions was made a bit more explicit in a 1959 section on what he called "secular parables of truth"[16] (IV/3.1, §69.2). Outside the church and apart from utterances that are self-consciously Christian, there are also certain "secular parables" being spoken. Such parables, according to Barth, can bear authentic witness to truth. That is, they represent genuine utterances about God which are "in material agreement" with the Word and which "illumine, accentuate, or explain the biblical witness in a particular time and situation" (IV/3.1, 115).

Barth denied that secular parables are merely affirmations of natural theology under a different guise. Natural theology attests the generic God of nature, the God of naked powers bearing down upon us, rather than the particular God of Christian revelation who is gracious.[17] Secular parables are non-Christian attestations of who this gracious God is. They are attestations of the God who (in Christ by the Spirit's power) is beneficently disposed to be "for" and "with" human beings. Barth is affirming that there are ways of saying something meaningful about that gracious reality without being confined to the nomenclature of the Christian cultural-linguistic system.

Here there is an opening in the seemingly closed and exclusivist theology of Karl Barth. The exclusivity of God's revelation in Jesus Christ is not nearly as important for him as the *concreteness* of that revelation. In Jesus Christ God's being is made manifest in act. But as Robert Scharlemann interprets Barth, if such a concrete manifestation "has occurred at least once, then it is a matter of indifference how many other times it has occurred or in what other ways."[18] The "name" of Jesus Christ is the concrete embodiment of who God is, namely one who is both "for" and radically "with" human beings in grace. Yet a Christian may believe in the concrete embodiment of divine identity in Jesus Christ without believing that non-Christian, secular parables are excluded from bearing witness to that gracious reality.

Barth refused in the *CD* to give any examples of persons who had actually uttered such illuminating parables. This he considered a matter for the church to discern, usually with the benefit of hindsight (IV/3.1, 132). Nevertheless, on occasion he did draw from certain secular critics of Christianity to raise questions about Christian theology itself. One such example was the atheist historian, Franz Overbeck (1837–1905), a friend of Friedrich Nietzsche, whom Barth read with particular interest as he worked on the revised second edition of the Romans commentary. Most mainstream thinkers regarded Overbeck as an entirely negative critic of Christianity. Yet, in a review of Overbeck's posthumously published papers, Barth strained to see if there did not exist, after all, a uniquely "theological" element in Overbeck's writings. Standing as it did on the boundary between skepticism and inspired criticism, Overbeck's thinking, declared Barth, was quite theological indeed. Lifting up Overbeck's twin claims, that nothing in history can tell us of God and that Christianity's historical prospects for survival stand in jeopardy, Barth observed that whereas some have tried to be theologians and have failed, Overbeck had repudiated all desire to be a theologian and may, inadvertently, have succeeded.[19] He succeeded because he pointed out with compelling clarity the conundrums that theology perpetually faces.

If in the *CD* Barth was reticent to name names, he did point to specific problems that secular sources can illuminate. This list is an impressive one, including the mystery of God, the peace of creation, the summons to gratitude, the unity of faith and life, the disquiet of life, and the phenomenon of human solidarity (IV/3.1, 125).

In light of the Christian belief in resurrection, says Barth, it is impossible to conceive of God *not* speaking outside the church's own parochial sphere. In the resurrection the church perceives that the risen Christ belongs to all. And so secular parables are just what we would expect from a God who desires to communicate grace through human witnesses. Of necessity, declares Barth, this divine capacity must extend outside the isolated sphere of the church (IV/3.1, 117–18).

Once again in IV/3.1, Barth resorted to the metaphor of the "center" to explain his meaning. The Word of God, he said, remains the criterion by which the truth of "secular parables" must be judged. The Word of God constitutes the truth both of the "center" of the circle and of the whole "periphery." "Center" and "periphery" dwell in a mutual coinherence of parts within a greater whole.

What if we were to integrate what Barth says about center and periphery in IV/3.1 with his earlier metaphor of the wagon wheel from the Romans commentary and from *CD* I/2? Then it would seem that the term "periphery" from IV/3.1 refers not to the "inner" periphery of the church's own proclamation but to the open-ended "outer" periphery, the undefined rim of the wagon wheel. On this reading, the open-ended "rim," which Barth had made clear was not to be closed up, includes "secular parables" too as part of the overall divine self-witness.

This calls into question the idea that Barth permitted nothing other than an "intratextual" or narrowly confessional approach to theology.[20] Perhaps most remarkable of all, even though secular parables are subordinate to the Word of God, which is their criterion of truth, they bear the same capacity (or incapacity) to speak truth as do explicitly Christian utterances. As with his view of any good Christian affirmation about God, Barth asserted that secular parables, if they be genuine, must speak about who God is in the "entirety" and not just in a way that is partial and obscure. Like true Christian utterance, secular parables do not express merely a portion of truth, but "they express the one and total truth from a particular angle" (IV/3.1, 123).

This brings us back to an earlier question. How can we square Barth's claim that God is never known in part but "only in the entirety or not at all" with his further claim that a plurality of different and seemingly "partial" perspectives, even some (we now learn) that are non-Christian, combine to form a composite portrait of who God is? What can it possibly mean, after all, to know God "in the entirety"? And how can such a knowledge become real, on his view, until the final words about God have been uttered? The answer lies in an open-ended and eschatologically directed interpretation of the one act of God the Creator, Reconciler, Redeemer.

3

THE MYSTERY
OF THE TRIUNE GOD

[God] is not a transcendent being . . . From all eternity [God] has determined to turn to humanity.

Karl Barth, *CD*, II/2, 547

One of Barth's major reconstructive moves was to breathe new life into the classical doctrine of the triune God, the God who has determined to be "for" and "with" humanity in Jesus Christ by the power of God's own Spirit. His reinterpretation of classical trinitarian thought undoubtedly is one of Barth's most enduring theological legacies. What needs to be examined is whether his reconstruction of trinitarian doctrine does in fact pave the way for the kind of open-ended and multidimensional possibilities suggested in the preceding two chapters.

THE TRIUNE MYSTERY

In Barth's hands trinitarian theology is both traditional and innovative at the same time. Drawing its breath from the ancient tradition, Barth's trinitarian theology sets forth what we might call a structural view of divine triunity, offering a set of formal rules, a grammar, by which to define the identity of God.

If trinitarian theology is to make sense for a new generation, this very same grammar, though definitive in form, must be kept open-ended in content. By "open-ended" I mean both that the triune act of God is an ongoing event received in the mode of promise (I/2, 55) and that our concept of this God is in continual need of reconstruction. Even though a theologian may speak from Christian conviction about the reality of God, he or she is never in a position to speak exhaustively about this mystery. To the extent that God's redemptive work is not yet finished, there is always more about God to be disclosed and more about God to be said.

Therefore, we should receive Barth's threefold concept of God the Creator, Reconciler, and Redeemer as a set of *formal* categories that invites continual inquiry into their *material* significance. For example, the concept of "creation," formally speaking, is the belief that God made all things, including human beings, what they are. But the material shape of that belief must be constructed on a radically different basis today, for example, in the light of "Big Bang" cosmology, the theory of evolution, and the human genome, than it was in, say, the Middle Ages. Similarly, "reconciliation" and "redemption" can be seen as formal Christian claims that all estrangement—whether between God and humanity, between one human being and another, or between humanity and the created order itself—has been healed (reconciliation) and that human beings have the possibility of becoming all that they were meant to be (redemption). Yet the material implications of reconciliation and redemption, such as how to construe them in relation to the environment, to the political economy, to the threat of warfare and holocaust, or to genetic engineering, call for continual theological construction.

To keep our understanding of creation, reconciliation, and redemption open-ended is only fitting, since "statements about God's triunity cannot claim to be directly identical . . . with revelation itself" (I/1, 308, rev.). Nowhere explicitly taught in scripture, trinitarian theology is the fallible, imaginative construction of the church's theologians. As such, it is able to point only indirectly to the mystery of its object, the God who is "the ground without grounds" (I/1, 307–9). Since the concept of God's triunity is fallible, it must not be simply reasserted as a relic from the past but must continually be the subject of "criticism," (Kritik) "correction," (Korrektur) and "development" (Entwicklung) (KD, I/1, 328, CD, 311).

God as ultimate mystery, in short, cannot be fully comprehended or exhausted in the term "Trinity." Barth would never agree, for instance, with Karl Rahner that "the Trinity" is itself the mystery of salvation.[1] God is mystery, but the mystery pertains to God and not to any particular doctrine about God.

For centuries theologians reduced the mystery of God to abstractions, as though God were a solitary individual, a self-contained and all-sufficient being, existing primordially without change, contingency, or need of any kind. This is the "God" so often caricatured as an "old man with a beard," the "God" who dwells in dispassionate and inviolate distance from the world. To put it in a more philosophical vein, this "God" traditionally has been said to exist eternally without change (God is immutable) and without feeling of any kind (God is impassible). This philosophical construct of "God," despite its ancient pedigree, is difficult to square with the God of mercy and compassion confessed in ordinary Christian conviction. It is no wonder, then, that often such a purely theoretical "God" has failed to inspire faith or trust in the modern era—no wonder that a critically-minded atheism has said "no" to this overly abstract "God" of theism.

In contrast to these classical abstractions, Barth reconceived God as dynamic and relational in character. In doubtless one of his simplest and yet most breathtaking analytical insights, Barth proclaimed that God is one whose very being (or character) is expressed in act[2] (II/1, §28). To have one's being in act is what it means to be truly free. To act with integrity is what it means to be sovereign. By contrast, human action is often only an ambiguous indicator of the agent's character. A human being may perform good deeds from mixed motives. Or a human being may perform what she thinks is a good deed only to have it go awry.

Unlike human action, God's action is a reliable measure of who God is. This is necessary, argued Barth, in order to render the most basic tenets of Christian faith intelligible. If Christians believe that God acted personally and definitively in the human being, Jesus of Nazareth, then God's being or identity must be capable of reproducing itself in the life and act of another.

Note how this deduction follows an "if-then" form of reasoning.[3] *If* it is true that in Jesus Christ knowledge of God is real and possible—a conviction that cannot be proved but only presupposed—*then* we need to construct a way of conceiving God that makes sense of this conviction. Barth does not argue for this first-order principle but presupposes it. *If* one accepts the premise that God has been revealed in Jesus Christ, *then* a constructive, second-order explanatory statement must also be adopted: namely, God's being (which is eternal) must be able to express itself ever anew (in history) in God's act.[4] Or to put it the other way around, God *is* in God's historic revelation *as* God is in God's self-being eternally (II/1, §28). God reproduces God's being in the world *as* a history.

It might help to translate this rather abstract language of "being" into the language of character. Barth is saying that, although it is a mystery and a wonder, the very *character* of God has been replicated and displayed in the suffering character of this finite human being, Jesus of Nazareth. God is nothing other than gracious in Jesus Christ. Nor is there some different and ungracious divine figure lurking in the shadows. *God is as Jesus is; God acts as Jesus acts.*

In short, revelation is a disclosure or identification of God's very own character. To encounter an act of God is to encounter God's own identity as made known in time. In a rubric borrowed from Huldrych Zwingli but also reminiscent of Hegel, Barth declared that "God is known only through God."[5] This means that only God is in a position to identify who God really is. If God is known only through God, Barth's reasoning continues, this must mean that God is simultaneously the Who ("Father"), the What ("Son"), and the How ("Spirit") of God's own revelatory activity. Or to put it another way, God is the selfsame "Revealer," the "Revelation," and the "Being Revealed" in the work of salvation.

These reflections are examples of redescriptive, conceptual analysis. They state what must be the case conceptually for knowledge of God to occur experientially. They do not, in and of themselves, locate any particular experience or occasion in which such knowledge actually *has* occurred. When knowledge of God does occur it is because the first two movements—primordial ground and present encounter—have come to fruition in subjective effect. The "Who" and the "What" must come to expression in the "How."

Emphasizing the "act" of God, as Barth does, shifts the emphasis away from the so-called "immanent Trinity" and towards the so-called "economic Trinity." Theologians have sometimes drawn this immanent-economic distinction in overly sharp ways, so much so that one wonders whether the distinction obscures more than it illuminates. The "immanent Trinity" has referred to God in God's own self-being, while the "economic Trinity" spoke of God's relationship to humanity in the economy of salvation. Such a differentiation, however, runs the risk of dividing God up into two "Trinities."

Perhaps it would be better to give up speaking statically about "Trinity" altogether and speak more dynamically about the "triune" act of God. This emphasis on "act" suggests that triunity is better addressed in adverbial than in nominal terms. Triunity, that is to say, signifies a way of modifying a verb. Instead of an abstract, reified "Trinity," Barth often spoke of God's *Dreieinigkeit*, which means "triunity" or "threefoldness." It has more to do with the qualitative configuration of an act than with an abstract or static "thing." This does not mean there is no "subject" in the act of revelation. But only through the *act* of this subject in the economy of salvation can we learn who this subject—God—is. In other words, God is the acting "subject" of every sentence in the divine story. Only "in act" can the identity of this Subject be known. "In act" this particular Subject is always reliable and worth trusting.

Barth would hear nothing of Martin Luther's fear, for instance, that somehow God's own character, God's own inaccessible selfhood *ad intra*, would ever contradict God's gracious action toward human beings *ad extra*. For Barth reconciliation in Christ is a genuine historical enactment of who God really is. As Eberhard Jüngel puts it, there is a "correspondence" (*Entsprechung*) between the economic and immanent triunity, a correspondence, that is to say, between the way God is in self-being (*in se*) and the way God is for us (*pro nobis*).[6] God does not remain aloof from the world in a genteel and disinterested satiety, but God is actively at work in the world. To put it plainly, God "is not a transcendent being. From all eternity [God] has determined to turn to humanity" (II/2, 547).

This "turning" toward humanity is not something statically "present," but it is enacted in the dramatic unfolding of a story. It is a story of a God whose own life and character, although an unfathomable mystery, are confessed to have become embodied in the life and death of Jesus Christ. Even though God is "imperceptible and incomprehensible in . . . essence, yet [God is] perceptible and comprehensible in [God's] work (III/4, 24). Through this human embodiment, God stands in a suffering solidarity with all human brokenness. This remarkable story, we must hasten to add, is not yet consummated but is still working itself out toward a distant finale. Through the efficacy of the Spirit, God's story is still being enacted in the power of the risen Christ.

This story is not simply a "narrative" that makes no claims beyond its own community; rather, it is (in the very sense given this word by Lyotard) a "metanarrative" that speaks of a divine drama enacted with the whole human race.[7] Yet it is a metanarrative about one whose identity remains veiled—it is a mystery—even in its unveiling. We can understand the entire Barthian project as one of thinking through this "identity" as triune mystery.

By substituting the word "identification" for the word "revelation," one will travel a great distance in understanding what Barth means by the revelatory event.[8] When Christians say that God was in Christ reconciling the world (2 Cor. 5:19a), they mean that an act of reconciliation was the unique way God's identity has been disclosed in the world. Until we can speak with some conviction about God's identity, until we know who or what we are talking about when we say "God," all the collateral questions—including all our menacing doubts over whether there even is a God—remain relatively hypothetical and unimportant.[9] As John Calvin put it, whether a "god" exists (*quid sit Deus*) is not nearly as important a question as what *sort* of God exists (*qualis sit Deus*). What is the character of this God? Is God beneficent or maleficent, interested in us or disinterested? What counts in answering these questions, said Calvin, is not abstract speculation into God's "essence" but sure and faithful knowledge of God's grace.[10] Similarly, in Barth's perspective, God is not just any old "god" but the incomparably unique God who has demonstrated solidarity "with" and "for" humanity in the life and work of Jesus Christ through the power of the Holy Spirit. The concept of "triunity" furnishes a shorthand interpretation of who Christians confess this God to be (I/1, 311).

There is more to speaking this identity than describing a tradition or exegeting a text. For Barth, "it is one thing to take one's bearings from the fathers," but quite another thing "to try as a matter of principle to think and speak according to their judgments and confessions . . . Nobody should maintain that he has learned to do this from me" (III/4, xiii). To be sure, much of Barth's theology is taken up with the analysis of Christian concepts. Still, there is something more to understanding the triune mystery than exegeting the Bible or repristinating the tradition. Precisely because the Christian story is about the disclosure of God's very own identity, it is not simply a "given" to be possessed or described.[11] Instead it is an unfolding event (*Ereignis*), a dramatic "giving" that has a beginning (God is our Creator), a middle (God is our Reconciler), and an end towards which it is still moving (God is our Redeemer).

God's activity in the world as Creator, Reconciler, Redeemer is the one work of the one God. It is often said that Barth is more Augustinian and Western in the way he accents the unity of God.[12] Western trinitarianism in its emphasis on divine unity is usually assumed to differ from Eastern

trinitarianism's preoccupation with God's threeness. Yet one must remember that the East too thought in terms of one dynamic power of God
(ἐνέργεια), an energy that is focused in one Will and one unfolding Activity. For the East, the threeness of God is unified in "perichoresis," meaning that there is a mutually implicating relationality and essential unity inhering among the three modes of God's being. Even in the East, therefore,
God is not three centers of willing, but everything God does is the work
of the one God whose one will and work are enacted in the historical
drama of "Father, Son, and Holy Spirit."[13]

Similarly, Barth did not understand the traditional language of God as
"Father, Son, and Holy Spirit" to indicate three subjectivities differentiated
in a literal sense. For that matter, he considered the biblical terms "Father,"
"Son," and "Spirit" themselves to be insufficient to grasp the divine mystery in all its fullness. "We do not know what we are saying when we call
God 'Father' and 'Son'" (I/1, 433). "We do not know what we are saying
when we call Jesus Christ the eternal Word of God" (I/1, 436). Why? Because the terms "Son" or "Word" are not made "only or even primarily" in
reference to Jesus of Nazareth in his capacity as a human being like us, but
in reference to God, who is not like us. God is one acting subject who acts
according to a threefold economy that is still unfolding in our midst.

For this reason Barth refused to heed Augustine's use of psychological
analogies to understand God's triunity. Augustine was mistaken to posit
"vestiges" of the "Trinity" located within the human psychological makeup
(e.g., memory, understanding, will), or otherwise present in history, culture, or nature (I/1, §8.3). Since God is dynamically and actively "becoming" in the world, the triune reality of God is like a rock against which all
our analogies fall apart (I/1, 113). What the divine Spirit makes visible in
Jesus Christ is not a static or reified "thing" but a dynamic movement, the
implications of which are forever needing to be plumbed.

Similarly, Barth eschewed the traditional term "persons" for "Father,"
"Son," and "Spirit." If each of the three modalities of divine action were
a discrete "person" or "personality" with a distinct center of consciousness, then we would be left with tritheism—three gods. Instead Barth
preferred to speak of God subsisting in three dynamic "modes of being,"
or *Seinsweise,* his German translation of the ancient Cappadocian term
τρόπος ὑπάρξεως. For Barth this terminology meant that God is not three
divine "I's" but a single "I" acting according to a threefold structure (I/1,
353–68).

This structural view of God's triunity has been severely criticized in recent years by those who find fault with Western trinitarianism in general
and who favor a so-called "social" model. Emphasizing the distribution of
God in three "persons," the social model tends to view God as a society or
communion of three divine co-equals. God is said to be three "persons" in

one divine essence. Social trinitarians argue that the Western Augustinian view followed by Barth emphasized divine unity to the detriment of relationality.

For example, one of the best-known advocates of social trinitarianism, Jürgen Moltmann, who is an heir of Barth's theology, embraces the explicit view that his mentor rejected: he conceives the plurality of God as three individual persons with three individual personalities or centers of consciousness. There are three subjects, three "I's" who dwell in a society or communion with one another.[14] Moltmann is joined, among others, by Robert W. Jenson who, while agreeing with Barth that God is best conceived as a single, dynamic being-in-action, differs from Barth in attributing to that one divine action three individual "identities." God is identical with what happens in Jesus Christ; identical with what happens when human beings are united to Christ in the Spirit; and identical with the eternal will of the one who is moving all things toward consummate glory.[15]

Social trinitarians charge that by speaking of God in the language of three "modalities," Barth conceived God according to the monolithic Enlightenment ideal of the autonomous agent writ large.[16] To envision God as a "self-imparting" agent, argues Moltmann, fails to acknowledge the relational language of the New Testament about God giving up the Son (Rom. 8:22; Gal. 2:20) and bequeathing to us the Spirit (John 20:21f.; Acts 2). The upshot for Moltmann is that Barth, like Schleiermacher, succumbed to the heresy of "modalism," or "Sabellianism." According to this view, the distinctions in God were only temporary and nonessential, having no permanence in God's eternal being. In modalism God is a singular and absolute monarch whose being is only incidently related to God's triune act.

This charge of modalism is a serious one, because it threatens to undo Barth's most basic principle: the being-in-act of God. But this charge does not do justice to three of the rudimentary premises that make Barth's theology what it is. First, Barth always regarded God's revelation as a self-imparting of God's own being or character. Revelation in Jesus Christ *is* the giving of God's own reality, albeit a giving in the mode of promise. Hence this revealing cannot be construed as the parceling out of bits and pieces of information *about* God. God cannot be broken up into "various quanta of deity" (I/1, 393). This appertains directly to the second point, that for Barth the being of God itself is never subject to division, contrast, or confusion. With Augustine he affirms that the outward works of the triune God cannot be divided (*opera trinitatis ad extra sunt indivisa*). Third, the New Testament language Moltmann cites must be understood analogically and not literally. It is one thing to speak of God as personal or as relational and quite another thing to say that God "is" three persons in relationship. God is not literally either one person or three. One can speak of God as personal without intending to reify God as though God were a finite individual, and still less a group of individuals.[17] We may speak of God as the inherently personal creator of the world, not because God is "a person" like us but because God is *more* than a person, the eternal and non-contingent source of personhood.

Barth's point is that the one God can have only one identity. And this identity is a disposition to be "for" human beings. This "structural" understanding of how God enacts God's life in human history unfolds according to the grand drama of creation, reconciliation, and redemption. In this triadic structure God is self-identically the ground, the encounter, and also the effect of God's relationship with human beings. We may plot this as shown in figure 3.1.

Examples of this threefold structure run throughout the *CD* and form the basis for what in later chapters I shall call the "triadic" structure of Christian experience. That God's triunity relates to human experience is of paramount importance. God is both the acting subject that enables humanity's redemptive experience and the very act itself. God is both the subject and predicate of God's own revelatory deed. One can hardly imagine a more radical way of formulating this than Barth's: God *is* what God achieves in human beings (*KD*, I/1, 315, *CD*, 299).

For example, in II/1 Barth declared (alluding to Luther) that God is the one whom human beings must fear above all things because they are permitted to love God above all things. The permission to love God follows the threefold pattern. It consists in (a) God being worthy of our love (prevenient ground); (b) God making God's identity known (encounter itself); and (c) God creating within human beings in the first place the possibility, willingness, and readiness to embrace this knowledge (emerging, subjective effect). Similarly, the obligation to fear God entails: (a) God's meriting our fear; (b) the fearful encounter itself; and (c) the effective opening of our eyes and ears to God (II/1, 33, 34).

Another example arose in Barth's discussion of how human knowledge of God is always a mediated knowledge. Human beings can never have an immediate "experience of God" but only an "experience of [God's] work and sign" (II/1, 57). In other words, an experience of God is always at the same time an experience of something else.[18] Hence knowledge of God arises only in "signs" and through "fragments" in which (a) God permits the humanity of Jesus to serve as a sacramental gesture of who God is (prevenient ground); (b) there is an encounter creating a reciprocal response in human beings (present encounter); and (c) God's identity is unfolded, as already noted in chapter two, through a diversity of cognitions that is progressing throughout human history (emerging, subjective effect) (II/1, 53–62). The same triune structure, to cite yet one more exam-

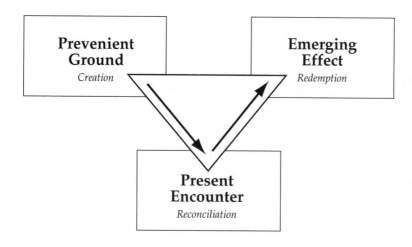

FIGURE 3.1

ple, governs human readiness to receive the ready grace of God. Such readiness rests on a human need (prevenient ground), on the knowledge of that need (encounter), and on a willingness to embrace God's grace (emerging, subjective effect) (II/1, 130).

Through this threefold structure of primordial beginning, existential encounter, and anticipated effect, God is "for" human beings, "with" human beings, and at work "in" and "among" human beings. Thus, trinitarian theology signals a threefold structure to all God's dealings with human beings. God is concurrently the prevenient ground ("Father"), the encounter itself ("Son"), and the subjective effect or efficacy ("Holy Spirit") of humanity's knowledge of God. God's act occurs in the threefold modes of "freedom" (the "Father"), a particular historical "form" (the "Son"), and "historicity" itself (the "Spirit")—all in one. Even though God abides apart from us (*extra nos*), God is nonetheless "for" us and "with" us in Jesus Christ (*pro nobis*), and is also at work "in" us and "among" us by the power of the Holy Spirit (*in nobis*).[19] In short, God is humanity's Creator, Reconciler, Redeemer.

Barth derived God's triune identity as an interpolation of the Christian "root" belief that in Jesus Christ "God reveals himself as Lord" (I/1, §9). The term "Lord" is a synonym for "sovereign." The divine sovereignty Barth envisioned is not the erratic despotism, capriciousness, or arbitrary power of a tyrant, for God's power must be measured by God's own self-identity in Jesus Christ. Mere arbitrary power would be demonic. What then does it mean to speak of a sovereign God in relationship to the world?

Barth aimed at underscoring God's dynamic relationship with the world (*ad extra*) while at the same time upholding God's own unique integrity (*ad intra*). By "integrity" I refer to God's own preeminence and stature. The tradition spoke of this as the "aseity" of God. It means that God is already self-contained and eternally complete in deity before creating the world. God did not "need" to create the cosmos or humanity in order to be God. The very concept of "creation" itself intimates such a prior, divine independence and actuality vis à vis the world.

Divine "integrity" must be conceived so as also to affirm divine "relationality." We may think of "relationality" as God's intrinsic desire to be gracious to the other, God's determination not to be God without us. God is not a self-enclosed monad but a God who is able to render God's being in reference to the "other" in act.

The symmetry between integrity and relationality is best observed in Barth's treatment of the divine perfections of "love" and "freedom" (II/1, §§29–31). Barth spoke of "perfections" rather than "attributes" to avoid the nominalist idea that these are traits one merely attributes to God arbitrarily. Rather, the "perfections" of God *are* God. In holding the perfections of love and freedom (or what I am calling integrity and relationality) together, Barth treated the perfections of the divine loving first, weaving them together in three pairings: grace and holiness, mercy and righteousness, and patience and wisdom. Both members within the three pairs are said to manifest the divine love, but the second member of each pairing manifests love in a way that points backwards toward the divine freedom. Thus love as "grace," "mercy," and "patience" embraces freedom as "holiness," "righteousness," and "wisdom" (see figure 3.2).

Although Barth does not make this explicit, the three pairings correspond to the trinitarian pattern of God's relationship with the world. The organization moves from primordial ground, to gracious encounter, to consummate effect. Thus the first set of perfections, "grace" and "holiness," bespeak God as the one who is the prevenient ground of all that is. "Grace" Barth defines as God's primordial turning toward the creature in condescension to establish fellowship. Since grace is enacted from a standpoint of "condescension," it is only the Creator God and not the creature who is capable of grace. In this very act of being gracious, God retains sovereignty over God's grace and thus is "holy." In the relationality confirmed in the fellowship of "grace," in other words, God still affirms God's own freedom and integrity by remaining "holy."

Similarly, the perfections of "mercy" and "righteousness" indicate the second aspect of the triune design, namely the reconciling work of

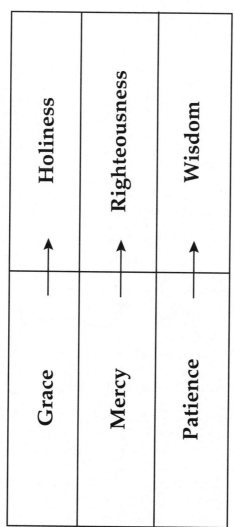

Perfections of the Divine Loving

LOVE   FREEDOM

Grace   →   Holiness

Mercy   →   Righteousness

Patience   →   Wisdom

Creation = Ground

Reconciliation = Encounter

Redemption = Effect

FIGURE 3.2

divine-human encounter in Jesus Christ, who is the "Son." "Mercy" is God's readiness, out of the depths of God's being, to share in sympathy the creature's distress. Like the incarnation itself, mercy is an "effectual participation" in human suffering. Significantly for this triadic interpretation, what Barth writes here concerning mercy anticipates the doctrine of reconciliation in volume four, emphasizing Jesus Christ as the "Son" and "Judge" who himself was judged in humanity's place. In a quiet whisper buried deep within an excursus, Barth dismissed several centuries' worth of traditional theology by claiming that in Jesus Christ the God of mercy "can feel and be affected"—this God "is not impassible" (II/1, 370–71). God is not impassible, for through the humanity of Jesus Christ God has determined to suffer with God's creatures. Still, God's suffering mercy remains free. It is "a self-chosen necessity" in which God's "mercy" is always displayed as "righteous"—a free and moral act that is entirely worthy of God.

The third pair of perfections of the divine loving, "patience" and "wisdom," is more indicative of the redemptive work of the Spirit, which is to enable human beings to realize their freedom for obedience (II/2, 409). In "patience" God gives God's creatures space and time, accompanying and sustaining them and allowing them to realize their own freedom. Now it may seem foolhardy for God to exercise "patience" in a world wracked by so much evil. Yet Christian faith embraces the belief that God's "patient" bearing with the world is nonetheless "wise." God is not the slave of God's "patience," for God's loving "patience" is also a freely chosen divine providence.

The perfections of divine freedom are also arranged so that one item in each pair gestures backward toward the divine love. The perfections are, yet again, an example of analyzing what must be the case conceptually to render the church's confession meaningful (see figure 3.3).

"Unity" and "omnipresence," the perfections of the primordial Creator, proclaim the uniqueness and simplicity of God. God is incomparably and undividedly who God is. But the freedom of God's unity is not detached from creation, for God is also "omnipresent" in love. Omnipresence means there is both "remoteness" and "proximity" in the divine life. This, in turn, undercuts both an abstract dualism that would too sharply separate God from the world and an equally abstract monism that would deny the world its own integrity. God is able to strike a togetherness with creatures, though always a "togetherness at a distance." Without this ability to be both freely remote and yet lovingly proximate, there could be no creation of the world and no incarnation in Jesus Christ.

By the same token, God's "constancy" and "omnipotence," the second set of perfections, indicate that God can do a "new thing" in the reconciling work of Jesus Christ and still be God. Even in assuming the humanity

Perfections of Divine Freedom

FREEDOM	LOVE
Unity $\longrightarrow$	Omnipresence
Constancy $\longrightarrow$	Omnipotence
Eternity $\longrightarrow$	Glory

Creation = Ground

Reconciliation
= Encounter

Redemption = Effect

FIGURE 3.3

of Jesus, God is able to remain wholly and reliably who God is. Barth can speak of God's ability to remain "always the same in every change" as a "holy mutability" (II/1, 496). God's "constancy" is not a static or impotent unchangeableness, because God is always able to exercise new possibilities of redemption. Thus God is also "omnipotent," or "all-powerful" in the sense of having all the power that is true power, namely, the power to act in ways that are conciliatory and redeeming. In contrast to the brand of orthodoxy that placed omnipotence at the head of God's attributes and construed omnipotence as God's arbitrary ability to do anything God wished, Barth placed omnipotence deep into his presentation and reconstrued it as a power that works in the midst of suffering. God is not "omnipotent" if that means having all the power there is. For God has vested power in God's creatures, although it is a power that bears fruit only if it aligns itself with the redemptive power of God. Absolute power, in other words, would be evil per se.

The divine perfections culminate with the third pairing of freedom, "eternity" and "glory." Like "patience" and "wisdom," these are the perfections of the divine freedom that point to the redemptive direction toward which the Holy Spirit is moving all things. Just as in "patience" and "wisdom" God gives the creature space and time, so in "eternity" and "glory" God is the beginning, succession, and consummation of all things. "Eternity," which can be conceived either as God's pure duration or as simultaneity, is the inward efficacy of God that enables God to be outwardly "for us" in time as Creator, Reconciler, and Redeemer. "Glory," on the other hand, reminds us that God's freedom is also love, for God's "glory" is to be made manifest to God's creatures. "Glory" is like a light that is its own source, that reaches out, that is self-identical in its manifestation, and that is recognized and acknowledged by creatures in gratitude (see figure 3.4).

If we accept that God is making the divine identity known in the world through this grand gesture that begins in "grace" and culminates in "glory," the question remains: how is it possible to absorb this identity at a single glance? Is it possible to discover the character of another all at once? This was the question, it will be recalled, with which we concluded the previous chapter. On the one hand, Barth argued that we can only know God's character in the "entirety" or else not at all. On the other hand, this divine self-identification occurs and is still occurring through a divine action that is stretched out over a past, present, and future—it takes time for us to know who God is. God has created us, is reconciling us, and is moving us toward redemption. In all three aspects of this unfolding drama, we are continually learning more of who God is.

How do we hold together the need to know God reliably today and the need to continue to learn about God tomorrow? The answer to this question lies in Barth's doctrine of election.

	PERFECTIONS OF DIVINE LOVE	PERFECTIONS OF DIVINE FREEDOM
Father	Love ⟶ Freedom	Freedom ⟶ Love
Son	Grace ⟶ Holiness	Unity ⟶ Omnipresence
	Mercy ⟶ Righteousness	Constancy ⟶ Omnipotence
Spirit	Patience ⟶ Wisdom	Eternity ⟶ Glory

FIGURE 3.4

THE MYSTERY OF ELECTION

The topic of election brings us to another side of Barth's trinitarian reflection, a side that is more synthetic in quality. By means of a formal and highly conceptual mode of analysis Barth could spin out hundreds of paragraphs of conceptual analysis before uttering a single declaration of ostensive content. When he did finally get to the "heart of the matter" (*zur Sache*), it was usually a statement about the divine election of grace in Jesus Christ.

Barth's doctrine of election helps us to find a way past one of the pivotal impasses in contemporary trinitarian thinking, namely whether trinitarian theology should be derived descriptively or constructively. Is the appropriate trinitarian path that of the analytical, rational description of Christian concepts? Or does theology need to strive for a more concrete synthesis rooted in the diversity of Christian experience?[20] Is triunity a particular description of God's gracious identity in Jesus Christ as witnessed to in scripture? Or does triunity represent a symbol that is constructively connected to other beliefs we hold about the nature of the world?

From the standpoint of the first approach—conceptual redescription—the crucial task of the mind is to configure one's thinking according to the biblical pattern of God's action in Christ by the power of the Spirit. It is "crucial" in the literal sense that it pertains to what happened regarding Jesus on the *cross*—God's triunity is visible in God's solidarity in the Spirit with the suffering Jesus. It is crucial, too, in that it marks a "crossroads" of decision between rival hypotheses about God. This approach rules out speculation into God's "essence" and seeks instead to examine the particular claims of the Christian gospel on their own terms. The theologian formulates an analysis of the threefold way God encounters humanity as a God of grace in Jesus Christ. Trinitarian doctrine, on this view, tries to state an organizing, conceptual framework by which the cruciform language of the gospel faith can be understood. It generates a "grammar" for speaking of the divine identity.

Nevertheless, there is more to Barth's approach than the strictly descriptive and confessional. Formal analysis is not enough. One must also arrive at the thing itself, which for Barth was summed up in election. Barth defined election as the "very center" of the divine self-revelation. Election is the veritable "sum of the gospel." "If there is any mystery of God . . . then this is it" (II/2, 159). The doctrine of election moves Barth's theology beyond the analytical and toward the synthetic.

Barth believed the doctrine of election in its traditional form needed a complete overhaul. "As I let the Bible itself speak to me" on this issue of divine election, "I was driven irresistibly to reconstruction (*die Neuerung*)

(*KD*, II/2, vii, *CD*, x). This reconstruction is summed up in the affirmation that, in Jesus Christ by the Spirit's power, God is fundamentally "for" human beings. The divine "for" is comprehensive in its scope. *Everyone* is elected to be reconciled with God in Jesus Christ, although whether everyone will fully *realize* her or his election is another matter. If the doctrine of election meant, as it did for John Calvin and so many of his heirs, a "double predestination," namely a divine determination of some people for salvation and others for rejection, then it was ill-conceived and even hideous. Barth considered God to be a humane God—a God who is committed to humanity and to humanity's cause.[21] The most devastating flaw in the Calvinistic doctrine of predestination, according to Barth, is that it violates our deepest humanistic commitments—says Barth, we simply cannot believe it (II/2, 161).

In stark contrast to Calvin's "double determination" of human beings to heaven and to hell, Barth's doctrine of election contemplates a "determination" (*Bestimmung*) of a quite different sort. It is not, in the first instance, a determination about the eternal fate of God's creatures but it is God's own *self*-determination (*Selbstbestimmung*). To be "self-determined" is to act freely and without coercion. In election, God acts in conformity to God's character; God is "determined" to be who God really is. Like the commander of a peacekeeping force who vows not to abandon a city until all its inhabitants are safely out of danger, God has determined, in grace, to take up humanity's fledgling cause. To put it another way, God is gracious enough *not* to be God without humanity. God has claimed a stake in humanity's future, for election is God's primordial resolution to be "for" human beings no matter what the cost.

The use of the word "determination" (*Bestimmung*) rather than "choice" regarding God's election is significant. The verb *bestimmen* can mean to fix, designate, settle, appoint, establish. The noun *Bestimmung* means both determination and destiny. In the latter sense it includes one's sense of purpose or vocation. It can include both a determination of something at the beginning or the resulting effect that becomes visible at the end. Election as "determination" embraces both. It is an eternal determination at the beginning that reaches a concrete result within human history.

At stake in the distinction between "determination" and "choice" is the way one construes what it means to be authentically free. Often we assume that true freedom means freedom to choose x or y, what philosophers call the freedom of deliberation, or contrary choice. Freedom for Barth, however, means something altogether different. To be mired in deliberating among contrary choices is not freedom at all but bondage.

For example, imagine that I happen to see your wallet fall out of your pocket, and I stoop to pick it up. Standing there with the wallet in my hand, I start to deliberate whether to return it to you or to keep it for myself. Such deliberation and choosing would not present an instance of "freedom" but an illustration of conflictedness, moral confusion, and a propensity to self-aggrandizement. If on the other hand, I pick up the wallet and do the right thing, returning it to you without an instant's hesitation, this is an example of what it means to be free. In the second case, rather than an uncertain deliberation and choice, I am simply "determined" to act in accordance with what I know to be the right and the good.

Similarly, God does not deliberate and then choose to be gracious, but God "determines" to be the gracious one God already is. This determination is not simply an abstract decision but a concrete act that manifests itself in history. Election is not an arbitrary "decision" but a concrete deed.

The affirmation of the "concrete" and rejection of the "abstract" is pivotal to Barth's theology. "To abstract" is to draw or pull something away from something else. To view something abstractly is to view it in disconnection from other things that are properly a part of it. For example, to define a person as a "taxpayer" or a "criminal" is to view her in abstraction from all the other relationships that make her the person she is. It is to treat her not as a human being but as a function of a particular way of thinking. How can I be "for" someone when I have reduced them to such an abstraction?

Or to give an example drawn from the history of doctrine, the Pelagian or Arminian theologian is thinking abstractly when he argues that persons should make autonomous, "neutral," and arm's length decisions for or against the ways of God. Barth would say this is simply nonsense. No one can be "neutral" about God or about one's neighbor and then decide yes or no. One is either "for" them already or one is not. To view a thing abstractly, then, is to view it apart from what it really is in the whole of its relationships. To view something "concretely," on the other hand, is to see it in connection to everything else that makes it what it is.

Perhaps another illustration would be helpful. It is possible to "freeze-frame" a motion picture and view it one image at a time. Each individual frame has its own integrity and may be viewed in isolation; but no frame is fully intelligible apart from running the movie from beginning to end. Individual frames are considered "concretely," that is to say, only in their relation to the movie as a whole. Similarly, an individual person or isolated event, from Barth's point of view, needs to be seen in its "actuality." It is considered "concretely" *only* when it is viewed in dynamic relationship to the drama of salvation in all its comprehensiveness as creation, reconciliation, and redemption.

In keeping with this relational viewpoint, Barth denied that it is possible to conceive of a human being "in itself" or even of deity or godhead "in itself" (*Gottheit an sich*) (*KD*, II/2, 123, *CD*, 115). "There is no such thing as godhead in itself. Godhead is always the godhead of the Father, Son, and Holy Spirit" (II/2, 115). Nor is God a remote God in and for God's own self (*für sich und als solches*). God is only who God is in the determination to be "for" humanity in Jesus Christ. Or to put it another way, there is a link between what a reality is "in itself" and what it is "for us." What this link means in the case of God is that God's relationship to humanity in Jesus Christ is irrevocable. Apart from Jesus Christ and apart from the covenant people of God, "God would be a different, an alien God" (II/2, 7). There is no will of God different from the divine will made manifest in Jesus Christ. In language similar to Hegel, Barth declared that God's own character "in itself" is defined by who God is "for us."

Barth's exegetical basis for this understanding of election was Eph. 1:4, which says that people are elected *in* Jesus Christ. The figure of Jesus is the hinge upon which election turns, both ontically and noetically. Noetically, it is in Christ that one learns of this grace. Ontically, it is in Jesus Christ that God accomplishes this grace. Jesus Christ is the joint where the "electing God" and the "elected human being" are sealed in their togetherness (II/2, §33.1, 103).

First let us consider Jesus Christ as the "electing God." This does not mean—note carefully—that the human being Jesus of Nazareth is somehow equated with God per se. Rather, Jesus is the electing God in that by his own human *action* he is the sole object of the divine good pleasure, the "will of God in action" (II/2, 104). There is no will of God different from the will of Jesus Christ. In the life of Jesus, there is a divine and human togetherness-in-act. On the one hand, Jesus was determined to be truly human, meaning that he was truly obedient to God. On the other hand, God was determined to be truly God, determined to be true to God's own gracious character. More will be said about this uniqueness and divinity of Jesus in chapter five.

Jesus is also, in the second place, the "elected human being" (II/2, 116). Jesus is the one who is well-pleasing in God's sight. Yet this election is not an elevation to a peculiar status but an appointment to a peculiar suffering. There is both a luminous "yes" and an ominous "no" occurring in election. In election God utters a "yes" to humanity—all human beings are elect in Jesus Christ, even though not all human beings happen to live out their election. Nevertheless, in election God also utters a "no." God says "no" to the evil inherent in our fragile human existence. But even more remarkably, God also chooses to bear the brunt of that "no," absorbing its blows within God's very own being. Let us consider each of these, the "no" and the "yes" in its turn.

First, regarding the negative side—the "no"—God in electing human beings had to surrender something of God's own power and impassibility. The God who (according to traditional Christian confession) is impervious to evil elected to become passible—not only affected by but also subject to evil (II/2, 163). Note the peculiarity of this "had to." How can we speak of such a necessity being imposed on God? Is not God beyond all necessity? Barth resolves this by speaking of God's "self-chosen" necessity. But this still presents a conundrum. If it is self-chosen, then how can it truly be a "necessity"?

This is another place where God's "integrity" and "relationality" must be held in careful balance. For God to be "for" human beings means that God engages in a self-limitation to create them and place them in a world of freedom.[22] Yet this injects an element of contingency into the cosmos, together with the possibility (though not, in Barth's view, the necessity) of evil. By allowing this contingency, God no longer retained all the power there is—creation means the empowerment of God's creatures as well. By allowing this element of freedom and contingency in the cosmos, God not only empowered God's creatures but God put God's own honor at risk. "What a risk God ran when [God] willed to take up the cause of created humanity even in [God's] original righteousness, when [God] constituted and ordained [God's own commitment] to solidarity with human beings!" (II/2, 163–64, rev.). The honor of God was placed into question by the emergence of this impossible possibility of evil. The "had to" of creation, in its turn, made necessary a different sort of "had to": the "had to" of God's reconciling action in Jesus Christ.

Now, by virtue of election, God has joined God's own glory into the advancement of humanity's cause. But most astonishing of all, by saying "yes" to humanity, God in Jesus Christ has allowed human beings to point their own accusing fingers at the electing God and to declare God guilty of humanity's own self-contradictoriness. As Barth puts it rather homiletically, "Judas who betrays, [God] elects as an apostle. The sentence of Pilate [God] elects as a revelation of [God's] judgment on the world. [God] elects the cross of Golgotha as [God's] royal throne. [God] elects the tomb in the garden as the scene of [God's] being as the living God" (II/2, 165).

In the end, by making common cause with the sufferings of this particular Galilean peasant, Jesus of Nazareth, God adopted the remarkable strategy of reconciling and redeeming human beings through a life that was not merely oppressed by evil but actually overcome by it (II/2, 163). God sought to surmount the problem of evil by submitting to its most forceful blow: the slaughter of one of the innocents.[23]

How to think through the problem of evil thus became, understandably, a major component of Barth's overall theological vision. As we shall see in the next chapter, Barth defined evil as that to which God says "no." But what becomes visible in election, astonishingly, is that God has already redirected this "no" from the very beginning, allowing the indictment, in the person of Jesus Christ, to be laid at God's own feet.

There is also a second, positive side of election—God's "yes" to humanity. Election tells us that God was not satisfied to remain God without God's creatures. Instead God determined in a primordial way to reach out to and to allow the existence of the "other." With this act, God would no longer be God apart from this "other." Both for God and for human beings, this act carried radical consequences. For God, this meant an overflowing of the divine glory outward, so to speak, in a communication of the divine being toward the other. For humanity, it meant receiving the call to freedom, the call to partake in a share of God's own glory. Being invested with this possibility of contingent freedom meant that humanity was "foreordained to danger and trouble" (II/2, 169). God's great gamble in this situation of disturbance and chaos was the mission of Jesus Christ to overcome evil by achieving true humanity.

To some this talk of God's eternal risk-taking may seem an overly mythopoeic way of speaking. Be that as it may, Barth's doctrine of election is a way of summing up the dramatic two-way movement at the heart of Christian proclamation—the faithfulness of the electing God, and the faithful response of Jesus as the elected human being. The strict Calvinists were not wrong to make predestination "double"; but they were utterly wrong about what the twofold movement meant. It encompassed, first, a predestination of God to be gracious and, second, a predestination of humanity to be chosen and redeemed. Election means grace. It means that God is "for" humanity and, as we shall see in the next chapter, that human beings should be "for" one another.

To know God in the "entirety," to return to our earlier question, is to know the truth of this divine election of grace. It is to know that God is "for" human beings. According to Barth, this election is accomplished and can only be known in reference to the "center" which is Jesus Christ. Recall, however, from the previous two chapters that this "center" itself is known only from the vantage point of the "periphery." And the periphery includes a plurality of perceptions spread out over time. Moreover, that periphery, as stated in IV/3, includes non-Christian utterances as well, utterances that are truly able to convey who God is. How do we make sense of this?

The only way to make sense of it, I submit, is to see that the metaphor of "center" and "periphery" unlocks a more open-ended and synthetic way of understanding God's triune "yes" in election. To know God in the "entirety" is to know God in the "concrete" and not in the "abstract." To know God's "yes" is to know God's character as a character of grace—that is what it means to know God in the "entirety." One may know this grace and still not know all there is to know about this grace. Not unlike a child who knows the love of the parent but has not yet experienced every aspect of that love, so one may know God truly but still need to know more about God.

This knowing "more" about God is the responsibility of Christians, but it is not limited to Christians. In this christocentric rethinking of election, the "name" of Jesus Christ signifies God's "yes," and the obedience of Jesus Christ is this divine "yes" enacted in history. Yet the logic of Barth's treatment of "center" and "periphery" includes the possibility that even non-Christian utterance can embrace and proclaim the truth about this "yes." This means that, even with no explicit mention of Jesus of Nazareth at all, a non-Christian can utter true insights concerning this "yes" from the "periphery." If we take the metaphor of "center" and "periphery" seriously, there must be myriad ways of saying who God is in Jesus Christ no one of which can exhaust the mystery of who Jesus Christ is as God.

The election of God is also the command of God (II/2, §36). And obedience to this command requires a broad-ranging inquiry into what God is doing in the world. The ethics of the divine command is of decisive significance in Barth's theology, as will be explored in more depth in chapter seven. If election is the divine determination, "I will be your God", ethics is the completion of the circle, "You will be my people." God's election to be "for" humanity becomes actual on humanity's side only to the extent that humanity, in turn, makes its own election to be "for" God. To be complete, election requires not only God's action but humanity's action as well. "God is what God achieves in human beings."

It has seldom been noticed that regarding ethics, Barth in volume II/2 calls for an expansive and unobstructed scrutiny of human existence in the round. Contrary to stereotype, Barth advises the theologian to cast a wide net in discovering what one ought to do. Theology must be "absolutely open" to all that it can learn from human ethical inquiry generically, no matter what the source (II/2, 535). In ethics Barth not only *permits* the possibility of non-ecclesial sources but positively *invites* them, declaring that sources outside the church are essential for the pursuit of the theologian's task. Theological ethics is an interrogation that establishes a continuous relationship with "the human problem as a whole" (II/2, 540–42). "Its starting point is that all ethical truth is enclosed in the command of the grace of God" (II/2, 527). As such, the ethical problem is a global human problem manifest in philosophy, politics, education, and so on. In keeping with this, there must be an open-endedness to ethical reflection.

The curious fact is that Barth himself engaged in precious little sifting of the sorts of wide-ranging data he proclaimed to be necessary for the ethical task. His reflections were meant to place the Christian in the position for ethical action, but that action itself, and the comprehensive inquiry that precedes it, remains the responsibility of each Christian believer.

To draw these thoughts to a conclusion, Barth's doctrine of election opens up a synthetic side to his otherwise strictly analytical approach. This synthetic possibility, I submit, is implicit in everything Barth wrote, though he himself did not bring it explicitly to fruition. The synthetic side invites an inquiry into the significance of God's "for" and God's "with" in the diverse contexts of human experience. No single vision is ever sufficient to convey the full extent of the mystery that confronts us in Jesus Christ by the power of the Spirit. In Jesus Christ the cloak of the divine trinitarian incognito is lifted. We know through Christ that God is "for us," even though the veil of the divine mystery remains. It remains hidden even *in* the Christ occurrence. And the meaning of that mystery, which has its own integrity apart from human history, is being made actual (*wirklich*) in relation to the whole of human history through "the activity of God as Creator, Reconciler, and Redeemer" (II/2, 5).

God's act of creation, reconciliation, and redemption requires of the theologian more than description and analysis; it must also lead to action. "I will be your God" anticipates the "synthesis" in human experience in which we respond, "We will be your people." This ethical response will be treated in Part 3, while the threefold pattern of creation, reconciliation, and redemption will be the subject of of Part 2.

PART TWO

THE MYSTERY OF GOD:
CREATOR, RECONCILER, REDEEMER

Hidden in their being, both God and humanity are revealed . . . not in themselves, not directly . . . but in the Word of God in Jesus Christ. Without ceasing to be a mystery, they are an open mystery in Christ; imperceptible and incomprehensible in their essence, yet perceptible and comprehensible in their work.

Karl Barth, CD, III/4, 24

4

GOD "FOR" US

The work of the Son of God includes the work of the Father as its presupposition and the work of the Holy Spirit as its consequence. The first article is to a certain extent the source, the third article the goal of our path. But the second article is the Way upon which we find ourselves in faith. From that vantage point we may review the entire fullness of the acts of God.

Karl Barth, *Dogmatics in Outline*, 71

Amid the bombed-out ruins of the University of Bonn just months after the end of the Second World War, Karl Barth stood before a group of German students to deliver a summary of his mature theology. These lectures, which he had been invited to present by the institution from which he was summarily dismissed in 1934 for refusing to swear an oath to Adolf Hitler, are, unlike most of his corpus, a model of brevity. Entitled *Dogmatics in Outline*, the lectures are no substitute for the virtuoso performance of the *Church Dogmatics*, but they do provide occasional clues into the grand design of his larger work.

One such clue occurs in the pivotal chapter entitled "Jesus Christ." As one might expect, God's reconciliation in Jesus Christ formed a central theme of the lectures. Reconciliation is not an isolated event, sequestered from everything else in the scheme of salvation history. Reconciliation, Barth told his audience, contemplates creation as its great "presupposition" (*Voraussetzung*) and embraces the redemptive work of the Holy Spirit as its "consequence" (*Konsequenz*). The first article (creation) is the source, the third article (redemption) the goal, and the second article (reconciliation) is "the Way upon which we find ourselves in faith."[1] Barth's remarks about faith's "presupposition" and "consequence" stood, rather cryptically, at the lecture's conclusion. As we shall see, the same language recurs at some interesting turning points in the *CD*.

Barth once used the same word "presupposition" as a synonym for Immanuel Kant's notion of a "postulate." According to Kant, "God" may be treated either as a "regulative idea" of theoretical reason or as a practical "postulate" of morality. A "regulative idea" is an idea that can be conceived in thought but never really known as a thing in itself. We are in no position either to prove the "idea" of God or to disprove it. On the other hand, a "postulate"—or in Barth's vocabulary a "presupposition"—is something that, while it is not immediately present in experience, still remains necessary in order to make that experience possible. Thus, belief in God may be "postulated" or "presupposed" as a necessary condition to render our moral life intelligible. Indeed, Kant considered the postulate of God to be a veritable "need" of moral reason.

Without belief in God, morality would lose its moorings and all coherence.

On Barth's reading of Kant, postulates or presuppositions are never simply "given" to human experience. Instead, they make themselves visible through the exercise of moral freedom. The truth of a "presupposition," said Barth, is brought to fruition (*vollzogener*) by means of ethical action.[2]

This in turn sheds light on what Barth means by a "consequence." A "consequence" is the practical action which flows from one's presuppositions. As we shall see in greater detail in later chapters, a "consequence" is something not yet present in experience but something that one expects to follow as a result of what has already been occurring.

Thus, reconciliation in Jesus Christ is a present reality that sets the "Way" upon which the person of faith must travel. Reconciliation looks over its shoulder to belief in creation as an "origin that lies not in darkness" but that is posited as a "presupposition."[3] Following Kant, this means that even though the fact of creation cannot be proved directly from immediate experience, it is still a necessary condition to render belief in God the Reconciler possible. Moreover, reconciliation looks forward to "the goal of our path," to redemption which is to emerge as a "consequence" of our present act of faith.

To speak of creation and redemption, the great origin and goal of Christian faith, as a matter of "presupposition" and "consequence" means that they are not simply "given" to our present horizon. Instead we know them more in the modes of remembrance and hope. To be reconciled to God means living as people who have come from God who is our Creator and are returning to God who is our Redeemer.

This framework of presupposition and consequence as it operates in the *CD* helps to verify another one of Walter Lowe's insights about the Romans commentary. Modern Western metaphysics, Lowe argues, has often understood itself according to a three-part story based on implicit Christian assumptions. Beginning from a point of original unity, an *archē*, history is said to have lapsed into a radical and alienating falling away from that unity, only then to proceed to a finale of ultimate reunification, a *telos*. Often both the points of initiation and conclusion, the *archē* and the *telos*, were thought to be ready-made and known in advance; they were thought to constitute a "presence" (in Derrida's sense) by which all things in life were rendered intelligible.[4] Lowe invites us to read the theology of Barth's Romans commentary as an effort to break open this tripartite "diamond," or what William James used to call the "block universe."

Although Barth's theology retained the language of *archē* and *telos*, as any Christian theology arguably must, it did so, Lowe argues, in order to problematize the points of origin and conclusion. Neither *archē* nor *telos* are "present" to us in Barth's theology as something foundational and "given." Apart from grace, there is no direct connection between the brokenness that afflicts our present moment and these presumed points of perfect beginning and consummate ending.[5]

In the light of Lowe's suggestion, the reflections in these next three chapters consider Barth's mature theology of God the Creator, Reconciler, Redeemer as an open-ended triad. It is a triad that finds its center in reconciliation as an ongoing process that takes creation as its presupposition of intelligibility and redemption as its hoped-for consequence. As in traditional theology, everything for Barth comes from God and is returning to God (*an der Gott herkommenden und zu Gott zurückkehrenden*) (*KD*, III/2, 214, *CD*, 179). Still, Barth's construal of the triad is open-ended because we have neither the *archē* nor the *telos* as something "given" to be possessed. In this chapter, I apply this open-ended style of interpretation to Barth's theology of creation (III/1), the human creature (III/2), and providence (III/3).

GOD THE CREATOR

For Barth creation is a world of grace. God is never neutral concerning our prospects, for God is "for" us. And therefore creation confronts us as "benefit" (*Wohltat*) (III/1, §42.1). Despite all apparent evidence to the contrary, the Christian confesses the goodness of the created world.

We receive and recognize this graciousness in creation, however, not directly but only indirectly. Worldly phenomena pose themselves as a riddle lying all around us. It is quite plausible that apart from Christian revelation one would construe these worldly events as a congeries of impersonal powers arising from mere chance rather than from a divine intentionality to be "for" human beings. Indeed, some aspects of worldly phenomena— one thinks of the various "dead ends" and mass extinctions of evolution— lend themselves quite well to just such a profane interpretation. To view the world in a different way, to see it as the result of a divine creativity, requires one to construe the evidence in a different light, the light of grace.

To understand the cosmos as a "creation," then, requires a constructive act of interpretation. Even though the world we call "creation" is a genuine reality (*verwirklicht*) (III/1, §42.2), we do not enjoy an unmediated (*unmittelbar*) knowledge of its reality as such. While we do have an "unmediated supposition" (*unmittelbar meinen*) of its reality, this supposition still coexists with a pervasive "nihilism" which is forever pressing in upon us. We must live by the "healthy supposition" that we indeed are confronted by a gracious reality, but we lay no claim to "certitude" of it. "Always beneath our feet there yawns the gulf of the possibility that our healthy opinion might be deceiving us . . . " (III/1, 345). Only the dynamic and ongoing event of the living impartation of the Creator's "yes" can ever let us move from appearance to reality, from mere human consciousness to the truth of being itself.

In certain respects, Barth was intensifying a trajectory that began with Kant and was later carried forward by Schleiermacher, a trajectory that refused to reduce the "world" or "creation" to something given to human consciousness. For Kant we can "think" the world but we cannot "know" it as such in immediate experience. Similarly, Schleiermacher, by looking solely to the phenomena that presented themselves directly in religious consciousness, found it necessary to shift the focus of modern theology away from creation, which is inaccessibly in the past, and toward providence—or what he called "preservation"—which is experienced in the here and now.[6] Barth himself went yet another step beyond Schleiermacher by questioning whether there is any "immediate" consciousness of God at all. Over and above the supposed givenness of Schleiermacher's immediate consciousness of God, Barth argued, one would still need to hear afresh the dynamic Word of the Creator's "yes."

Barth demurred from his predecessors in yet another way as well. Not only did he underscore the problematic quality of "creation," but he refused to restrict the doctrine to a "cosmology" or "worldview" (*Weltanschauung*) about the fixed "origins" of the cosmos. For Barth it is a mistake for theology to rely upon a general "worldview" of any kind, whether secular or even Christian in derivation. Some critics have interpreted this denunciation, mistakenly, as a retreat into obscurantism or fideism. They perceive Barth as attempting to place Christian belief within a protective tower, free from any alien influence.

Barth's nay-saying to the many worldviews, however, also could be read as a way of freeing theology to new ways of thinking rather than an exercise in anxiously protecting the old. Instead of protecting theology, the move of thoroughly relativizing all "worldviews" might actually challenge theology to rethink its cherished assumptions. Admittedly, there is much in Barth's rhetoric—for example, his railing against non-christological starting points—that seems to support the view that his theology aims to be narrow and exclusivist. Nevertheless, a deeper reading reveals another motivation behind his denunciations, or at the very least a different direction in which Barth's thought may be pushed, a direction that, if followed, would lead to an alternative approach for how one ought to pursue constructive theology.

In *Dogmatics in Outline*, Barth advised his audience to "bracket" all "worldviews," even those that are supposedly *Christian*. For how can the mystery of God be captured through the formulae of any humanly-conceived master plan? If one chooses to pursue a "worldview," one's thinking will tend to settle upon "what is" (*vom Seienden*), upon the apparent givenness of the world. If, however, one aspires to think about God—that is, to do theology in the strict sense—one must stand aloof from the fixities of one's inherited mindset and prepare oneself instead to acquire a new framework for thought.[7] Barth problematized the "worldviews" because he opposed turning any of them into a premature "foundation" for thinking the divine mystery.

In the *Church Dogmatics* Barth offered a rather ingenious argument against prematurely baptizing one's preconceived "worldview," an argument drawn from the practices of modern scientific inquiry itself. Recognizing the prestige enjoyed by science, Barth argued that not even the natural sciences themselves purport to espouse a "worldview." Rather, the sciences require observation and description of the phenomena of life in ways appropriate to the object under inquiry. If the scientific disciplines, so highly-reputed in our age, pursue their work free from the agenda of a "worldview," then why should not theology follow suit (III/2, 12–13)?

Whether the sciences today understand themselves to be as bias-free as Barth's claim suggests is debatable, since philosophers of science now recognize that scientific inquiry is intimately linked to a particular point of view and context.[8] Be that as it may, Barth's message was not that science, or theology, or any other human inquiry, is able completely to prescind from the presuppositions of a "worldview." He knew quite well that human beings are incapable of thinking without the assistance of inherited concepts. Rather, his point was that "worldviews"—even so-called Christian worldviews—are merely provisional and have no veto power when it comes to the ultimate questions of life. All "worldviews" are fallible. Even science poses an imperfect mode of investigation. Indeed, what we think of as the "laws" of creaturely activity, those laws into which the sciences so diligently inquire, are only "noetic assertions," the "ontic" content of which is impossible to guarantee (III/3, 126).

If the analogy between theology and science can run in one direction, it arguably ought to run in the other as well. If scientific assertions are thoroughly fallible and thus not able to "ground" theology, then theological assertions, too, must be made without guarantees. Theology, like any scientific endeavor, is an inquiry that builds upon a set of revisable presuppositions that it must test in the living.

Whereas the natural sciences depend upon the neutral assumption that the natural order and its processes are intelligible, the presupposition of theology is the committed assumption—or faith—that life depends upon an intelligible divine source. Theology, just like the other sciences, investigates a definite subject matter; but unlike them, its subject matter, the mystery of God, is by definition a reality that is not exhausted in the "phenomena." To think about God, therefore, is to remain open to new thoughts and new ways of being in the world. Rather than read Christian faith through the lens of any single "worldview," one should problematize all the "worldviews" in light of the impenetrable affirmation that God the ultimate mystery is also the "Creator."[9]

Barth never worked out with any precision how to distinguish between concepts drawn from a secular "worldview," on the one hand, and concepts necessary, on the other, for constructing what in "Fate and Idea" he called the "conceptual world" (*Begriffswelt*) of theology. Maybe we should avoid any conception of God in relation to the world whatsoever. After all, Barth denied any need for theology to focus on the world's scientific "origins," and he could even claim with a straight face that the scriptures themselves are loath to embrace a "cosmology." The biblical account of creation merely "uses" ancient near Eastern cosmologies but without explicitly "adopting" them (III/2, 7–11). But then perhaps this distinction between "use" and "adoption," however doubtful it may be from the standpoint of the biblical text itself, can point us to a different way forward. Maybe it is permissible for theologians to utilize various cultural concepts on an ad hoc basis, so long as they leave such concepts provisional and subject to further revision.[10]

Interestingly enough, Barth did not foreclose the possibility that some future philosophical or scientific theory would develop a new concept for describing reality, a concept that would serve theology's purposes quite well. He even went so far as to toy with the philosophical concept of "pure becoming" as a possible candidate. In the end, however, he deemed it inadequate (III/1, 340–43). Here again we see Barth opening the door to a dialogue with non-ecclesial sources of truth but, alas, declining to enter in. Still, even though Barth himself failed to pursue a thoroughgoing conversation with the natural sciences, he did hold open the possibility of such an interchange, so long as it did not compromise the theologian's ultimate goal of keeping theology "theological."[11] The test for any such approach, he said, would be its "non-neutrality"; it would need to have the capacity to account concretely for creation as a "benefit" of God's grace.

Hence the doctrine of creation is conceived by Barth as but one part of the ongoing, beneficent act by which God effectuates God's eternal choice to be graciously "for" and "with" human beings in the unfolding history of creation, reconciliation, and redemption. To isolate "creation" from its future trajectory is to "abstract" it from the whole of its relationships. If the doctrine of creation is to be viewed in the "concrete," given the meaning assigned that term in the preceding chapter, it must be seen in connection to everything else that makes it what it is. If "we do not know what we are saying" when we call God "Father," do we know any better all that it means to call God "Creator"? Creation cannot be "freeze-framed" in isolation from the historical flow of the grace of reconciliation and the hope of redemption.

This is the reason Barth advanced his often-disputed opinion that the Christian creed's "first article" belief in creation can only be grasped in the light of its "second article" confession of Jesus Christ. It is only in Jesus Christ that we catch our first glimpse of what it truly means to be a creature. He believed, in fact, that we cannot even know *that* we are creatures, let alone what creaturehood itself means, apart from the dynamic event of salvation in Christ. It is only from the standpoint of being reconciled to God in Jesus Christ that we can view our creaturehood as reconciliation's presupposition.

If one wants to label this approach "christocentrism," it is not the sort of static christocentrism, focusing narrowly on a Jesus whom we think we already know, of which Barth is so often accused. For the "center" being contemplated here, as intimated before, is open-ended, continually gathering new meaning as it moves forward from its "presupposition" to its inexorable, but as yet unrealized "consequence."

Barth captured the relationship between the first article as "presupposition" and the second article as dramatic turning point on its way toward redemption as "consequence" in an epigram that guides his entire theology: "Creation is the external basis of the covenant, and covenant is the internal basis of creation" (III/1, §41). Insofar as it is external, creation provides a point of beginning; it is the stage upon which the drama of life unfolds. Yet creation is by no means a beginning point that is merely neutral; it is no "outer courtyard of the temple" that can ground a strictly "natural" theology. Since the covenant forms the internal precept of creation from the outset, creation already contains a trajectory toward redemption. God is not simply neutral regarding God's creatures, and so Christians must confess that the spheres of nature and history already exist for our "benefit" (*Wohltat*). They already contain the hidden seeds of the reconciling and redeeming covenantal enactment. The natural and historical events which comprise creation are never neutral but bear the character of "promise." The act of God is both the seed planted in election and creation and the growth itself in reconciliation and redemption.

Barth tried to conceive the act of God by reconstructing Hegelian categories. To compare Barth and Hegel is useful, since Hegel is a classic exponent of the threefold "diamond" that Walter Lowe has argued Barth is set on denying. The comparison is also instructive, because contemporary post-Barthians such as Jürgen Moltmann, Eberhard Jüngel, and Wolfhart Pannenberg are drawing upon Hegel today in ways that tip the balance toward divine relationality and thus away from Barth's effort to hold God's relationality in a careful equilibrium with God's integrity.[12] For Barth, the mystery of God's being must still retain a logical priority over God's act in history. "Though the work of God is the essence of God, it is necessary and important to distinguish [God's] essence as such from [God's] work, remembering that this work is grace, a free divine decision . . . " (I/1, 371).

In Hegel, by contrast, the integrity and relationality of God become confused. Hegel traced the odyssey of what he called "Absolute Spirit" as it made its way through history from a first moment of implicit unity in which the infinite and the finite were conjoined, to a second moment of breach and alienation, and then on to a third moment of sublation (*Aufhebung*) in which the original unity, implicit from the start, was said to become explicit in human consciousness. This threefold movement is a classic statement of Lowe's "diamond" in that the triumph of Absolute Spirit as it proceeds along its trek Hegel believed to be assured from the beginning. Therefore, all the setbacks, tragedies, and defeats encountered along the way were rendered tolerable in light of the third and consummate movement. All of history's tragedies were merely mopping up exercises along the way to the absolute attainment of a final end. It was against the triumphalism inherent in Hegel's "diamond" that William James protested so vehemently at the turn of the century, deriding it as a "block universe" in which all the answers to all of life's riddles are presumed to be known in advance, and in which evil is but a subordinate moment to be explained away in the grand march of historical progress.[13]

Hegel posited a dialectic arising between the Absolute as it exists implicitly "for itself" (*an sich*) and as it exists explicitly "for us" (*für uns*). To contemplate something "for itself" is to think of it in abstraction from its relations, whereas to consider it "for us" is to consider it in the unfolding of its actuality. The career of the Absolute in history represents for Hegel a movement from the implicit to the explicit, from the abstract to the concrete. The Absolute is not content to remain "for itself"; but only as it actualizes itself does it become what it deigns to be both "for itself" or "for us." In other words, there can be no separation between the Absolute "in itself" and the Absolute in its being "for" the world. This emphasis on concreteness Barth shared with Hegel.

Yet unlike Barth, Hegel considered it impossible to posit a concrete moment when God, or in his terms "Spirit," possessed a reality that was separate from the world. Accordingly, the term "Creator," when understood as a being conceived in separation from the "creation," was to Hegel thoroughly misleading and should be jettisoned. To make this more understandable, imagine an artist "in herself" who may possess all the innate skills, together with an aesthetic vision inspiring enough, to give promise of producing a great work of art. Yet it is only in applying brush to canvas, only in creating the product itself as already imagined, that her art becomes a reality either for the artist herself (*für sich*) or for us (*für uns*). We can think of her as already being an artist implicitly but as needing also to become one explicitly through an artistry that she carries to concrete fruition.

Hegel's view is that God the "divine artist" cannot really be conceived as an artist at all, apart from the work of art. But this raises a problem: if we must always think of God concretely in relationship to the creature, then does this mean that God "needs" the creature in order to be God? Some have argued—for example, Johann Gottlieb Fichte in the nineteenth century and Wolfhart Pannenberg in our own day—that relationship to an "other" is a constitutive and necessary aspect of being personal. They would question the "modern" view by which a person, or self, is defined or centered strictly in relation to itself. On some versions of "postmodernity" selves are "decentered." They become who they are only through their interaction with others. Hence there is no such thing as an isolated, autonomous "self" or "subject" that always possesses the same "essence" irrespective of context. Rather, on a postmodern view, persons are "constituted" in and by their relationships.[14]

If we extend this view of decentered selfhood to God, God could not properly be considered a personal God absent a relationship to that which is "other" than God, namely, the creature. Thus, even though Hegel was a modern philosopher, he contributed to a distinctively postmodern way of thinking about personhood. Similarly, Barth also conceived the divine life in terms that are contextual and relational rather than essentialist and static. As we learned in the previous chapter, God's being "in itself" (*ad intra*) and God's action "for us" (*ad extra*) may be distinguished in the abstract, but in the concrete light of Jesus Christ they must always be considered together. By holding God's eternal being and God's historical action together in this fashion, Barth wished to assimilate historicity and relationality into the concept of God, and he did this in a manner strikingly similar to Hegel.

Nevertheless, Barth believed that Hegel jeopardized God's prior actuality or "aseity" vis à vis the world. Barth endeavored to affirm God's personhood and relationality, but in a way that was careful not to compromise God's integrity. In other words, God is genuinely identified in God's work but is never exhausted by that work. For Barth, God is already personal in God's own being. God already is the divine artist par excellence, so to speak, even apart from making the world as God's own work of art. God has no need of the world in order to be God. Still, God has determined not to be God without the world. God has constituted the world as the dynamic arena of divine and human interaction.

In short, Barth was struggling to forge a dynamic and relational view of God that also preserved the integrity of who God is. God is who God is, but God must also realize or enact who God is in human history. The glory of God's integrity is not diminished but is enhanced by the relationality of God's action.

Barth extended his dynamic and relational view of God's trinitarian being-in-act to include a dynamic and relational view of created existence as well. In order to understand this, let us turn to consider how Barth conceived God's purposes for human life.

THE HUMAN CREATURE

The issue of how to achieve our true humanity is one of the decisive themes in Barth's theology. To be truly human, in analogy to being truly divine, is to have one's being in act. It is to live a life of integrity and committed relationality in respect to the "other." We shall return to this theme in chapters seven and eight.

Martin Luther once commented that human life is "not righteousness but growth in righteousness, not health but healing, not being but becoming, not rest but exercise."[15] Luther's sense of life being set in motion toward a goal aptly characterizes Barth's view of what it means to be a creature in relation to the grace of God the Creator. Being a creature is an existence in grace; it is not a unique "status" but a deed. The meaning of human existence he characterized as a "history"—not a state of being but an ongoing endeavor. The preferred image is not that of an isolated point but of a connected line (III/2, 157).

As is the case with our perception of deity, our cognizance of our humanity is not a "given." What it means to be human is thoroughly problematic. Any attempt to capture it conceptually is either "not yet" or "no longer" a theological anthropology (III/2, 132). We experience our humanity in inescapable antitheses, knowing ourselves only in fragments (III/2, 47). Four such fragments are discussed by Barth as examples of the "phenomena" of the human. These comprise the secular philosophies of naturalism, idealism, existentialism, and the theistic anthropology of Emil Brunner's neo-orthodoxy (III/2, §44.2, 75–132).

First, "naturalism" seeks to explain humanity by merging human beings into their environment. This reduction of humanity to a material "something" which can be objectified resembles the mistake of the one-sided "realism" Barth had flagged in "Fate and Idea." Barth detected this materialistic reductionism at play in both the ideologies of capitalism and totalitarianism. In their mutual fixation on material well-being, both have the effect of deflating true human freedom.

The second, "idealist" reduction (think again of "Fate and Idea") reacts to materialism by trying to comprehend humanity's essence in terms of "will," "freedom," "purpose," or the like. In the end, idealism amounts to nothing more than humanity's own self-knowledge asserting itself; it is but a pale shadow of the true freedom and action and purpose of *God*. Whatever freedom idealism can imagine, it does not rise to the "freedom for obedience" that life with God entails.

A third and better approach is visible in the historical questing of "existentialism." It moves beyond idealism's focus on a truncated freedom and beyond realism's supposed "self-contained and complete reality" to contemplate what Barth considers the real "subject" of historical questing—human being in the concrete. But Barth wondered whether existentialism's concentration on the jarring, anguished moments of life was sufficient in itself to yank humanity into relationship to God. Even world wars do not seem to faze human beings, lamented Barth, and for that matter, he supposed, neither would the day of judgment itself (III/2, 114–15). It is not possible, he concluded, to reach God simply by way of surveying the negations and aporias of the world.

Finally, even the theistic anthropology of a Christian theologian such as Emil Brunner ends up treating humanity's relationship to God as another "neutral" attribute belonging to humanity itself as a possession rather than a free and liberating act of God that constitutes us in our selfhood.

These "fragments" lifted up by naturalism, idealism, existentialism, and neo-orthodox theism can tell us only about the "phenomena" of the human. They tell us little about the thing itself; they do not press forward to an understanding of what Barth called "real" humanity.

"Real" or "actual" (*wirklich*) humanity, true human selfhood, is not something to be taken for granted. It is a gift of grace. God's gracious act is what *constitutes* true selfhood. The "real" human being is not reflected in humanity "as it is," for the "real" humanity is always humanity "as it ought to be." Real humanity is the human being actualized by God. We cannot be truly human apart from God.

But where has such real, actualized humanity become visible? According to Barth, it has become visible in Jesus of Nazareth. He alone lived his life not for self-aggrandizement; he alone was wholly turned toward God. Therefore, it is from looking to Jesus Christ that Christian theologians must derive any true knowledge of what it means to be human. Just as God may be known through God alone, so humanity too is known only through God (III/2, 152).

Notwithstanding the incompleteness of the knowledge derived from naturalism, idealism, existentialism, and theism, it is a mistake to think we learn nothing from these sources at all. Such a misreading of Barth could easily occur if one listened only to the critique leveled against the "phenomena of the human" in §44.2 but neglected the later section on "real humanity" in which, having relativized the adequacy of all information about humanity, Barth then revisited the "phenomena of the human" in a more positive light (§44.3). In typical Barthian fashion, what he snatched away with the right hand he then returned with the left. Regarding the earlier critique, Barth said, "our purpose was simply to refute the claim that [non-theological knowledge] could be a genuine knowledge of a real object *independently* of a prior knowledge of real humanity" in Jesus Christ (III/2, 199, emphasis supplied). There is no knowledge of humanity "in itself" apart from an appraisal of humanity in relationship to God and God's action in Jesus Christ.

Having made that critique, Barth then went on to appreciate the positive contribution of data derived from secular sources. Once we have placed the role of secular sources in proper perspective, Barth insisted, they are indeed able to uncover what he termed "real indications" of humanity's condition. Through these secular sources "one can arrive at a non-theological but genuine knowledge of the phenomena of the human" (III/2, 198–99). In sources such as these, then, we can discover a "technical capacity" to realize our humanity, even if apart from grace the goal itself eludes us.

The realism of the natural sciences, to begin with, rightly points to humanity's place not as an isolated self but as a creature situated in the cosmos. Idealistic ethics, on the other hand, celebrates our human capacity to differentiate ourselves from the cosmos. On an even higher level, existentialist philosophy accents humanity's relationality and openness toward something beyond us. Theistic anthropology, finally, points to humanity's fitness for a theonomous as opposed to an autonomous existence (III/2, 198–202). True, none of these disciplines is competent per se and by itself to disclose the true humanity that resides in Jesus Christ. But in principle each of these disciplines could contribute to theological understanding.

That Barth himself was overly cautious about delving into what such secular sources can contribute need not prevent others from doing so and completing the task which he left unfinished. Even though secular knowledge provides no firm basis for a so-called natural theology of God, there is still something worth discovering and knowing in all these various ways of being human (III/2, 207).

The key for Barth is that without God's action, humanity is unable to be what it ought to be. Only the recognition that "God is" enables a genuine "I am" (III/2, 178). To be genuinely human is to live by grace. Through ourselves alone, we human beings cannot explain ourselves. Only through God can such an explanation arise—and specifically through the history God enacts with humanity in Jesus Christ. Adumbrating his later use in volume IV (The Doctrine of Reconciliation) of the Lukan parable of the prodigal son, Barth maintained that the real human being is the one who, like the repentant prodigal, "arises and goes to his Father" (III/2, 177). Jesus Christ alone is the creature who has truly been caught up in such a movement of personal responsibility before God. Jesus Christ alone, by the power of God's Spirit, has proved capable of doing this and of fulfilling his humanity (III/2, §44). Therefore, if we want to know what it means to be human, we should look to the real humanity exhibited by Jesus Christ in his *act*.

"Act" emerges once again as the crucial Barthian category. "Action" for Barth, as for Kant, is not reducible to the mere contingency of our ordinary modes of doing. "Action" is performed at a more intentional and deliberate level than mere "behavior." To eat an everyday meal of bread and drink may rest on the level of ordinary "behavior." To celebrate as a Christian believer the symbolically charged "Lord's Supper," on the other hand, is more on the nature of a true "act." For to "act" is to pursue a deliberate and thoroughly free deed. It is to enact a project that contributes to our destiny. It is to perform deeds that are redemptive.

In addition, action is the mode of existence by which we discover who we truly are. According to Kant, we do not know ourselves directly, for we are never in a position to experience directly all of who we are.[16] Yet who we are is disclosed indirectly by the free actions we perform in the world. Barth pursues a similar line of analysis, for it is only in "action" that our freedom, and thus our authentic humanity, emerges. "It is as one acts that a human being exists as a person" (II/2, 516). "Action means not only to choose and realize this or that, but to choose and realize oneself in this or that" (III/4, 13).

In action, moreover, certain things become visible which "thought" by itself cannot fathom. As noted above, Kant believed we could "think" certain realities, such as God, freedom, and immortality, even though we could not directly "know" them. Yet we can "postulate" them, or in Barth's language "presuppose" them, as conditions that render our moral lives intelligible. Similarly, for Barth we are able to "think" the reality of God, but we can only know God through the prism of our moral deeds, or to put it more pointedly, through obedience to the divine command. Obedient action is the concrete, connected deed of the "real, actualized" (*wirklich*) human being (III/4, 5). In short, it is only as a person acts that she or he is a person at all (II/2, 516). It is only in the "prism" of our own action that we are able to perceive the act of God (I/1, 14).

That divine and human action must coincide makes sense in light of the coming together of a dual action in Jesus Christ. We already saw in the preceding chapter that Jesus Christ is both "the elect human being" and "the electing God." The divine initiative in election coincides with the human appropriation of election as response. Similarly, Barth defined the uniqueness of Jesus' humanity as another sort of action—an action that, once again, brings divine and human action in concert one to the other. Barth defined Jesus Christ as both a "human being for *God*" (III/2, §44.1) and a "human being for *others*" (III/2, §45.1). These are not two essentially different and juxtaposed aspects of Jesus' humanity but a way of viewing the singularity of his action from two perspectives.

In the first place, Jesus Christ is a human being "for" God. While God has taken the initiative in being "for" humanity, Jesus in his turn is the one human being who has responded by being truly "for" God. The fact that Jesus is "for" God defines his uniqueness. Jesus alone among human beings is "for" God in the most radical sense. Indeed, for Barth, Jesus' stance toward God is both what expresses his true humanity and also what constitutes his true divinity. Note the radicality of the claim: *Jesus is divine precisely by virtue of his being truly human.*

Jesus is just like other human beings in sharing our common creaturely constitution (*Beschaffenheit*). Jesus and other human beings embrace a common "being," even though Jesus is the only one who has realized that being "in act." He lives out his humanity in a unique way by taking up a qualitatively different creaturely stance (*Stand*) (*KD*, III/2, 62; *CD*, 53). Jesus' uniqueness rests not in his being superhuman but precisely in the fact that he alone has truly realized his humanity. Jesus fulfills his humanity through a free obedience to the will of God. This novel stance of obedience is not superhuman, but it does express what we might call an uncommon humanity. In his humanity Jesus does what he does as a genuine human being and not a demigod. Jesus enacts what all human beings were created to fulfill, for all humanity is supposed to be "for" God in just the same way as Jesus. Jesus has achieved the "real" or "actual" (*wirklich*) humanity that all the rest of us are meant to become. Therefore, Jesus as "human being for God" points the way forward to the fulfillment of our own human destiny.

That Jesus embodies divinity precisely through realizing his own true humanity does not mean that God and humanity have all of a sudden become identical in Jesus, or that anyone else could fulfill Jesus' role as the divine-human mediator. God is still mystery; and Jesus, in his true humanity, still reflects God only indirectly. The analogy between the humanity of Jesus and the deity of God, Barth says, is an analogy of *relationship* (*analogia relationis*) and not an analogy of *being* (*analogia entis*) (III/2, 220–21, 323–24). Since humanity and divinity are of two different natures, there can be no identity of being occurring between them.

Nevertheless, through his relationship with God the "Father," Jesus' uncommon humanity is able to point sacramentally to the reality of God. "It is in the humanity, in the saving work of the human Jesus, that the relationship (*Beziehung*) between God and humanity becomes visible and in which alone it consists and becomes actual (*wirklich*)" (*KD*, III/2, 262, *CD*, 219–20). Jesus is *for* God in conformity with the same love and freedom in which God achieves (and is thus "for") God's own purposes. To put it another way, Jesus, as the "human being *for God*," reflects the "inner sphere" of God's own relationship to self *ad intra*. For God too is "for" God's own glory and purpose. The analogy of relationship means that God is as Jesus is, and God does as Jesus does.

Jesus as "human being *for others*," in the second place, reflects the "outer sphere" of God's relationship *ad extra* to the "other" (III/2, 218–19). Jesus is a human being who, in addition to being radically *for God*, is also fundamentally engaged *for others*. And his being "for" others is an extension and reflection of his being "for" God. Indeed Barth sees a "real" and "radical" connection between the two (III/2, 211–12). Jesus draws his life from God and, through his obedient suffering unto death, gives it back to his fellow human beings. In this way the reality of God is mediated to the whole human race, albeit indirectly through the humanity of Jesus. That Jesus sets himself on a course *for others,* Barth believed, creates a new ontological reality in the human situation. Now there is one who has done the will of God "on earth as it is in heaven."

From Jesus' committed stance directed "for" the other, Barth proclaimed that all human beings could discern the "basic form" (*Grundform*) of their own creaturely existence. In a volume published in 1948, following the years of carnage that marked World War II together with the horrors of the Holocaust, Barth proclaimed in *CD* III/2 that humanity's "basic form of existence" should consist directly and plainly in our own "co-humanity."

We have our humanity (or lack thereof) in the sheer fact of living inescapably *"with"* one another. Given the atrocities perpetrated in this century, admonished Barth, we need an anthropology that will not compromise this basic, if all too fragile, co-humanity (III/2, §45.2). In contrast, say, to the capitalist individualism that is simply out for itself, on the one hand, or the fascist reduction of others to mere extensions of one's own schemes or projects, on the other, genuine co-humanity calls for mutuality, for reciprocity, and for the recognition that "I am as thou art" (III/2, 248).

Barth reached this conclusion through a fascinating, though really quite simple, theological deduction. In order for Jesus to be "for" us, reasoned Barth, he must first be "with" us. "Where one being is for the other, there is necessarily a common sphere or form of existence in which the 'for' can be possible and effective" (III/2, 223). By being "with" us, Jesus' example showed us that we cannot escape being "with" one another.

In keeping with the main idea set forth earlier in "Fate and Idea," a true understanding of this co-humanity must avoid either idealist or realist distortions. Against the Enlightenment "ideal" of the isolated "self," and against the perverted extreme to which it was carried in Nietzsche's "humanity without a fellow-humanity," Barth argued that we are inextricably bound to one another as fellow human beings. Co-humanity is a far cry from Nietzsche's seductive vision of the isolated and self-sufficient human being. What Nietzsche wished at all costs to avoid, charged Barth, was any figure of a humanity that suffers on behalf of others (III/2, 231–42).

Against this extreme form of idealism, Barth opposed any understanding of the "I am" as an absolute or isolated subject. But, against realism, he rejected the equal and opposite error of submerging the individual into the anonymous confluence of the masses. Against any allegedly "realistic" appraisal that would surrender the individual to the inhuman forces of totalitarian bureaucracy or pit them against the inhumane grinding of the unfettered machine of capitalism, Barth argued that no person—no one—should be turned into a product or pawn of the community.

This respect for the other, this "I am as thou art," can be summarized by four characteristics. First, one will always look the other in the eye. This is a departure from all bureaucratic, compartmentalized, and detached approaches to life. The announcement, "That is no concern of mine . . . ," chided Barth, is almost always wrong. Second, there must occur the mutuality of conversation—real listening and real speaking. The empty banter of so many everyday conversations reflects empty people, with no sense of who, and whose, they really are. Third, there must occur the rendering of mutual aid. For being "with" the other means standing by the other. There can be no evading the cry for help. Every need presses for recognition. To be truly human is to be in solidarity with others. Finally, being "with" one another occurs with mutual gladness—there can be no neutrality about the other's future.

The cogency of the distinction Barth drew between Jesus' being "for God" and "for others" depends on an implicit distinction-in-unity he drew between human "nature" and human "destiny." This distinction parallels his even more pervasive distinction-in-unity between being and action. Whereas Jesus' engagement "for God" and "for others" gestures ahead, so to speak, towards humanity's redeemed destiny, Jesus' solidarity "with" other human beings points backward towards humanity's created nature. Jesus' action—and by analogy all genuine human action—occurs between primordial and eschatological horizons. We may diagram the relationship as shown in figure 4.1. Let us consider both sides of this equation.

On the one hand, Jesus' being "for" God is the definitive expression of humanity's eschatological "destiny" which is to be redeemed. The Christian witness, on Barth's read, claims that Jesus is the only one who is unreservedly "for" God and "for" others. Jesus exists "for" God and "for" others not just incidently but intrinsically as a matter of his character and mission. This is not merely some ephemeral, inward attitude on Jesus' part but his real and radical engagement for the other. The rest of us have yet to be "for" one another in this most radical way; to be "for" one another, and also "for" God, forms the "real" or "actual" humanity to which God calls us. "Real" or "actual" (wirklich) humanity, in short, lies yet ahead of us.

On the other hand, Jesus' being for other human beings is also the definitive expression of humanity's primordial "nature," its native endowment to be a creature in solidarity with other creatures. In advance of what humanity will one day become, there is already a basic "form" or infrastructure of humanity as it is, here and now. In the present moment, human beings are untranscendably "with" one another. Right now, like it or

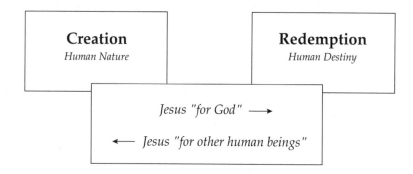

FIGURE 4.1

not, our condition is one of mutual relationality, a relationality that inheres not merely among those in the church but among all human beings. Believing in election means that one cannot choose to eliminate anyone from one's horizon of responsibility and concern. If God is "for" us, we must be not only "for" God but also "for" one another.

This last point needs to be appreciated by all those who delight in caricaturing Barth as though he had no interest in issues of theological anthropology. In particular, a misconception has spread among English-speaking interpreters over Barth's teaching concerning the traditional concept of the *imago Dei*, the image of God in human beings. Influenced by Emil Brunner, this misreading has claimed that the early Barth preached the complete annihilation of the image in human beings, while the later Barth reversed his stance in *CD* III/2.[17] But, in fact, Barth never denied that humanity is the image of God. "Humanity would not be humanity if it were not the image of God" (III/1, 184, rev.). Nor did Barth ever deny an objective relationship between God and the creature. He denied only that this relationship was "given" as something inherently self-evident to human understanding. What he rejected was any concept of the image as an intrinsic "faculty," "capacity," "neutral condition," or "given" which is accessible to human beings by their own devices apart from God.[18] The image is described instead as "the act of decision *for* God."[19] All Barth's early language about the marring of the image refers to the image understood only in this peculiar sense. Remarked Barth in his Göttingen lectures: "That [the image] is lost to us and no longer visible does nothing to alter its reality and possibility."[20]

Humanity is the image of God only when it is determined to be "for" God in response to God's being "for" humanity. The proper analogy by which to understand the image, according to Barth, is not that of a fixed state of being (*Zustand*) but of a dynamic movement, a circular arrow moving toward the human side from God and returning from the human side toward God to make the circle complete (III/2, 162–63). Hence the image is a dynamic historical relationship. The image is something which humanity is, but only in promise and in hope. From one point of view, the image is an eschatological reality that points forward to redemption; it is not what "I am" but what "I am becoming." Nevertheless, from another point of view, the image still belongs to "original humanity" (*ursprünglich Mensch*) as a genuine and primordial "analogy" to God.

To sum up, to the extent that the image is a divine *promise*, it is never to be withdrawn and is never destroyed. To the extent that the image is human *hope*, humanity waits for the proper manifestation of it. The image as hope rests in Jesus' relation to God and to his fellow human beings.

Jesus' relationship to God not only illumines human nature and destiny from above but it shows how that nature and destiny stand in relationship to the triunity of God. That is, Jesus' relationship to God and to others tells us what it means to be divine, what it means to be human, and also how divinity and humanity are related. First of all, we have just seen that human beings have both a "basic form of existence" which is presently visible and an "actual" humanity toward which they are destined. Now Barth believes that both the "basic form" and the "actual" humanity reflect, in different ways, the trinitarian reality of God. This may seem rather astonishing in light of the caricatures in which humanity is thought to occupy an insignificant place in Barth's thought. To speak of the way humanity is actually able to reflect the reality of God may sound strangely un-Barthian, but it is actually Barthian in the highest degree.

To substantiate this claim, Barth draws an easy to overlook technical distinction between divine "relationality" (*Beziehung*) and divine "fellowship" (*Gemeinschaft*) (*KD*, III/2, 384–91, *CD*, 319–24). The difference between relationality and fellowship, which on its face seems hopelessly equivocal, is explained by making reference both to humanity's primordial "nature"—its "basic form"—and to its eschatological "destiny"—its "actual" humanity.

First, God's "relationality" (*Beziehung*) is God's inherent capacity to subsist "with" God in integrity. In God's own integrity God subsists in "relationality" *ad intra*. Barth speaks of God being "God *with* God." It is this "relationality" that God allows to be reflected *ad extra* in humanity's own "basic form" of existing "with" one another. What Barth calls "generic humanity" (*Mensch überhaupt und im Allgemeinen*), or humanity as it subsists "with" other human beings, is modeled after (*nachgebildet ist*) the divine likeness of the human Jesus, the one human being who is "for" other human beings (*KD*, III/2, 390, *CD*, 324). The modeling works like this. Generic humanity is modeled after the way the human being Jesus of

Nazareth who is "for" his fellow human beings is also "with" them. Jesus himself, in turn, is modeled after God. Therefore, the way generic humanity lives together "with" its fellow human beings is an indirect reflection of God's own image (III/2, 324).

Second, God not only lives in "relationality" but in "fellowship" (*Gemeinschaft*). Divine "fellowship" is God's activity of being "God *for* God." Barth thinks of relationality (God *with* God) as more quiescent, whereas fellowship (God *for* God) is more active. Fellowship is the active work by which God enacts who God is. God's action of "fellowship" *ad intra*, in being "God *for* God," is reflected *ad extra* in the "real" humanity of Jesus. Recall that Jesus' real humanity consists in his stance of being "for" the other— both God and neighbor—and this is also humanity's own implicit destiny and goal. Now "relationality" (being "with" one another) signals a reciprocity inhering among human beings, while "fellowship" (being "for" one another) bespeaks a grace already extended to human beings from God and a grace that they in return are to extend to one another. Whereas relationality is our nature, fellowship is our destiny. One is primordial, the other eschatological. The two are related like this. What Barth calls the "basic form" of humanity (being "with" one another), which Jesus embodies, is a present reality, here and now. "Actual" or "real" humanity (being "for" God and "for" one another) is something Jesus has already accomplished but which the rest of us anticipate as a future possibility and goal.

After delineating these (admittedly) cumbersome technicalities, we come finally to appreciate Barth's main point. Through this rather contorted use of prepositions and analogies, Barth is able to show—albeit at a highly formal level—how human nature and destiny reflect the very nature and destiny of God. What becomes clear to one who wades through this tangled net of Barthian reasoning is that human "relationality" reflects the divine "relationality." "The being of humanity in encounter"—i.e., being "with" the other—"is a being in correspondence to God" (III/2, 323). What Barth does not say specifically in the texts we have been summarizing, but which seems implicit nonetheless, is that the telos or goal of human "fellowship"—the goal of being "for" the other—also reflects and corresponds to the divine "fellowship." (See III/2, 319–24.) Humanity reflects the divine fellowship, he says, not in present possession but "in hope" (III/2, 324). More will be said about the importance of hope in chapter eight.

The reason for Barth's reticence in making this last point explicit is undoubtedly his belief that such human fellowship is a commandment yet to be enacted rather than a "given." Thus he can make the remarkable claim: "Humanity is essentially *for* God because humanity is essentially *from* God and in God" (*KD*, III/2, 82, *CD*, 71, emphasis supplied). Jesus Christ already *is* this "real" human being as the "Son of God," and human beings are meant to *become* this "real" humanity as the "children of God."

For now human beings have fallen away from the proximity or context (*Zusammenhang*) of their covenant destiny. They do not live in complete darkness, however, since they are still living in the creaturely "form" of humanity. That is, they are living inexorably "with" one another, together with all that this relationality implies ethically. What human beings still need is for this open "form" of their existence to be filled in with the divinely determined "content" of true fellowship.

Therefore, both the "basic form" which is now, and the "actualized," "real" humanity which is coming, together comprise what it means to live *from* God and *for* God, and hence to be truly human. Although Barth does not spell it out clearly, the analogy he draws between God and humanity, using the christological lens of Jesus' humanity "with" and "for" others, may be represented schematically as shown in figure 4.2.

At least one more ambiguity remains in Barth's treatment of these relationships. What is clear is that, regarding the relationship between "God with us" and humanity "with" one another, both Jesus and the rest of humanity reflect God in fundamentally the same way: the human Jesus has his "being" in common with the rest of humanity. What is also clear is that, regarding the relationship between "God for us" and humanity "for" God, Jesus as "human being for God" mirrors the being of God "for us." Jesus is truly human in that he, like God, has his being "in act."

What is left vague is whether we human beings who seek to follow Jesus are ever able to be "for" *God* in quite the same way Jesus is. Barth does say that humanity is never "for" God in the same way that *God* in Jesus Christ is "for" them. Yet if this, in turn, were to imply that ordinary human beings can never even *strive* toward being "for" God in the same way that *Jesus* is "for" God, then a basic gap between Jesus' humanity and the humanity of all others would arise. Arguably in that case, Jesus would be a superman or demigod rather than a "true human being." Consequently, his role as divine-human mediator would be destroyed. The human side of the Chalcedonian two natures formula would thereby have been abrogated.

The best way to make sense of Barth's anthropology, as the above table indicates, is to understand the power of human beings to be "for" God as a mark of human *destiny* rather than a present possession of human nature. Being "for" God is an eschatological goal made possible by the work of the Spirit in Jesus Christ. The human Jesus is "for" God now in the same way that all potentially shall be "for" God at the eschaton, when God is "all in all."

Thus, to be "for God" is not a human attribute per se—it is not a "given." For the call to be the "covenant partner of *God*" is a possibility that is actualized only by the redeeming power of God's Spirit. To be "for

Divine Trinitarian Relationality Ad Intra

DIVINE BEING	DIVINE ACT
God "with" God $\longrightarrow$	God "for" God

Divine Trinitarian Relationality Ad Extra

DIVINE BEING (Incarnation)	DIVINE ACT (Atonement)
God "with" Humanity $\longrightarrow$	God "for" Humanity

Christology

BEING	ACT
Jesus "with" Humanity $\longrightarrow$	Jesus "for" Humanity and "for" God
(Commonality with Others)	(Uniqueness from Others)

Anthropology

HUMAN BEING	HUMAN DESTINY
Humanity "with" Humanity $\longrightarrow$	Humanity "for" God
(Basic Form of Humanity)	(Goal of Actual Humanity)

FIGURE 4.2

others," however, stands already within human reach. Already in their very nature, human beings have the capacity to act as covenant partners with one another.

To sum up, this means that we human beings have our being as a dynamic reality outside ourselves; it is constituted *extra nos.* Unlike the modern anthropology in which human beings are self-grounding and self-constituting, in Barth's anthropology human beings are constituted outside themselves. As we shall see in chapters seven and eight, we discover who we are by living "ec-centrically," that is, from a center that is "other" than self.

The reliability of this interpretation of Barth's anthropology is fortified by the way Barth defines human life in reference to the traditional maxims of Augustine regarding sin. Augustine defined human life as proceeding in four stages. Before the "fall" human beings were capable of sinning *(posse peccare)*, even though they had not yet sinned. After the fall, they became so corrupt as to be no longer capable of *not* sinning *(non posse non peccare)*. Notwithstanding the dire nature of their plight, the work of God's grace in Christ could empower them not to sin *(posse non peccare)*. This regeneration of their powers, in turn, would make possible an ongoing pilgrimage which would one day culminate in heavenly glory. In that fourth and final stage, human beings are no longer capable of sinning at all *(non posse peccare)*.[21]

In *Dogmatics in Outline* Barth seized Augustine's fourth stage, which is thoroughly eschatological, and turned it into the *normative* definition of humanity. To be truly human, according to Karl Barth, is to be *incapable* of sinning. That is what it means to be free: to be determined as God's covenant partner, to be in a state of no longer having to be torn between this or that. One need not "deliberate" over what to do, but one is "determined" in what to do. To be capable of such determination, which is the same thing as being *in*capable of sinning, is to have God as the hidden subject of all one's being and doing. Only with God's empowerment is human being and acting rendered "actual" *(wirklich)*; only God makes possible a "genuinely and truly human being and acting" (I/2, 151, rev.). Once again, this reinforces the fact that for Barth human beings have their true existence "out in front of" themselves.

Notice that Barth's anthropology, as formulated in *CD* III/2, accomplishes four things. First, it presents a way of understanding human existence as a being-in-act. Realizing our humanity is always a task and not a "given." It is a deed on our part that is constituted in advance by grace on God's part. This means we are *not yet* fully human. But like God's own being-in-act, humanity's being-in-act is not without definition at the beginning. Just as divine election stands at the beginning of God's work, giving it integrity, so humanity has a "basic form of existence" that enables it to be what it is truly meant to be.

Second, Barth's anthropology allows him to derive the meaning of the image of God from the person of Jesus Christ. Humanity is to reflect that which is already refracted in the life of Jesus. Implicit in this scheme, third, is a way of speaking intelligibly about the divine-human union in Jesus Christ. According to Chalcedon, Jesus Christ is both truly human and truly divine. In the framework just outlined, Jesus is truly divine by virtue of living in a genuinely human way and truly human by virtue of having walked the path of obedience which is the actual (wirklich) destiny of all humanity. The fact of his having embodied "true" humanity constitutes and preserves Jesus' uniqueness, while the fact that what he embodies is still "humanity" continues Jesus' solidarity and sameness with his fellow human beings. More will be said in the next chapter about how this anthropological conviction shapes Barth's christology.

However, this scheme does even more than help to render an intelligible christology. Barth has also managed to preserve, fourth, the uniqueness of God vis à vis humanity by locating God's connection to humanity in the dynamic act of Jesus Christ and the continuing actions of God's people, rather than in something statically fixed or "given." God is at work giving humanity its vocation and luring humanity toward its ultimate goal. Humanity moves toward this goal by coming to participate in the divine providential history of grace.

PROVIDENCE

What we have seen thus far is that neither "creation" nor "humanity" are concepts simply "given" in advance. Their meaning needs to be constructed, and the meaning Barth constructs for them is not simply protological but eschatological in scope. Creation finds its intelligibility ahead of itself, so to speak, in a redemption that is still coming. Because creation is not neutral, world-occurrence is not impervious to God's covenantal designs. Or put more positively, Christians believe God is providentially at work in the world.

Nevertheless, Barth does not formulate his view of providence along the triumphalistic lines of traditional theology. In keeping with the postmodern emphasis on mystery, the precise mode of God's work in the world remains for Barth an ultimate enigma. Barth's reflections on providence are some of the most important in the CD. They comprise the whole of volume III/3 and are later amplified in the last half of the final volume (IV/3.2). Barth's key concept is that the mystery of God's providence cannot be properly "described" but only "indicated" in fragments of incomplete detail (III/3, 45).

Barth discusses providence as a formal "concept," a material "belief," and a comprehensive "doctrine." As a "concept," the idea of "providence" is distinct from that of "creation," which is the one-time initiation of all things. He would have nothing to do with the proposal of Moltmann and others that there is a "continual" creation.[22] For Barth creation is the "external basis" of providence, meaning that the created order provides the context in which the history of God's providence unfolds. Creation signals the coming into being of a world with its own laws and its own integrity. The concept of providence implies that God never simply leaves the world to its own devices. Providence is the concept of gracious interaction between Creator and creature. As such, it is connected to the even more primordial concept of election.

Election, which belongs to the eternal determination of God, as we have already seen, is the proper "presupposition of all the movement of creaturely life" (II/2, 184). It is "the secret of everything that takes place in this world." Every event looks back to "the decision of God which eternally precedes it" and all events "culminate in the history of salvation" (II/2, 185). Therefore, to allude to our earlier terminology, election stands as both a "presupposition" and a "consequence," or "result." It is like a grammatical perfect tense: it is a past act that bears continuing consequences (II/2, 187). In God's own integrity God has willed to be gracious, and the results of that gracious decision continue into the present and carry human beings into the overflow of the future. If God's election in Jesus Christ is "presupposed" by the theologian, this does not imply (at least not in Barth's special vocabulary) a supposition that is already fixed in one's understanding as though it were something "given"—quite the contrary. As reported in chapter two, the task of theology is to disclose "how far" and "to what extent" theology's "presuppositions" are true.

Providence is the outworking of that presupposition in human history (III/3, 5). Providence asks us to believe in God's active and faithful provision for all God's creatures. Accordingly, Barth considers Genesis 22 to be the quintessential biblical passage on providence: God's remarkable provision of a "ram in the bush" as the substitute for Abraham's bone-chilling sacrifice of Isaac.

Thus, the concept of providence has nothing to do with identifying God with the reality of world-occurrence "as it is" (IV/3.2, §72.1). That would be, once again, to reduce theology to mere "fate." This does not mean that God is remote from historical reality. Indeed, God is implicated in all of history, for God's relationship to the world is radical in its extent. Karl Barth is no less committed than John Calvin to the belief that in "everything which may happen" a person "has to do with God." No event or situation wrests itself free from God's claim upon it (III/3, 53). God would not be God "if there were a single point where [God] was absent or inactive" (III/3, 133). But this does not mean that God is simply identified with what happens. Even though election sets the "context" of history, it does not fatalistically determine its outcome.

Nevertheless, because of his high view of divine sovereignty, Barth predicts that critics will mistake his own doctrine of providence for but another totalistic and deterministic vision of the *deus ex machina*. But this is far from Barth's intention. The history of God in the world is a "hidden history." It is not to be confused with a general doctrine of world-occurrence. Calvin and the Protestant scholastics, who saw all events following more or less directly from the hand of God, come in for a blistering critique for precisely such a reductionism (III/3, 30–33). Providence is "neither felt, seen, known, nor dialectically perceived . . . but can only be believed on the basis of this Word of God" (III/3, 19).

This leads us to the second aspect of Barth's analysis, providence as Christian "belief." Providence as belief is not directed to the data of human experience nor to events as they occur in the world. Rather, it is directed to God. Once more, providence is not "fate," because it does not teach that "what will be will be," but it looks toward that qualitative element in world-occurrence that is covenantal and salvific in character. Neither does it swing to the other extreme of "idea." Covenantal history cannot be captured in any idealistically-conceived "worldview." The "worldviews" tend to treat the world either as a "great thought" or a "great machine." Too often they try to compress the God-world relationship into the portrait of a "godless world" (e.g., Arthur Schopenhauer) or a "worldless God" (e.g., Marcion) (III/1, 334–40).

To be sure, everyone has some working view of how history operates, and some of these viewpoints can be quite sophisticated and illuminating, others less so. The theologian will inevitably be informed by one or more such historical worldviews, whether drawn from Marx, Comte, Toynbee, Voegelin, or whomever. Without these concepts human beings would be without practical orientation in the world. But these viewpoints are usable only provisionally as a "working hypothesis" (III/3, 20–21). No such hypothesis is sufficient by itself to orient theology, for all our concepts of history are fallible and in need of revision.

This provisionality applies not only to our apprehension of secular history but to sacred history also. Since God is ultimate mystery, God's action in itself is never direct or immediate. God always acts through means (III/3, 64). In the world as it is, all that can be seen directly is ambiguity and confusion. In the midst of this ambiguity and evil, however, God utters a profound "Nevertheless" in the reconciling work of Jesus Christ (III/2, 44).

Knowing that God is working to reconcile the world in Christ is more important to Barth than the modern preoccupation with the "mode" of God's relationship to the world. Against this modern trend, Barth audaciously announces that the mode by which God interacts with the world is "irrelevant" (I/1, 94), for in any event it is inconceivable (III/3, 67). Attempts to fathom the divine-human relationship inevitably fall into the typical realistic or idealistic distortions (III/3, 22). They tend either to focus upon the realism of events or upon the idealism of the interpreter of events. Or again, they contrast the notion of a higher realm that is future with a realm of confusion that is present (IV/3.2, 702ff.). We must not try to make the world conform to these preconceived abstractions. What makes for a seer or a prophet, in the biblical sense, is not the ability to accurately read the events of the present or the future. The prophet speaks not *from* history but *into* history, seeing all events in relation to the qualitative command of God making itself felt "in" and "among" all events (III/3, 24). "Seeing into" such events is what the doctrine of providence is all about. It requires one to remain alert to the unheard of "new thing" in humanity's midst (IV/3.2, 708).

Notwithstanding the impenetrability of the divine hiddenness in history, Barth asserts that a certain analogy exists between the way God acts in Jesus Christ and the way God continues to operate in the world in general. Just as there is an "analogy of relationship" (*analogia relationis*) at play in the question of what it means to be human, there is an "analogy of operation" (*analogia operationis*) visible between God's work in Christ and God's working in general (III/3, 102). The analogy between general history and covenantal history is not an intrinsic one, for there is still no *analogia entis* between them. But world history in its totality receives its light from the hidden threads of the covenant. Or to use Barth's own metaphor, creaturely occurrence is enabled, by grace alone, to "mirror" God's covenantal activity in Christ (III/3, 50).

This leads us to the third point, providence as a matter of Christian "doctrine." Providence, in its capacity as part of the grammar of faith, is defined as God's preserving, accompanying, and ruling God's creatures. First, "preservation" is another way that God is *for* the creature, confirming the creature's life in its present existence. It is God's preservation that enables the creature to actualize its existence within its set limits. Like God, the creature is not an isolated monad; it is no "unhappy circle which has no periphery" (III/3, 85). Every creature stands in relationship to every other creature and, reflecting God's preservation of its own life, each creature should affirm the lives of every other creature. In their irreducible fragility, all creatures stand in need of preservation from the threat of nothingness (*das Nichtige*) and chaos.

Second, "accompanying" means that God is *with* the creature, consenting to the creature's autonomous actuality. God is irrevocably "for" us, just as a parent is "for" his or her wayward child. But, like a parent, God can be "for" us while not necessarily being "for" all our childish schemes and activities. God permits our freedom. God desires our obedience.

When we render that obedience, our freedom becomes freedom in the truest sense. All action that is truly free must be positively related to God's own action. We must conceive the activity of God and that of the obedient creature together "as a single action" (III/3, 132). Divine and human co-agency is at the heart of Barth's theology.

Barth relates his own thoughts about divine and human co-agency to the venerable doctrine of *concursus divinus*.[23] This doctrine tried to speak of how God "concurs" with creaturely activity in the most encompassing way, while also maintaining the liberty of the creature. Barth does not attempt to describe God's "concurrence" with the creature, as had the seventeenth-century scholastics with their theories of "influx" and the like.[24] Barth is convinced that resolution of these issues lies beyond human comprehension. This means that the differences between Calvinist, Lutheran, Catholic, and Arminian positions, for example, remain forever undecidable (III/3, 130). One can only render an account "to" God's work and not "of" it (III/3, 109). Nevertheless, God would not be God "if there were a single point where [God] was absent or inactive" (III/3, 133).

In trying to conceive this Barth alludes again to the realism-idealism interplay. Our conception of God's act must dissolve neither into the "resignation" of fate nor into the "rebellion" of idea. In contrast to any flat-footed realism, God's ways with the world must not be conceived materially, as though God and God's cause were mere "things." In contrast to a high-minded idealism, we should not make divine causation into a concept that subordinates both God and the creature to a "total scheme of things." The best we can say is that whatever the creature does, God's activity "precedes" the creature's action, "concurs" in it, and "follows up" with it long after the creature has ceased to act. God "precedes" the creature's activity by "predetermining" the laws of nature and the form and limits within which the creature may act, though it is not a predetermination of the creature's actions as such. God "accompanies" the creature by being coactive with the creature. God's coactivity occurs through the Word and the Spirit. God is a genuine "cause" in the world, though the concept of causation is only analogically useful. God "follows up" on the creature's deeds long after the results have left the creature's control. That God is still at work when we can work no longer is a cause for confidence and hope. The *how* of this divine operation remains a mystery of grace, not subject to human conceptuality (III/3, 140). However one decides to conceptualize God's work, it is a work that always reflects who God is in Jesus Christ.

Third, divine "ruling" means that the purposes of God make sense of the cosmos. The classical conviction is that God alone rules. From this Barth deduces that God alone is the very goal toward which God's ruling pushes. Everything proceeds from God and returns to God. This means there is an eschatological focus to providence. God is moving the creature towards a goal. Yet the conviction of God-ruling is based on more than conceptual deductions. The evidence of God-ruling occurs in certain constant features visible in our history. This evidence includes the fact that the scriptures, the church, and the Jewish people have been preserved through the centuries (III/3, 200–26). Interestingly, Barth believes God-ruling also is made manifest in the limits of birth and death that circumscribe human life. Contemplating these limits prompts Christians to be open to the encompassing and sustaining work of God (III/3, 226–38).

Mention of the limits of human life brings us to the most acute problem raised by the doctrine of providence. This is the question of how to relate the rule of God to evil, that is, to all the experiences of meaninglessness, tragedy, and chaos that afflict human existence. By uttering a divine "yes" to creation, God has justified and sanctified creation. Nevertheless, the way in which humanity knows God's work in creation is not mediated through this "yes" alone. God leaves humanity torn between the "no" and the "yes," even though Christian theology presupposes that the "no" ultimately serves the "yes." But this, mind you, is a presupposition which humanity must cling to against the weeping misery and tragic disquietude of a world which lies hidden in evil.

This topic has presented itself classically in the theodicy problem, the question of how an all-powerful and beneficent God could permit so much evil in the world. Either God's power or God's goodness seems to be compromised. If God is beneficent, then God must surely abhor evil. If, at the same time, God holds all the power there is, then why not stop evil?

Barth deliberately avoids providing an answer to the question of evil in the terms of classical "theodicy."[25] Evil cannot be domesticated by theological or philosophical systems. Most theodicies err by presuming already to know what the terms "all-powerful" and "beneficent" mean in the abstract, apart from God's self-identification in Jesus Christ. For that matter, they also suppose a too-easy definition of "evil" itself. Let us consider each of these.

First, regarding divine "beneficence," Barth resists the common assumption that a good God would simply want to eliminate evil by divine fiat. To the objection that evil seems ultimately to be God's own doing, hence calling into question God's beneficence and love, Barth's answer is that the objectors have misconstrued how God's beneficence manifests itself. God works through a love that has taken the pangs of evil upon itself. God "lets a catastrophe which might be quite remote from [God] approach [God] and affect [God's] very heart" (III/3, 357).

Second, regarding divine "power," we observed in the previous chapter's discussion of election that, in choosing to create the world, God relinquished a degree of power. God has all the power that is appropriate for a gracious *Creator* (as opposed, say, to a dictator) to have; but God cannot retain all the power there is and also allow time and space for the other. Barth went so far in the volume on election as to posit a qualified sense in which God actually wills evil, in the sense of permitting evil to continue; but God can never will evil in the same degree that God wills good. "God wills evil only because he wills not to keep to himself the light of his glory but to let it shine outside himself" (II/2, 170). To permit freedom is to risk permitting creatures the possibility of doing that which is excluded from the divine will. To the objection of classical theodicy that evil's apparent "necessity" limits the divine "sovereignty" or "freedom," Barth would answer that this again presupposes an "abstract" notion of freedom and not the concrete freedom which defines itself only in reference to the work it accomplishes in Jesus. While evil exists only "under the decree of God," it is also a catastrophe which God has taken into God's own heart. God has taken evil on as God's own cause to defeat it.

A third definitional problem pertains to the concept of evil itself. Classical theodicy tends to conceive "evil" only in reference to human wants, wishes, and desires, rather than in reference to the encompassing purposes of God. Barth joins evil squarely to God both ontically and noetically, though solely in a negative sense. Noetically, evil is connected to God, for only in the light of God do we perceive evil for what it is. Evil bears no "accessible relationship" (*zugängliche Beziehung*) to the creature that can be discovered by the creature on its own (*KD*, III/3, 404, *CD*, 350). Only in the light of God can one see evil for what it really is. Ontically, evil is related to God as that which God opposes. Evil is *das Nichtige*, or "nothingness," a contradictory disruption or "foreign body" (*Fremdkörper*) that lives parasitically in the arena of creation. If creation is that to which God says "yes," evil is that to which God says "no." It is that which God "passed over" in the act of creation (Gen. 1:2). The origin of nothingness, then, lies in God's primal renunciation. To that extent evil depends upon God, even though God did not specifically create it. Its existence is improper—and yet, it has all the demonic reality of a cancer.

That evil is "real" poses a tension, or perhaps even a contradiction. Evil has no right to exist, but it does exist. This "nothingness" is by no means "nothing." Thus it is probably wise to follow Arthur C. Cochrane's suggestion that we translate the German *das Nichtige* by using the term "Nihil" rather than "Nothingness." The Nihil is not merely Augustine's philosophically conceived and rather abstract "lapse into non-being." Instead, it is the virulent, the diabolical, the chaotic, the absurd. It can only be explained, if at all, in an indirect way. Perhaps it is a mistake to try and explain the Nihil at all, lest by naming it we delude ourselves into thinking we can master it.

Still, it is necessary to say something in order to distinguish evil from the good of creation itself. Indeed, the Nihil is not the same thing as what

Barth calls the "shadow side" (*Schattenseite*) of creation. The "shadow side" includes the creaturely realities of pain, disease, natural disasters, decay, and, above all, death itself. These are not per se evil but are a natural part of created existence. They contribute to the functioning of the "whole" that God has pronounced "good." Even disease and death are a necessary part of life, part of the struggle that makes life what it is.

Yet the shadow side is not without its own contradictions. On the one hand, Barth considers the "shadow side" to be a mark of creation's perfection, because it makes everything dependent upon God for security in the midst of jeopardy (III/3, 296). Yet, on the other hand, the "shadow side" is "so to speak adjacent to and turned towards the Nihil" (*KD*, III/3, 335, *CD*, 296, rev.).

Thus the disease and death of the "shadow side" are not good in themselves. Recall that for Barth there is no reality that is accessible "in itself." Instead, everything must be considered in light of its relationships. It is only when considered in the light of the "whole" that creation—and its "shadow side"—may be said to be "good." For the present, the Nihil too is a "necessity," even if an improper one. God permits the Nihil but, avers Barth, God is not responsible for its "nothing character" (*der Nichtigkeit*) (*KD*, III/3, 330, 424–25, *CD*, 292, 367).[26] The Nihil remains a mystery that arises on what Barth, following Luther, calls the "left hand" of God.

That Barth persists in defending the "necessity" of evil is sure to leave many of his readers perplexed. I mentioned earlier William James's complaint about Hegel and his ilk that their explanations for evil threatened to project a "block universe" in which evil was not so much "explained" as simply "explained away." In opposition to such totalistic explanations, James opted to believe in a "finite" God who resided in an "open" universe. Only a universe in which the struggle against evil was ongoing and real, in which there were real winners and real losers, and in which the outcome was not already known in advance, could enable James to make sense of the facts of existence as he saw them.

Is there any such "openness" to the universe as Barth conceives it? It seems to me James's question is a good one to pose to a theologian such as Barth who, not unlike Hegel, invests so much in the task of conceptual analysis. Perhaps the reflections of theologians and philosophers about evil are persuasive to those in positions of power and influence, but what can they mean for those whose lives are riddled by the setbacks, the tragedies, and the defeats of the Nihil? What do they say to those who suffer the base deprivations and massive cruelties inflicted by human beings against one another?

Presumably, Barth's response is that the divine "yes" heard in the experience of grace makes bearable the nihility and the shadow side of life, and that this same "yes" enables human beings to consent to the divine purpose in the world. After all, the Nihil is just what God was opposing in deigning to become a creature in Jesus Christ. But is God's solidarity with us in Jesus Christ enough? Perhaps it is enough to sustain human hope in the midst of the bourgeois struggle for meaning and affirmation, but is it enough to proclaim this and this alone over the smoking ash of Auschwitz? Does it perpetuate the "block universe" to continue Barth's orthodox claim that in the death and resurrection of Jesus Christ the Nihil is already brought to naught by God anyway? Can this give any comfort to those for whom the Nihil is not "nothing," but for whom it is an offense and a violation of their humanity?

Throughout this study I have accented the possibilities for a more open-ended reading of Barth's theology. In his discussion on the Nihil, Barth declares that a general revelation of how God is working to bring evil to naught has yet to occur. Indeed, the problem of evil provides "an extraordinarily clear demonstration of the necessary brokenness of all theological thought and utterance" (III/3, 293). We do not yet see how evil is overcome. For now, we still see in a mirror dimly. Barth's sober counsel is that we must neither underestimate evil nor overestimate it. Unlike James's reviled "block universe," in which a dispassionate God simply proclaims the universe "good" from without, the God to whom Barth gives witness is earnestly at work making the world "good" from within. Amid the suffering work of this God, a truly Christian theology must permit one to hear and to heed the "cries of the wounded."

In Christian perspective those cries are nowhere heard with more poignance than in the forsaken cry of the crushed and broken figure on the cross. Barth's hope in a postmodern world is that in Jesus Christ God is working to destroy evil, but only by means of suffering it. By the power of the Holy Spirit, God stands with humanity in a suffering solidarity—dividing the hostile waters of chaos, subduing Leviathan, and making possible the reconciliation of human beings to life's goodness. Only by suffering evil, and continuing to suffer it, will God destroy evil and reconcile the world.

5

GOD "WITH" US

> The central statement of the christology of the early church is that God becomes one with humanity: Jesus Christ, "true God and true human being."
>
> Karl Barth, *CD* I/2, 125 (rev.)

Reconciliation in Jesus Christ, God's becoming human in order to enable humanity to become reconciled with God, is at the "center" of Christian faith. In Jesus Christ God is "with" us. This insight forms the middle point or "center" of the "triad" of creation-reconciliation-redemption (IV/1, 110–11). This "center," which always remains ultimate mystery, would not be what it is apart from creation and redemption, the two horizons that form its "circumference" (IV/1, §57.1). Like creation, reconciliation is not an end in itself. Instead reconciliation is a new *beginning*. It is a transformation on the way to salvation (IV/1, 109).

Barth followed the apostle Paul in understanding "redemption" or "salvation" as a predominantly eschatological reality. Thus, reconciliation, as a turning point on the way to salvation should not be thought to establish a "final and stable relationship" in which God and humanity can finally co-exist in quiet and contented peace (IV/1, 110). Reconciliation does not mean, "I am saved," but that "I am saved by grace." Reconciliation opens one up for God; it causes one to look eagerly forward to what one will become in the Spirit, even as one looks with gratitude backward to one's point of origin as a creature in Jesus Christ.

In this dynamic movement from the *extra nos* to the *pro nobis* to the *in nobis*, creation belongs to the primordial regions of protology, while redemption (to anticipate the theme of the next chapter) belongs to the hidden sphere of eschatology.[1] Suspended in between creation and redemption is the present historical action by which God reconciles human beings in Jesus Christ. This is an event that occurs, and is still occurring, in the here and now of history, an event that lies poised between promise and fulfillment. It is an event in which God is restoring estranged creatures to fellowship with God and with one another, and in so doing, is moving them toward what they were truly meant to be: fully human.

This event of reconciliation, of humanity restored to fellowship with God, finds its focus in the uncommon humanity of Jesus of Nazareth, a humanity so extraordinary that Barth designates it a "sacrament" of the living God. The God "with" us of reconciliation in Christ makes the God "for" us of election and creation concrete. For of what use would be a divine ally who, as Creator, was predisposed to favor us, but who was either unable or unwilling to come to our aid? You and I may be vaguely "for" the inhabitants of some foreign land that is afflicted by war or famine; but this by itself is of small comfort to them as they endure their distress. Reconciliation in Christ declares that God is *with* us in Jesus Christ, actively embracing our precarious cause as God's own.

If God is truly "with" us in the humanity of Jesus, does this mean that we have finally located a point of "presence," a divine comfort that is "given" to humanity in a straightforward way? And not only "given," but given exclusively in Jesus Christ? If so, then how are we to square this givenness and exclusivity with all the talk we examined earlier about the radical "openness" of the Christian "center," talk which seems to flow from the very core of Barth's theology? Is there a contradiction between the theocentric recognition of mystery and the christocentric emphasis on grace?

The answer to this question depends on how one understands Barth's concept of the "center." For Barth Jesus Christ is the central embodiment of divine mystery, for "a church dogmatics must . . . be freely determined christologically as a whole and in all its parts, as surely as the revealed Word is identical with Jesus Christ" (I/2, 123, rev.). Anyone who quarrels with that conviction is disputing not only Barth but the very raison d'être of historic, mainstream Christianity. One could argue, after all, that "christocentrism" is a redundancy, since all Christians orient themselves by what God has done in Jesus Christ. Still, Barth effected a fundamental shift in that christological "center," a shift away from a static to a dynamic christology. Jesus Christ is not to be conceived as a static "given" but as a dynamic "act." To put the Christian message in its most succinct form, *"God acts as Jesus acts"* (III/2, 62).

The significance of Jesus Christ, to unpack this a bit more, is that in his life there occurs a coincidence, though not an identity, of divine and human action. "God does what this human being does. Or rather, this human being does what God does. But either way this life is fulfilled in a personal act" (IV/3.1, 41). In Jesus Christ, "God himself in person is the subject of a real, actualized [*wirklichen*] human being and acting" (I/2, 151). In Jesus Christ, God and humanity "live together . . . in the indestructible conjunction of the differentiated act in which both Creator and creature exist" (IV/3.1, 40).

Whatever Barth's "christological concentration" might have meant, it did not mean a "Jesus-olatry" nor any "abstract Jesus worship" (I/2, 136). We simply cannot get behind the mystery of Jesus' existence (I/2, 128). For it was not deity "in itself" that was made flesh in Jesus Christ, since deity "does not exist at all in itself as such." Instead deity exists within the world only in the dynamic mode of being-in-act (I/2, 133).

Thus the melodic sound of Barth's *christo*centrism is juxtaposed against but without contradicting the countermelody of his *theo*centrism. The point of focusing on Jesus Christ, as we saw earlier in the discussion of election, is to upset all neutral and abstract conceptions of God—as for example all dispassionate ways of construing divine omnipotence—in order to reshape them according to the free and gracious history that God is enacting in the world through Jesus Christ.

Rather than standing for a narrowing of theology, christocentrism stands for a widening in which all our preconceived notions of who and what God is must be thoroughly reconstructed in the light of Jesus Christ. This, in turn, entails three denials. First, centering on Christ does not turn christology into a "central dogma" or systematic principle of theology. Christocentrism is not a "system" in the sense of a "structure of principles" that are "self-contained and complete in themselves" and that rest on some "fundamental view of things" (*Grundanschauung*) (I/2, 861). Thus, christocentrism is not a preconceived "foundation" already well-known from which everything else can be deduced. No such systematic "center" or "foundation" is permissible in theology, not even a foundation that is christological, for this would foreclose the "free investigation" into the Christian message that the mystery of God requires (I/2, 868). Christian theology is "not dealing with a Christ-principle, but with Jesus Christ himself as attested in Holy Scripture" (IV/3.1, 174).

The two other denials revolve around the sacramental reality of Jesus Christ as truly divine and truly human. Regarding Jesus' true divinity, Barth denied—and hence his christocentrism could not mean—that the humanity of Jesus held deity as its own possession. The divinity of Christ, in other words, is not something simply obvious, or self-evident, that attends the person of Christ. There were many in the New Testament who knew Jesus but had no awareness of his divinity. Next, regarding Jesus' true humanity, Barth denied any "christomonism" that would make the deity of Christ such an all-encompassing factor in the event of salvation that it simply eliminated any genuine human action[2] (IV/4, Fragment, 20–33).

In order to understand these last two denials, let us consider in more detail Barth's understanding of the true divinity and true humanity of Jesus Christ as presented in volume four of the *Church Dogmatics*.

Barth's doctrine of reconciliation unfolds in three "aspects" (*Aspekte*) that in turn broaden out into three angles of viewing the one event of atonement. These three aspects follow, once again, the pattern we have noted before of "presupposition" and "consequence." What happens in Jesus Christ is, from one perspective, a humiliation of God, a downward movement which occurs in Jesus Christ, "the Lord as Servant." From another perspective, however, reconciliation is the elevation of humanity, an elevation accomplished in Jesus Christ, "the Servant as Lord." The downward movement is the presupposition of reconciliation, while the

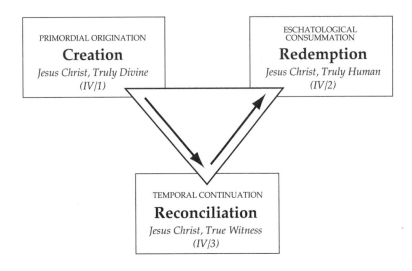

FIGURE 5.1

elevation of humanity is the consequence. Whereas traditional Reformed theology thought of these two movements as two "states"—the so-called "humiliation" and "exaltation" of Jesus—Barth repudiated such static formulae and preferred to speak instead of two dynamic "directions."

These two directions are then "held together" in a third "aspect" (IV/1, 136). As will become even clearer in the next chapter, this third aspect—indicated by the rubric of Jesus Christ, the "True Witness"—forms the centerpiece and connecting link between the first two. The reality of Jesus Christ as "True Witness" is not a third "thing" over against "the Lord as Servant" and "the Servant as Lord," but it offers a concrete way of viewing the first two in their unity. The first two, apart from their unity in the third, are merely an abstraction (IV/3.1, 41).

Respectively, these three aspects embrace divine action as presupposition, human action as consequence, and divine and human togetherness-in-action. These three also form a second triad within the larger triad of creation-reconciliation-redemption (see figure 5.1). As will become clear later on, the midpoint of the Reconciliation triad—Jesus Christ as "True Witness"—also stands at the "center" of the whole *CD*. In order to substantiate this interpretation, we shall examine these three aspects each in its turn.

JESUS CHRIST, TRULY DIVINE

Reconciliation begins with the "downward" movement from God to humanity in which God, operating in the mode of the divine "Son," becomes incarnate in Jesus Christ (IV/1, §59). This downward action of a God who reaches out to humanity fulfills the first and initiatory intention of the divine-human covenant in which God avers, "I will be your God."

Barth's intention was to achieve a dynamic and historically oriented reconception of the Nicene and Chalcedonian "two natures" christology. But, interestingly, it is "not the dogma itself" that Barth found instructive in classical christology. Although the ecumenical councils remind theology of the "direction" in which it must look, they do not absolve theology from "following [its] own path." Accordingly, Barth considered his own conclusions to be "formally independent" of Nicaea (IV/1, 200). What counts is not the dogma but the recognition (*Erkenntnis*) that is "presupposed and confirmed in the dogma"—namely, that in Jesus Christ one encounters the act of God (IV/1, 161, rev.). Indeed, Barth was attempting to move beyond Nicaea's static talk of "natures" or "substance" altogether. To achieve this Barth pondered the reality of Jesus Christ, first, under the "aspect" of the downward movement in which God the "Son," who is also the sovereign "Lord," deigns to become a human "servant" (IV/1, ch. XIV, §§59–63).

Barth's opening reflections on God's downward movement bear the caption, "The Obedience of the Son of God." The first subsection, in turn, is entitled, "The Way of the Son of God into the Far Country." The image of a "son" venturing out into the "far country" alludes to the well-known story of the "Prodigal Son" in Luke's gospel. There a miscreant son demands his inheritance and leaves the sanctuary of his father's house to pursue his own independent designs in a faraway land. Some time later he repents, having squandered his livelihood, and returns to the merciful forgiveness of his father.

Although this parable is primarily about human sin and the need to repent before a loving God, Barth reinterpreted it christologically. That the son takes leave of the father and then returns suggested to Barth a typology (IV/2, 21–25). It would be stretching the exegesis, Barth acknowledged, to draw a simple equation between the character of Jesus, who is righteous, and the prodigal, who is unrighteous. Nevertheless, the career of Jesus follows a similar movement of leave-taking and returning. Who other than Jesus, after all, can claim as the parable says of the prodigal to have been "once dead" but "now alive"? Who but Jesus has truly been "lost" in reference to God "but now found"? The "son of God" has, by assuming human nature in Jesus Christ, journeyed into the "far country" of human dissipation and sin. If Jesus Christ is not himself a prodigal, he nonetheless traces the footsteps of a prodigal, in order to accomplish the reconciling mission of the "Father."

Lest it be thought that Barth meant to reify this talk of "Father" and "Son," or to repristinate classical orthodoxy, the term "Son" remained for him an imprecise pointer that "does not correspond to its object" (IV/1, 210). No such "correspondence" is even possible, since the "object" in question is the dynamic history of *God*—God's act of reconciling the world in Christ. Barth declared, "the history in which God is the living God . . . can only be *indicated* but not *conceived* by our terms son and father and spirit" (IV/1, 210, emphasis supplied). In no way, then, does the revelation from God to humanity in Jesus Christ dissolve the mystery of God's being. Like all theological language used to express this mystery, the term "Son" can be used only "with great reserve because of its inadequacy" (ibid.).

Nevertheless, the term "Son" still "points," according to Barth, and it points Christians in a direction they must follow. Its inadequacy notwithstanding, the concept of Jesus' obedient "sonship" points the way to understanding his deity. How so? In what, specifically, does Jesus' "true divinity" consist? For Barth the deity of Jesus Christ is not something straightforward and "given," but it consists in the manner of his *action*.[3] It consists in Jesus' willing obedience to fulfill his mission—nothing more, but also nothing less. "What distinguishes the man Jesus as the Son of God is that . . . this man wills only to be obedient—obedient to the will of the Father, which is to be done on earth for the redemption of humanity as it is done in heaven" (IV/1, 164). Anything more or less would fail to be truly human.

The placing of such emphasis on the human obedience of Jesus in this first "aspect" of reconciliation is significant, for the purpose here is to gather up Jesus' divinity and to portray God's grand gesture from "above to below." Yet the very first words Barth uttered about the person of Jesus Christ when first he turned, after a methodological introduction, to the substance of christology itself (*zur Sache*) were an affirmation of the indubitable *humanity* of Jesus (IV/1, 159–60).[4] Barth carried these reflections in IV/1 to a quite astonishing conclusion. If Jesus is indeed a true human being, and if God is authentically revealed in this person, then, by inference, one must conclude that there is a "humanity of God" in the humanity of Jesus (IV/1, 124–25). As Barth put it in a lecture at the Aarau conference of 1956 on the "Humanity of God,"

> How could God's deity exclude his humanity, since it is God's freedom
> for love and thus his capacity to be not only in the heights but also in the
> depths, not only great but also small, not only in and for himself but also
> with another distinct from him, and to offer himself to him?"[5]

This is the great mystery of the Christian faith.

In the very humanity of Jesus, we are dealing with God. When God and humanity are co-actors, it changes something about a person's "being and acting." It is precisely because God is the subject, the co-actor, in Jesus' being and acting that "they are genuinely and truly human being and acting." God's coaction, far from removing Jesus' humanity, establishes it. "Jesus is not a demigod. He is not an angel. Nor is He an ideal man. He is a human being as we are, equal to us in the state and condition into which our disobedience has brought us. And in being what we are He is God's Word" (I/2, 151).

It is precisely in being truly human, then, that Jesus shows forth the truly divine. Jesus's humanity is not that of an automaton, but he is one who freely wills, who prays, who acts. His act is a genuinely free act, because it is an act of "witnessing to the reign of God" (II/2, 179). In Jesus we are confronted by a human being who lives and acts on a "qualitatively different plane" (*über qualitativ Anderer auf dem Plan*), though still a truly human plane (*KD* IV/1, 174, *CD*, 160). This is true whether or not Jesus had any so-called "messianic consciousness," a fact that can be neither proved nor disproved (IV/1, 161–62). Jesus' uniqueness consisted not in somehow possessing the "essence" of God but in his complete and unreserved obedience to the will of God.[6]

This new form of human obedience was illustrated with dramatic clarity in such biblical portrayals as Jesus' baptism, his temptation in the wilderness, and his prayer in Gethsemane. For instance, Barth interpreted Jesus' prayer and his obedience in Gethsemane as an echo in human history of the eternal election by which God determined to be gracious to human beings (IV/1, 238–39). Or again, regarding Jesus' baptism and temptation, Barth considered it significant that Jesus of Nazareth entered his ministry in the mode of "a great sinner repenting." Indeed, what separates Jesus from others, what makes him in his capacity as truly human also truly divine, is his assent to the justice of God's "no" against sin, on the one hand, and, on the other hand, his own human endeavor, by God's grace, to say "yes" to all God's purposes (IV/1, 225–73). In short, Jesus is as God is; Jesus does as God does.

Because Jesus is as God is and does as God does, Barth can call the humanity of Jesus the "sacrament" of the living God. Barth could speak of God being mediated and revealed in all created being (I/2, 162). Yet whatever we may make of such a general revelation of God, it is nothing like the way God's reality is mediated in the sacramental action of Jesus Christ. Barth defined a "sacrament" as a "sign" that bespeaks the mystery of God's grace (I/2, 228). His understanding of the "sacramental" way in which God mediates grace is akin to his thoughts about the various worldly "parables" of grace.

In the Romans commentary, for example, Barth announced that every aspect of reality points beyond itself parabolically in a cosmic "symbol-system" of grace.[7] Although no human action is good in itself, all action has the potential to be a "parable" or a "token" of the action of God.[8] Every human being "presents us with the problem of the hidden God."[9] In the *CD* Barth continued this affirmation of God's hiddenness within human reality. There is a sacramental character attending every human being. My neighbor, with whom I share a common need, acquires "a sacramental significance" and is "a visible sign of invisible grace, a proof that I, too, am not left alone in the world, but am borne and directed by God" (I/2, 436). Moreover, every reception of revelation must occur within the sphere of sacrament and be marked by definite (*bestimmt*) sacramental "signs." Such signs include the two liturgical sacraments of baptism and the Lord's Supper, which Barth thought of, following Calvin, as adjuncts to preaching (I/1, 56). In addition, the sign-giving of God stretches well beyond the liturgical sacraments to include such things as the history of the Jewish people, the history of the Church, the historic preservation of the scriptures, and even the way that human life is circumscribed by birth and death (III/3, 200–38). Yet all these signs find their meaning in the one sign par excellence of God's grace.

Jesus' being and act bear consequences not only for the being of humanity but for the being of God as well. Barth asserted that Jesus' obedience unto death provides the unique way for *God* to be "obedient" as well (IV/1, 164). Barth admits that the concept of an "obedient" God is one to which we are unaccustomed. We think of God owing obedience to no one. Yet divine "obedience" does not mean that God is somehow less than God but quite the opposite: God is said to be "obedient" in a *free* obedience through which God lives up to what God has already determined to be in election.

This recapitulates the same perplexing question raised earlier in chapter three of how what happens in Jesus Christ can have an effect on the life of God. To what extent are the sufferings of Jesus *constitutive* for the divine life, or to what extent do they merely *exemplify* something already real and true in God's own eternal being? The answer we gave is that God's character is genuinely embodied and exhibited in God's work but not exhausted in that work. God's own identity is genuinely enacted through the historical life of Jesus, but God's life subsists in a primordial reality that precedes those historical outworkings. God has determined to be "for" human beings primordially, and also, without any diminution of God's deity, to be "with" human beings historically.

Some of Barth's more adventuresome heirs maintain that what happened in the history of Jesus was actually "constitutive" for who God is. God becomes a different God as a result of what happened in Jesus. Arguing in this vein, Jürgen Moltmann offers in his book *The Crucified God* a midrash on the New Testament witness to the death and resurrection of

Christ, interpreting what happened at Jesus' crucifixion as an event that casts its shadow back on the "inner" triune life of God. Through the event of the cross, according to Moltmann, the contradictory features of history—the difference between the world as it is, with its oppression, suffering, and death, and the world as it ought to be—is permitted to impress itself into the very life of the Godhead.[10] The pathos of this contradiction is reflected in Jesus' cry of dereliction (Mark 15:34, par.), which for Moltmann poses the unavoidable question of theodicy, the question to which all of Christian theology is either explicitly or implicitly a reply.[11] In the "inner trinitarian event" of the cross, God the "Father" deliberately delivered up God the "Son" to a ghastly and violent death for the sake of all (Rom. 8:32; 1:18ff.; John 3:16). We would consider this divine abandonment demonic, explains Moltmann, were it not that Jesus is never merely a passive object in his death but also an acting subject who gave himself up freely for humanity's sake (Gal. 2:20). It is not clear, however, how the victim's assent to this hideousness in any way removes the offense of its being (according to Moltmann) divinely determined. In any event, the abandonment by the "Father" and the being-abandoned of the "Son" create a "rift" in the life of God. In this negation the "Son" suffers the pain of Godforsakenness, and the "Father" suffers as well the loss and death of the "Son." Even at the point of abject separation, however, the "Father" and the "Son" are, through the mediation of the Spirit, united in their solidarity with the world.[12]

Eberhard Jüngel has gone even further than Moltmann, making the beguiling suggestion that God's self-identification with the crucified Jesus entails the very death of God in that event.[13] In both these proposals, self-renunciation and self-surrender bleed over into self-contradiction as the defining characteristic of God's trinitarian life.

Though inspired by Barth's own theology of God's being-in-suffering with God's people, both of these rather extravagant proposals tend to restrict the life of God to the things that happen in human history. In pursuit of the praiseworthy goal of eliminating the old despotic view of divine aseity, Moltmann and Jüngel have pushed Barth's theology in a direction that (arguably) compromises God's freedom and self-consistency. We must wonder how theologians can possibly know in this much pictorial detail about what is going on eternally between the "Father" and the "Son."

Barth's own reflections are more circumspect. He would agree that God has freely chosen to be "with" us in solidarity through all our suffering and pain, something we know because the character of God is reflected and expressed in the suffering character of the crucified and risen Jesus. God indeed identifies with this crucified one. But Barth drew shy of the blank claim that God is in any sense a "crucified God," or a God who undergoes death in any literal sense. The Christian hope, rather, is that the character of God is not only a character that suffers but a power that, however hidden in its operations, can nonetheless act and can save.

In his own day, Barth rejected the notion of the seventeenth-century theologian Johannes Coccejus (who, incidently, had a significant influence on Moltmann) that salvation involves an inner-trinitarian "pact" between the "Father" and the Son."[14] There is no need to speak of any inner-trinitarian "decision" or "transaction," according to Barth, for God and humanity have already been placed in relationship through election (IV/1, 63–66). To speak with Coccejus in this way, Barth alleged, is simply "mythology." Presumably, Barth today would see a similar mythic quality in some of the recent positions of Jürgen Moltmann and perhaps Eberhard Jüngel as well.

The key affirmation for Barth is that God's new reconciling act of grace in Jesus Christ is more than an arbitrary and therefore potentially reversible deed. This genuine irreversibility is what it means to say that the "Son" has made his way into the "far country." It is the "Son's" obediently entering into the "far country" and becoming a "servant" that demonstrates his deity, for through the mission of the "Son," God in person has undertaken to reconcile and redeem humanity for the sake of God's own glory. That God goes to such great lengths to be "with" us defines the radical extent to which God is primevally "for" us.

God's unheard-of plan was to make humanity's plight God's own plight (IV/1, 215–16). All this may sound just as "mythological" and speculative as what Barth rejected in Coccejus and what he surely would have rejected in Moltmann. At the very least it is highly metaphorical. The key to understanding it, however, is to focus on the category of "act." The type of action one perceives in Jesus Christ, Barth is claiming, is just the sort of action one learns to expect from God. For Barth this is the truth behind the ancient "Monothelite" controversy in which the Sixth Ecumenical Council at Constantinople (680 C.E.) denied as heresy the belief that Jesus had only one will, holding instead that Jesus Christ had both a divine and a human will (II/2, 605). Although to speak of Jesus Christ having "two wills" may seem strange, the point is that in Jesus Christ there occurs a striking coincidence of divine and human willing. In Jesus Christ the will of God was done on earth as in heaven.

Perhaps substituting the word "character," once again, can augment our understanding. The trustworthy character of Jesus Christ reflects the equally trustworthy character of God. Through the gracious activity of Jesus Christ, people discover the unique identity of God. Jesus' fidelity to the "other" reflects the very fidelity of God. But something more occurs in Jesus Christ as well. What happens in Jesus Christ is a reversal of roles between divinity and humanity, effectuating a new situation: a reconciliation.

Through the person of Jesus Christ, God the divine "judge" of humanity submits to the full weight of humanity's own judgment. He is the "Judge Judged in Our Place" (IV/1, §59.2). Jesus' "sinlessness" consisted in his willingness to accept God's verdict against sin. "Put in the sinner's position [Jesus] bowed to the divine verdict and commended himself solely to the grace of God" (I/2, 157). We noted earlier that God assumed a risk in creating a world that was exposed to the possibility of evil. The evil of the world brings a certain jeopardy to the honor of God. The great reversal in Jesus Christ is that God assumes the judgment and responsibility for this evil. The "no" directed against sin and evil is now redirected towards God. Only by becoming "with" us even to the point of identifying with sin and death could God be truly "for" us in the event of reconciliation (IV/1, 228–31).

This great reversal, in which the righteous one is declared to be unrighteous, results in the exaltation of humanity. Jesus not only shows us the condescending grace of God but also accomplishes the elevated form of a new humanity.

JESUS CHRIST, TRULY HUMAN

There is only one God and only one act of reconciliation, but this one act of God must be viewed from a second angle. If the first part of reconciliation brings divinity to bear in human history ("I will be your God"), the second part brings to fruition for the first time a completed and "real" humanity ("You will be my people"). God stoops downward, so to speak, to embrace humanity, but human beings must also be elevated to a place of true fellowship with God and with their fellow human beings. The first aspect of reconciliation envisions the primordial Creator God who graciously deigns to be reconciled with the creature. The second glimpses the creature in a situation of renewed fellowship with this God who is the Reconciler.

Barth agreed with Schleiermacher that Jesus constitutes the first instance in history of a completed human existence. Nevertheless, he rejected the idea that Jesus accomplished this task through a realization of his own inherent human capacity for God (I/2, 134–35). Since for Barth there can be no inherent human capacity for God, he understood Jesus' accomplishments, like Calvin understood them before him, as resulting from the constant power of the Holy Spirit. Jesus' life of perfect obedience is a thoroughly human accomplishment, though it is enacted through the initiative of the power of God. Jesus Christ for Barth is both one hundred percent human and one hundred percent divine. Every act of Jesus is thoroughly human and divine at once. This double agency occurs in such a way that the divinity does not abrogate the humanity, nor vice versa, for

Jesus is completely like us in his human nature, differing from us only in the fact that his is a human nature now exalted to its true destiny.

Barth considered the distinctive humanity of Jesus under four aspects. First, the New Testament presents him as a human being par excellence, the "Royal Human Being." To be confronted by Jesus was to be transformed. It was impossible to be neutral in his presence. He demanded decision, *metanoia*. His character was, moreover, unforgettable in its freedom, for he was totally free to do the will of the God whom he called "Father." From these factors emerged his unique and abiding identity as the "Son." This filial identity abides, because "he is the one who still *is* what he *was*" (IV/2, 163, emphasis supplied). The New Testament could speak of him in no other way than as the one who is not dead but still alive (IV/2, 156–66).

Jesus' distinctiveness consists, second, in his own human existence agreeing with the existence of God. Jesus lives *kata theon*, meaning in a way analogous to the mode of existence of God. Jesus "reflects" God as God's image. As one who is ignored, discounted, and despised, Jesus shares the "strange identity which falls on God" in the world. In radical solidarity with the God who is poor in the eyes of the world, Jesus ignores the high and mighty and sides with the weak and lowly. In addition, Jesus cuts a revolutionary figure in connection to the so-called "orders" of life. Not ranging himself or his disciples on the side of any exigent program, party, or political principle, Jesus breaks all the constraints of the world as it is. To the extent the world is fallen, Jesus, like God, opposes it. But above all, the first and last word about the human being Jesus of Nazareth is that, like God, he is radically *for* the other, imparting blessing and reflecting God's elemental "yes" to humanity and the cosmos (IV/2, 166–92).

Jesus' human distinctiveness, third, is carried out in the entirety of his life-action (*Lebenstat*) (IV/2, 192–247). By "life-action" Barth understood the whole *Gestalt* of his person and work, neither of which is separable from the other. His life-action includes, on the one hand, his "word" in the broadest, most comprehensive sense. The New Testament has little desire to preserve the actual words of Jesus—the Aramaic Jesus spoke is now largely forgotten—but it does portray him evangelizing, teaching, and suffering. Jesus' life-action embraces then, on the other hand, his concrete activity. Jesus' activity in behalf of God's reign reflects a divine power at work which puts things in a new and different light (IV/2, 219–20). Jesus' actions are always done for the needy: to bring release from suffering; to embody the mutual commitment of the covenant; to bring about radical solidarity with humanity; and to realize the freedom of grace (IV/2, 221–33).

Finally, Jesus' human distinctiveness comes into focus through the reality of the cross. Jesus' whole life is, in a sense, a cross. Yet the gospels do not dwell on this as though it were a tragedy or a profound misfortune. Rather, it is from the cross that Jesus is crowned as the "Royal Human Being."

The combination of "True Divinity" and "True Humanity" is not meant to be a paradox: "the incarnation is inconceivable but it is not absurd" (I/2, 160). It is only by being truly human that Jesus is truly divine and vice versa. Jesus is just as human as anyone else, but in realizing his humanity Jesus is "the same as us in quite a different way from us." Jesus enacts a completed and realized humanity, whereas the humanity of everyone else is truncated and distorted. Jesus is like all other human beings in that he shares their *nature*; but he is different from them in that he enacts a new and different *destiny*. It is a destiny to which all human beings are appointed, even if they are far from completing it apart from grace. The key to understanding this, once again, is to realize that, in Barth's theology, it is only the act of God that enables *any* person to realize her humanity. In Jesus Christ "God himself in person is the subject of real human being and acting. And just because God is the subject of it, this being and acting are real. They are genuinely and truly human being and acting" (I/2, 151).

The last point is an ontic point from which flows a corresponding noetic point. We are in no position to read our own humanity into Jesus, for it is we who need to be told by him what is truly human (IV/1, 131). To be instructed about this by Jesus is to encounter him in his prophetic office, to which we now turn.

JESUS CHRIST, TRUE WITNESS

The two grand gestures of reconciliation—"I will be your God," and "You will be my people"—are not complete without a third feature which ties them together: "Jesus Christ, the True Witness" (IV/3, §69). Just as the first two aspects emphasized the traditional "priestly" and "royal" character of Christ's work, so the third accents Christ's prophetic office, the function of proclaiming the truth and making it effectual in the lives of God's people. Jesus not only embodies true divinity and true humanity, but he makes these realities known in their togetherness.

This third theme forms the climax of Barth's presentation of reconciliation and also, as things turned out, the conclusion of the *CD*. Speaking of it as the "climax," however, can be misleading if the third angle of viewing reconciliation is thought to follow after the first two as though in a linear sequence. The third aspect is not third in sequence, for Barth spoke of the third theme explicitly as solidifying a union: it forms a mediating or intervening link between the first two. It is the "source of the first two, and it comprehends them both" (IV/1, 135).

Viewed from this third angle, Jesus Christ is *both* divine and human and not some "third thing" between them, not some hybrid but the concrete coming together of the two in manifest truthfulness. This coming together is not merely conceptual, but it is a concrete historical occurrence. It is not God's grace in and of itself, nor the work of grace in humanity, nor the sum of the two side by side, but both in their concrete togetherness in Jesus Christ.

This third aspect is nothing less than the effectual bringing together of divinity and humanity through the power of the Holy Spirit. This togetherness is first actualized in the humanity of Jesus, which is the central sacramental sign of God's "yes" toward the world. But this togetherness also has implications for the lives of all other human beings. Whereas the first two movements signify the "what" of the covenant, the third, unifying movement pertains to the "how" of the covenant. The "how" of salvation points us in the direction of redemption. The "what" of the first two aspects were capsulized in two rubrics: the "Judge Judged in Our Place" and the "Royal Human Being." In the pivotal third aspect, Jesus is understood as "Victor." The "how" of reconciliation depends on the victory of God in Christ.

God's victory in Jesus Christ, contrary to much traditional doctrine, did not occur all at once. Reconciliation is not simply a "triumphant affair."[15] First of all, it occurs over time in the form of a life-changing transformation that can be "narrated." Note, however, that this narrative is not strictly limited to this or that line of narrative embedded in scripture. After all, it is Karl Barth himself who is doing the narrating in *CD* volume four, piecing together insights from scripture into his own rendition of the story of grace. The Word of light, second, can unfold only gradually. Recalling the question of William James, whether history is a real drama, we note that for Barth there is a real conflict between good and evil. The evil that opposes God must be taken seriously, otherwise we would not be narrating a real history with real risks and surprises (IV/3.1, 172). That God overcomes opposition "is . . . not something self-evident, given or necessary, but a new and special and wonderful thing" (IV/3.1, 167). It is good news.

Nevertheless, and this is the fourth point, the work of Jesus Christ does indeed work to overcome the opposition, for "God is not God in vain." The victory is sure, even if it can only be understood dynamically and teleologically. It is a work that reveals itself only "in the totality of its occurrence" (IV/3.1, 183–212). There is still a real openness to this history, for the empirical shape this victory will take is for now seen in a mirror only darkly.

The prophetic work of Christ echoes at another level the interplay that we have previously seen between realism and constructivism. On the one hand, the ontic reality of this prophetic work takes precedence over the noetic circumstance of anyone actually knowing the reality (IV/3.1, 213–14). Ontically speaking, Jesus brings salvation for all, though noetically the covenant has not yet been "concluded" with all (222). Yet, on the other hand, the ontic reality does actualize itself in a noetic reality. Salvation becomes real only insofar as it establishes human knowledge of God in the world

(214–16). Even though there is an asymmetry between the divine initiative and human response, the human side of the equation is given its own integrity in the event of reconciliation. "Whether we think down from Jesus Christ to his people, or up from his people to Jesus Christ, we must respect and bring out the relationship and reciprocity which always characterize the intercourse between God and humanity" (215). The reconciliation that takes place—the transformation of the human person—is not merely neutral, as though one decided whether to embrace reconciliation at a critical distance, but it is dynamically engaged under divine authorship (216–18). An encounter occurs that can be neither critically depreciated (à la idealism) nor objectivistically inflated (à la realism) (218–20). The action of Jesus Christ is a genuine human action in which a human being becomes "in the full and not merely the conventional sense of the term a Christian" (220).

Thus the prophetic work of Jesus Christ is, speaking realistically, a "divinely posited fact," something that has happened once and for all in the "then and there" of Jesus of Nazareth, bringing into being a new human mode of existence. God says to humanity in the prophetic act of Jesus Christ, "as I know you, you already are" (250). At the same time, it is strange to call this work a "fact," for it is a "fact" that is still running its course. Speaking idealistically, it is an occurrence that is not grounded in the world as it is, but one that rests in the ongoing work of God in the "here and now" of a history advancing into the future. Yet neither is it purely ideal, for "it takes its place within reality" even though it is not the work of any worldly reality (226). It is a history that cannot be summed up through any "ism" of the real or any "ism" of the ideal but only in the salvific "name" of Jesus Christ.

What occurs in the third aspect of reconciliation is an overcoming of the opposition God meets in the human person. God stands against the opposition of human beings, though God remains "for" and not against the human being per se. Human beings mount their opposition to reconciliation in three forms that Barth analyzes, yet again, by alluding to the interplay between realism and idealism. First, human beings oppose genuine reconciliation in grace through their desire for the givenness of "fate" (*Schicksal*) or a "supreme" being. Before such a "supreme" being there is no genuine reciprocity (252–53). Second, human beings oppose God in the opposite, more idealistic way by substituting a "worldview," a "little prophecy" of their own creation for the truth that is Jesus Christ. But this too eliminates reciprocity, for it amounts to humanity's meager attempt to understand itself through itself. A third form of opposing God is by way of "religion." This is the worst path of all, for even as it makes a move toward true divine-human togetherness, toward the genuine encounter of the Word, in the end it settles for "just a grey mist of puffed up mediocrity, of pathetic tedium and of important unimportance" (258–59; cf. I/2,

§17). Religion cannot provide the synthesis of "fate" and "idea" that only God's Word in Jesus Christ can provide.

Jesus "the Victor" must overcome these oppositions, but he does so in a victory that is not yet concluded. The reconciliation that is set in motion by Christ is still straining forward, as yet incomplete. Although the Christian may have certainty that victory is to be consummated in Jesus Christ, that consummation is not yet realized. Its realization is grounded neither realistically in the historical progress of humanity in general or of the church in particular, nor idealistically in the inner certainty of faith. No, the realization of divine and human togetherness is located in Jesus Christ who is the Word of God and (as such) the act of God, making prophetic appeal to the "real" human being who exists, as it were, out in front of us. Humanity is reconciled with God but not yet redeemed. Humanity is on the road but is not yet at its destination.

To sum up, the triadic union accomplished in the third aspect of reconciliation is not a superfluous add-on to the first two movements but constitutes their concrete "center." The triadic (rather than linear) interpretation offers the best way to make sense of the doctrine of reconciliation and to appreciate its pivotal place within the overall structure of the *CD*. In particular, it offers a more pneumatologically oriented way of reading Barth, for the third "aspect" functions in a way analogous to the Holy Spirit's role in Western theology as the *vinculum pacem* or *vinculum amoris*— the bond of peace or love—between the work of the "Father" and the work of the "Son."

PNEUMATOLOGY IN THE DOCTRINE OF RECONCILIATION

It is often alleged, especially by critics of the Western and Augustinian version of trinitarian theology, that the Holy Spirit is simply superfluous to Barth's theology, since to them Barth's focus on the encounter between the "Father" and the "Son" looks more "binitarian" than "trinitarian."[16] Yet the triadic interpretation we have been pursuing highlights the genuinely trinitarian shape of the theology of reconciliation. Not only are the "Father" and "Son" players in reconciliation but the Spirit is as well.

One little-noticed fact about the three christological moments of reconciliation is that Barth concludes each one with a lengthy pneumatological subsection, the purpose of which is to mark a transition from christology to the practical theme of the Christian life. Thus, the subsections entitled "The Verdict of the Father" in IV/1, "The Direction of the Son" in IV/2, and "The Promise of the Spirit" in IV/3, all shift the focus from christology to pneumatology. Barth was explicit that all three are meant to correspond

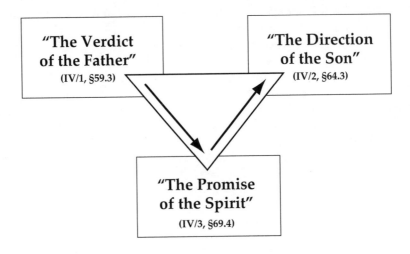

FIGURE 5.2

to one another. In each the purpose is to ask "how far" the being and action of Jesus Christ "can actually have effects, results and correspondences" in the realm of human experience (IV/3.1, 276).

"The Verdict of the Father," which reflects the humiliation theme in IV/1, highlights the "priestly" work of the Holy Spirit. It is the Spirit who effectuates and announces this "verdict" of judgment. Similarly, "The Direction of the Son" in IV/2 features the "royal" work of the Spirit. It is the Spirit who, in the manner of a sovereign, furnishes this new "direction" and thus sets human beings along the path leading to the ultimate goal of their existence. This transition from christology to pneumatology is often overlooked because the first two pneumatological subsections omit the term "Holy Spirit" from the titles. One must plow through voluminous pages of text before the pneumatological theme of these sections becomes apparent.

It is only in the third pneumatological subsection, labeled "The Promise of the Holy Spirit," that the title itself makes the transition from christology to pneumatology fully explicit. The primary mode of the Spirit's "presence," as we shall see in the next chapter, is that of "promise." The mode by which God encounters us is that of a "coming presence" (I/2, 95). Thus the third subsection coinciding with the "prophetic" office provides a fitting epithet with which to conclude the discussion of the Spirit's work in reconciliation.

If the pneumatological subject matter of these three subsections is obscured, what is equally hidden is that the third movement in IV/3, "The

Promise of the Spirit," operates as a "link" between the first and the second (see figure 5.2). Again, by making the last subsection (IV/3) a "link" between the first two, Barth was organizing the discussion according to a triadic rather than a strictly linear pattern.

The Verdict of the Father

"The Verdict of the Father" in IV/1 is an announcement of divine decision, a verdict from God. It states a negative judgment upon human sinfulness and a positive declaration about the uniqueness of Jesus Christ. This decision of God, though implicit in election, is finally made real through the event of Jesus Christ's resurrection.

How can this event which took place thousands of years ago become efficacious for contemporary human beings? How can that which is known to us only in historical recollection upon scripture and tradition become a contemporary "presence"? (IV/1, 288). Although the resurrection is an event that happened at a specific time and place, its power reaches out into the present and beyond the present toward the future.[17] Jesus of Nazareth traveled the solemn road to Golgotha once at a particular point in time, but as the eternal Lord he travels that same road again and again. It is not that the resurrection needs to be reenacted, but it does exert a continual impact that reaches into the future (IV/1, 313, 324). Thus when Barth says "resurrection," he does not simply refer to a historical claim by Jesus' disciples (though surely this is a part of it); but he envisions a dynamic and ongoing event that brings the benefits of the risen Christ to bear upon the future in the form of the Holy Spirit.

Barth interpreted the "coming" of the Holy Spirit in reconciliation as part of a threefold coming of Jesus Christ himself. The New Testament speaks of Jesus Christ's coming again as the *Parousia*. According to Barth, this does not simply refer to the so-called "Second Coming" at the end of history; rather, the "Second Coming" of Jesus Christ embraces a threefold movement that begins in the resurrection, continues with Pentecost, and moves on toward the end of time (IV/1, 342). In trinitarian fashion, it is a single event that includes origination, continuation, and consummation. The resurrection itself is only the *beginning* of Jesus' *Parousia* in much the same way that creation is only the beginning of reconciliation and redemption.

Barth's position that the resurrection occurred objectively in history (III/2, 442–55) but that it is inaccessible to ordinary historical investigation (IV/1, 335) is well-known. But there is a way in which the resurrection does become historically accessible. Through the outpouring of the Spirit at Pentecost, the effects of the resurrection are made historically accessible. At Pentecost something happens to Jesus' followers that a historian can evaluate (IV/1, 335–38). This "presence," however, is still nothing self-evident or straightforward. Historians doubtless will continue to argue over whether the event happened the way the New Testament records it. It is not self-evident in the sense of providing a "foundation" that can triumphantly coerce Christian belief. Instead it remains something "hidden with Christ in God" (Col. 3:3).

The Holy Spirit is not a superfluous add-on, then, but the way God's power makes a real difference in the lives of God's creatures. The pneumatological is that which "effectuates" something in the creature. The verdict announced in the resurrection is "pneumatological" because of the effect it has on humanity; it effectuates a fundamental alteration in the human situation.

Why does Barth not indicate the pneumatological theme in the title? By the end of the subsection Barth has actually changed the language of the "Verdict of the Father" to speak forthrightly of the "Verdict of the Holy Spirit" (IV/1, 319, 320, passim). Perhaps the rhetorical purpose of making this shift in such a subtle way is to underscore that he has already been talking about the Holy Spirit all along. To speak of the Holy Spirit is to speak of things that have already been said earlier from the thematic standpoint of the "Father" and the "Son." To speak of the Holy Spirit is to view the act of God from the angle of an effectual transformation of human life. The Holy Spirit is necessary, for example, in order to make the resurrection an event accessible in history.

In short, the aim of "The Verdict of the Father" is to point backward toward resurrection as the inaugurating event of the Christian life, just as one must look backward to view the inaugurating moment of creation itself and forward to see the consummate occurrence of redemption. "The Verdict of the Father" points backward to something that is not immediately accessible but which is presupposed as the origin or source of the Christian life. Although Barth does not make this explicit, it points even farther back, ultimately, to an even deeper presupposition; namely, to God's primordial decision in election from which the resurrection verdict in time originated.

Just as the first subsection points us backward to the "no longer," so the second subsection points us forward to the "not yet." The Spirit not only offers human beings a gracious verdict that stands in their past but also provides the "Direction of the Son" that forms the possibility of their future.

The Direction of the Son

The second pneumatological subsection (IV/2) is entitled "The Direction of the Son," and it redirects our focus to something out in front of us. This section is even more explicit than IV/1 in its pneumatological significance. Though it has seldom been recognized as such, it is one of the most important sections on the Spirit in the whole *CD*.[18] Once again it conceived the power of the resurrection as the basis (*Begründung*) for the action of the Spirit in and among believers. The "resurrection" we now know is a broad concept that includes the continual coming of Jesus Christ. It is the power of a new determination (*Bestimmung*) of human existence.

Part of the burden of IV/2 is to conceive this restoration of the covenant experientially. This is accomplished not by introspective phenomenological analysis but by looking concretely to what is learned from Jesus Christ. Because, for our part, we "do not yet exist in a complete and unbroken perception of [Christ's] being . . . ," our perception is not yet an achieved state of being but an ongoing and yet-to-be-consummated event. It is "an infrequent, weak, uncertain and flickering glow which stands in a sorry relationship to the perfection of even the smallest beam of light." We are but "wanderers who pass from one small and provisional response, from one small and provisional perception and love, to another" (IV/2, 286). For now, we live in a tensive state of need and expectation. By our own human capacities what Christ is in himself and what we human beings are in Christ remain in the "supreme sense" *unknowable* (IV/2, 287).

Let us pause for a moment before this statement. Barth is saying that there is an ultimate hiddenness to Jesus Christ, a hiddenness that is brought about *by God*. It is not merely an obscurity resulting from human sin. For our sin in and of itself, remarks Barth cleverly, is not powerful enough to conceal Christ. Consequently, it must be the will of God to conceal Christ. And, says Barth, Christ will remain concealed until "his return in glory." Prior to that time, "we are neither commanded nor authorized to count on a removal of the concealment of Jesus Christ." In the meantime of history, Christ is not at our disposal in any "cheap and easy fashion." "Even in the most sincere and effective prayer He is not accessible and at our disposal in this way . . . for we are speaking of the One who is high and lifted up, and of the majesty of our being in Him and with Him" (IV/2, 287–89).

The concealment of Jesus Christ that Barth intends here is not some general epistemological or metaphysical concealment but concretely the concealment of the cross. The cross upsets any analogies we might draw between our human situation and God. For to Barth's way of thinking, the cross is *katalogon* rather than *analogon*. It is anti-analogy rather than analogy (*KD* IV/2, 318; cf. *CD*, 286–87). The cross, with its humiliation, is not what we naturally would have expected of God; yet in God's grace it is the turning point of history. It is, first, Jesus' way of fulfilling the humility and obedience required of one who is the "Son of God." It is, second, Jesus' way of assuming in the most radical way the desperate situation of humankind. It is, third, in the light of the resurrection, an event that bears the character of an act of God. Yet in this strange work of the cross, Christ still remains concealed, unless and until there is a removal of the veil.

Even to Christians God remains veiled within the meantime of history, because the self-unveiling of God's identity in Christ is not yet complete. In the event of reconciliation the unveiling has begun. But for the time being, "its removal has not yet taken place" (IV/2, 287). The unveiling is rendered complete only at the apex of God's work in eschatological redemption.

The unveiling contemplated in "The Direction of the Son" is accomplished by the royal power of the Holy Spirit. Yet it is an accomplishment that still awaits its eschatological fulfillment. For now, our access to the Spirit is doxological: we can know the Spirit, who is beyond our grasping and seeing, only in an act of worship. Even if for now there is still a concealment draped over our prayers, there is at the same time, in the very act of prayer itself, an implicit testimony that the Spirit is more than simply the great unknown.

Recall the earlier statement that God *is* what God accomplishes in human beings. The Spirit accomplishes a reiteration *within* human existence of what God *is* in God's own being—a fellowship between the "Father" and the "Son." In a statement crucial to the "triadic" interpretation I am advancing here, Barth says that the Spirit accomplishes an "intervention" (*Dazwischentreten*) between God and humanity (*KD*, IV/2, 379, *CD*, 339). The Holy Spirit is, so to speak, the "go-between" from God to humanity. Barth specifically disavows any modalistic way of conceiving this go-between activity, as though it were some mystical or magical "third thing" between Jesus and us. He advocates no "Sabellianism," as though God were reaching out to humanity only through an instrumentality and not through an extension of God's own being. The Spirit links the human being squarely to God.

There is something quite remarkable about this linkage. What Barth is saying is that there is to be a human sharing in the very reality of God. Whatever the term *"homoousios"* might mean in respect to the person of Jesus—whatever it means for Jesus to be of the "same reality" as God—there is to be a sharing of this "same reality," this *homoousios*, with the other. We human beings are permitted to share eschatologically in the same reality as God, a sharing that does not obliterate our humanity but, on the contrary, that finally makes us truly human. It is a sharing that accomplishes divine and human communion—yet always, it must be added, in the perduring presence of a difference.

How are we to conceive such a unity-in-difference, especially if what we are in Christ is, for now at least, still "unknowable"? Barth's answer is even more remarkable. On the one hand, when we speak of the Spirit, we are speaking of the living God. On the other hand, we are speaking of a work of God that must be mediated in a humanly accessible way. The Spirit's mission, says Barth, must be accomplished through an operation or working (*Wirkung*) from one human being to another. Although who we are in Christ remains a mystery, who we are as operated upon by the Spirit must be rendered speakable. If the Spirit works in an authentically human way, Barth is saying, then this work must be capable of being "defined" and "described" in thoroughly human terms. This is the case, because the manner of the Spirit's operation, according to Barth, is through the *humanity* of Jesus Christ. It is through the humanity of Jesus that the Spirit establishes relationship to other human beings (IV/2, 360–61).

Following the Chalcedonian two-natures pattern, the work of God is a genuinely divine work. Jesus Christ, the human being from whom it proceeds, is the Son of God. But it must also be a thoroughly and authentically human work. And if it is a human work, Barth argues, then it must be capable of description. So then, what description can Barth render of the Spirit? If the Spirit is God, and if God in turn is ultimate mystery, then what sort of characterization will suffice? Barth designates this thoroughly and authentically human reality given to us by God in Christ as simply a "direction." The Spirit offers us a "direction." The English, "direction," translates the German, "*Weisung*," which also means "wisdom." Barth specifically selects the same term, as we shall see in chapter seven, to indicate the Spirit's guidance in ethics.

The "direction" of the Spirit comes in three forms. First, it is a realistic work that offers an "indication" (*Einweisung*) of the determining ground of our freedom in Christ. Following the ancient Pauline and Augustinian model, the Spirit gives us a real indicative from which flows all genuine imperatives: "Give what you command, command what you will"; "be what you already are." Second, the "direction" of the Spirit contains a critical moment of warning and correction (*Zurechtweisung*). It sets a limit, lest one miss the only true path along which our freedom can genuinely be exercised. Third, the "direction" of the Spirit includes a positive and determinate instruction (*Unterweisung*) to be written upon the believer's conscience. The mention of "conscience" here is significant, since the "knowing with God" that "con-science" implies was defined, throughout Barth's writings, as a characteristic of redeemed humanity.[19] Only the redeemed human being can "know" in companionship with God. Insofar as the Spirit points Christians in this new "direction," it anticipates the eschatological redemption of all things in Jesus' "Second Coming."

This "direction" that newly determines human existence is *both* the presence and action of the humanity of Jesus Christ himself and the presence and action of God (IV/2, 322). This is not a contradiction but simply a recognition that the human encounter that arises between Jesus and human beings depends on something already lying in the background, that is, a "higher dimension," which is the reality of God at work in the world. "God himself is at work ruling in his holiness at the center (*in der Mitte*) of all world occurrence as it is directed by God" (IV/2, 335, rev.).

The history of God unfolds according to the triadic pattern, proceeding within Christian experience from a point of beginning to a point of eschatological conclusion (IV/2, 336–42). The first aspect of this unfolding history, says Barth, is the sheer existence of the person of Jesus. His existence constitutes the *beginning* of this history, but it also adumbrates an ultimate *goal*. This first element, which was the subject matter of IV/1, corresponds formally to the primordial being of "God the Father"—it is the "Verdict of the Father." Second, this history moves toward "The Direction of the Son" as goal. Although Barth discusses this goal second in the order of presentation, he makes clear that he considers it third in the logical order of substance. The third factor in this history is "the middle one," a link [*der mittlere*], or a power of transition [*Kraft des Übergangs*] connecting the first to the second, or, in other words, that connects the origin to the goal (*KD* IV/2, 376, *CD*, 337). It is the go-between power that overcomes the distance between the humanity of Jesus and the humanity of everyone else. While this factor is third in presentation, occurring as it does in IV/3, it is the second and "middle factor" in the unfolding of the divine history. Thus, it points most explicitly of all to "God the Holy Spirit," to the active connection between God's primordial being, on the one hand, and the goal of God's being-in-act, on the other, a reality that can be neither seen nor grasped but that is made actual in our lives only in the power of prayer. This intervening moment is not a pure "presence," but it is the "promise" of the Holy Spirit.

The Promise of the Holy Spirit

A final pneumatological section is captioned, "The Promise of the Holy Spirit." Here for the first time Barth renders the transition from christology to pneumatology fully explicit (IV/3.1, 274–367). It is as though he wished the Spirit's identity to emerge gradually in the course of his reflections.

The prophetic work of revelation indicated by the "promise" of the Spirit is an ongoing activity that lies situated between the Spirit's backward-pointing "verdict" and forward-moving "direction." In keeping with the triadic pattern, "The Promise of the Spirit" corresponds to the second or middle form of the unfolding history of God, namely the outpouring of the Holy Spirit (see figure 5.3). The prophetic work arises out of the "Verdict" and hastens toward the new "Direction." Says Barth, "As the revealer of His work [God] has not yet reached His goal. He is still moving towards it" (IV/3.1, 327). "Jesus Christ Himself is in transition, living, acting, speaking, and working under the same sign of promise" (IV/3.1, 361). This unfinished state of being is not to Christ's shame, says Barth, but to his glory.

Pentecost gives us what Barth labels the "middle form" (*mittleren Gestalt*) of Christ's coming. Living in the promise of the Spirit, we experience the operation of God in "the time between the times" (*in der Zeit der*

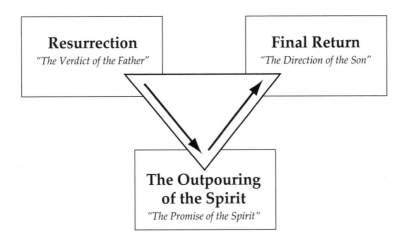

FIGURE 5.3

Mitte zwischen den Zeiten), an in-between time (*Zwischenzeit*) (*KD*, IV/3.1, 413, 416, *CD*, 358, 360). Barth can even speak of this promise of the Spirit, this prophetic aspect of the Spirit's work, as the "integrating moment" (*integrierendes Moment*) of the whole event (*Geschehens*) that includes the priestly and royal work (*KD*, IV/3.1, 413; cf. *CD*, 358). "Not only was God glorious in the past, and not only will He be glorious in the final fulfill-ment of His promise, but He is glorious *here and now* in the promise of His Spirit" (IV/3.1, 359, emphasis supplied). With this language Barth makes clear that the triad's third movement in order of presentation is actually its second movement in order of logic. The "Promise of the Spirit" char-acterizes Christian life here and now.

Usually this third movement is interpreted as following in a linear se-quence from the first two. But something more complex is clearly at work here. In the same way that reconciliation forms a middle movement be-tween creation and redemption, so also "The Promise of the Spirit" con-stitutes an intervening reality between "The Verdict of the Father" and "The Direction of the Son." The triadic pattern may be diagrammed as shown in figure 5.4.

What difference does uncovering this triadic pattern make? The differ-ence is that by means of this pattern Barth is already adumbrating the doc-trine of redemption and making it part of the organizing structure of his doctrine of reconciliation. The history of God is a movement along a path from the primordial past (grounded in the verdict of the resurrection), to

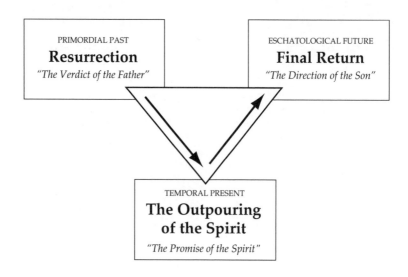

PRIMORDIAL PAST
Resurrection
"The Verdict of the Father"

ESCHATOLOGICAL FUTURE
Final Return
"The Direction of the Son"

TEMPORAL PRESENT
**The Outpouring
of the Spirit**
"The Promise of the Spirit"

FIGURE 5.4

the existential present (sealed in the promise of the Holy Spirit), to the eschatological future (gestured in the direction of the Son).

We must exercise caution in our use of the past-present-future scheme, however, since for Barth all three dimensions are mutually implicated in one another, meaning that the resurrection, the outpouring of the Spirit, and the final return are but three aspects of a single divine event. This one event is an occurrence that was inaugurated in the resurrection but still awaits consummation in the future (e.g., IV/3.1, 294–96). But then the very eschatological union of these three moments suggests that they be interpreted as a dynamic, forward-moving procession-in-togetherness. All three constitute different aspects of a single dynamic event. Each contains the other by way of anticipation or recapitulation, but all three are luring the believer along the road towards redemption.

To sum up, the formal theme of all three of these pneumatological sections is the Holy Spirit as the mode by which Christians participate in the grace of Christ. The material theme of each section, likewise, is the coming of Christ—the *Parousia*, in its threefold form of Resurrection, Pentecost, and Second Coming. Each of these subsections also marks a segue into subsequent discussions concerning concrete human existence—discussions pertaining to sin, soteriology, the existence of the community, and the existence of the individual Christian. Indeed, volume four contains more raw pages on these anthropologically and pneumatologically rich themes than on christology proper.

We are now in a position for the triadic pattern to pay a nice dividend. Once one recognizes the triadic structure of Barth's thinking, one is finally in a position to understand that his somewhat circuitous theology is trying to say something important about the postmodern shape of Christian experience. The crux of that discussion comes in the way Barth conceptualizes the Christian life as a dynamic movement of justification, sanctification, and vocation. As will become clear in the remaining chapters, Barth presents the Christian life as a tensive and open-ended existence lived out primarily in the mode of hope. The Christian life is never something self-evident but always something received in the form of an enigma and a task.

6

GOD "IN"
AND "AMONG" US

> In the . . . present . . . what took place once is still hidden from us . . .
> [W]e cannot see it as yet, either in the world, the church, or above all
> our own hearts and lives. What we see in these is the misty landscape,
> the luminous darkness, in which God is both known and unknown.
> In our time between the times the veil has not yet fallen.
> Karl Barth, *The Christian Life*, 168

Redemption is the third movement in the drama of salvation, a movement defined in the very first part-volume of the *CD* as the freedom by which human beings are enabled to become "children of God." Redemption, on this definition, was hardly an afterthought, as critics of Barth's theology often allege; instead, he conceived it as the very purpose or goal of God's grace from the outset.

In chapter four we discussed the passage from *Dogmatics in Outline* in which Barth described creation as the "presupposition" (*Voraussetzung*) of reconciliation and the redemptive work of the Holy Spirit as its "consequence" (*Konsequenz*). A "presupposition," following Barth's interpretation of Immanuel Kant, is not self-evident to present experience but is a hypothesis that validates itself in a particular way of life, and specifically in moral action. A "consequence" is that resultant moral activity itself coming to fruition as a result and a validation of one's presuppositions. The concrete experience of redemption as "consequence," then, is the culmination of God's action of creation and reconciliation.

On this view, reconciliation is the dramatic turning point at the center of divine and human history. It is an axis that presupposes creation as its *archē* and anticipates redemption as its *telos*, with all three movements—creation, reconciliation, and redemption—making up one dynamic activity of God. Without creation as "presupposition" and redemption as "consequence," reconciliation would not be what it is. For this reason Barth already began to discuss redemption, as we have seen, in his treatment of reconciliation. More importantly for our present purposes, creation and reconciliation are themselves incomplete if they fail to reach their culmination or "consequence" in human redemption.

Momentarily, I shall say more about the way this conceptuality of "presupposition" and "consequence" works itself out in Barth's reconstruction of the Christian experience of justification, sanctification, and vocation. But first, let us consider in more detail the place redemption plays in the *CD* as a whole.

REDEMPTION IN THE HOLY SPIRIT

In construing redemption as the third facet in the trinitarian economy of salvation, Barth was actually engaging in a rather striking reconstrual of the classical tradition. The terms "redeemer" and "redemption" have usually been used to signify the work of Christ. For an example of such usage, we need look no further than Schleiermacher, whose writings are peppered with references to "Christ the redeemer."[1] Thus, "redeemer" and "redemption" were used as christologically focused terms pertaining to the "second article" of the Apostles' Creed or the Niceno-Constantinopolitan Creed.

For Barth, however, redemption is a "third article" term pertaining primarily to the work of the Holy Spirit. Although reconciliation and redemption are not to be dissevered from one another, redemption is, nevertheless, more pneumatological for Barth than christological, more future gift than present impartation.

Redemption as the freedom to "become" children of God suggests a goal toward which human beings are moving (I/1, §12). To "become" God's "children" means to move toward complete fellowship with God. The Eastern orthodox tradition conceived this fellowship as "divinization" or "theosis," a "participation" in God's own being: "God became human," Athanasius said, "so that human beings might become divine."[2] To think in this way of an unmediated participation in the divine life was, from Barth's perspective, to push too far (IV/2, 377). Barth resonated much more readily with John Calvin's revision of the Athanasian dictum: "God became human so that human beings might become *children* of God."[3] There is a filial unity between God and humanity, to be sure, but it is a unity that is still in the process of being realized, a unity made possible only by God's prior initiative and not by any intrinsic human capacity.

This circumspect way of describing this divine-human intimacy flows logically from Barth's concept of revelation as a divine self-giving. For God to give God's own self in revelation requires that the very life of God be implicated in the inner workings of salvation history. Note the boldness with which Barth conceived this divine self-giving: "God's self is not merely God's self alone, but it is what God creates and achieves in human beings" (*KD*, I/1, 315; cf. *CD*, 299). God *is* that which God *accomplishes* in human life. A more daring statement of divine-human togetherness is scarcely imaginable.

But, then, does all this talk of a divine impartation occurring in the experience of redemption mean that we are now dealing with something "present" and "given" to humanity? Not if redemption is a peculiarly *eschatological* work of the Holy Spirit. And that is just what redemption is for Barth. It is a goal toward which human beings are pressing. It is never simply "given," as though somehow it could be completely possessed in the present. In the present, God's creatures have not yet realized their destiny as God's children. Not yet do they possess the fullness of life. For now they live as *heirs* who are still pressing toward it. To be sure, there will come a future point at which God is "all in all": Christianity was, and in Barth's theology still is, a "linear" religion. But from the standpoint of present experience, the answer to the question whether God is now "given" to humanity in redemption remains an unqualified "no."

Barth's argument for an eschatological interpretation of redemption was, in part, exegetical. The New Testament term for redemption, ἀπολύτρωσις, signifies a liberating or ransoming from slavery. This liberation cannot be interpreted as a present possession but remains to occur in the future (I/1, 409). To support this future-oriented interpretation of New Testament redemption, Barth cited passages such as the following: Rom. 8:23 ("we ourselves, who have the first fruits of the Spirit, groan inwardly while we wait for adoption, the redemption of our bodies"); Eph. 4:30 ("And do not grieve the Holy Spirit of God, with which you were marked with a seal for the day of redemption"); Col. 1:22 ("he has now reconciled in his fleshly body through death, so as to present you holy and blameless and irreproachable before him").

Similarly, the concept of "salvation" itself, on Barth's reading, is an eschatological event yet to be consummated. The "salvation" signified by the Greek word σωτηρία, Barth argued, was never believed to be a present possession; rather, for the time being, humanity lives a life that is suspended between promise and fulfillment. Again, he cited biblical evidence: Rom. 5:10 ("For if while we were enemies, we were reconciled to God through the death of his Son, much more surely, having been reconciled, will we be saved by his life"); Rom. 13:11 ("For salvation is nearer to us now than when we became believers . . . "); Phil. 1:19 ("for I know that through your prayers and the help of the Spirit of Jesus Christ this will turn out for my deliverance"); 1 Thess. 5:8 ("the hope of salvation . . . "); Heb. 9:28 ("so Christ, having been offered once to bear the sins of many, will appear a second time, not to deal with sin, but to save those who are eagerly waiting for him").

This future-oriented interpretation was not only based on exegesis, however, but was supported by the underlying *structure* of Barth's theology. His eschatological view of redemption matched his dynamic understanding of God as one whose being is in act. God's very own being is wholeheartedly engaged in the act of redeeming creation; yet this is an act still in the process of making itself known. His eschatological understanding also supported the belief we explored previously that divine and human activity must be understood concretely and never in abstraction from one another. The truth about God and humanity is summed up only in the whole sweep of salvation history, and thus it is known fully only in reference to God's consummate act of redemption. Only in the last scene does the whole shape of the divine drama finally become visible. This eschatological reorientation of redemption, moveover, supports Barth's overall view of the divine hiddenness. If God is a God of hiddenness and mystery, then the Christian life too must partake of a similar hiddenness and mystery. Redemption—the Christian life made real—is something as yet out in front of the Christian community, something still needing to be realized.

This eschatological structure of redemption sets up a deep irony within Christian experience. To know Jesus Christ, and to be caught up in the dynamic process of reconciliation, places the Christian believer in a state of tension. "In the . . . present . . . " the reconciliation that "took place once" in Christ "is still hidden from us . . . [W]e cannot see it as yet, either in the world, the church, or above all our own hearts and lives."[4]

To be brought within the sphere of God's grace, in other words, is to know that one's final goal has yet to be attained. This life, as we heard Luther say earlier, "is not righteousness but growth in righteousness, not health but healing." Since reconciliation is still working itself out and moving toward ultimate redemption, Christian experience displays a tensive and fractured quality. What we see in present experience is, to quote Barth again, but a "misty landscape, the luminous darkness, in which God is both known and unknown."[5]

The mystery of God is "veiled" in the humanity of Jesus. This veiling for Barth is also an unveiling, a hiddenness that discloses. Nevertheless, the veil has not yet been completely lifted, for it is still in the process of being lifted. "In our time between the times," says Barth, "the veil has not yet fallen."[6]

For this reason, it will not suffice to treat Christian experience as a self-evident and foundational source for theology. As noted earlier, this is where Barth differed most decisively from Schleiermacher. Human experience in itself is too ambiguous to provide such a foundation; and besides that, it is only in the transformative light of Jesus Christ that one can even learn what authentic human experience is. Still, for Barth, as for Schleiermacher, the Christian life is profoundly experiential. The key difference is that for Barth experience is not a "given" but a goal. It is not a "presupposition" of grace but a "consequence."

Accordingly, Barth conceived the Christian life not as a finished "state" (*Zustand*) of already being Christian but as an "event" (*Ereignis*) of still becoming one. Notwithstanding the objectivity of reconciliation, the fact of anyone's being redeemed, or of being found steadfast "in Christ," remains hidden under a cloak (*Verborgensein*). No one yet fully understands the significance of Jesus Christ. For the time being the best one can attain is a "discontinuous seeing" which results from the Holy Spirit's ever-novel in-breaking (*Durchbrechung*) into one's present situation (*KD*, IV/2, 317–19, *CD*, 285–87).

Now we begin to see more clearly why Barth made redemption a third article concept. In his 1928/1929 Münster and 1929/1930 Bonn lectures on "Ethics" and in his 1929 lectures on "The Holy Spirit and the Christian Life," Barth made it clear that the concept of being "redeemed" as God's "child" indicates a higher and more perfect status than that of being a mere "creature" alone. Even more perfect still is the status of being "redeemed" over that of being "reconciled" in Christ. Redemption indicates the fulfillment of one's destiny. It points to something consummate, final, and unsurpassable that is beyond God's reign in created nature (*regno naturae*) and beyond God's reign in the grace of reconciliation (*regno gratiae*). It points instead to the ultimate reign of God in glory (*in regno gloriae*).[7]

In the *CD* itself redemption is only seldom a discrete and extended topic of discussion. Barth died before the projected fifth and final volume on redemption could be written. Nevertheless, the concept of God's ultimate eschatological reign in redemption pervades Barth's thinking. In the Romans commentary, for instance, he had made the well-known declaration that a Christianity that is not "wholly and utterly and irreducibly eschatology has nothing whatsoever to do with Jesus Christ."[8] Sometimes it is claimed that in his later work Barth abandoned this radical eschatological proviso. While it is true that eschatology and protology are held in a more careful balance in the mature writings of the *CD*, the later Barth still could declare that "there is nothing absolutely false in these bold words" from *Romans*, so long as the appropriate place of protology is not eclipsed in the process (II/1, 634–35).

The key point is that the eschatological significance of redemption, even though seldom made an explicit theme in the *CD*, is still intended to cast its shadow back upon everything else. Each theological statement throughout Barth's theology is fraught with eschatological significance. Each looks forward to the future redemption in the Holy Spirit. Still, redemption itself "is not a relation which we can survey in its totality" (I/1, 462). It is something we anticipate with faith and not with sight. Barth will speak of redemption in the Holy Spirit as something one holds only in "promise." "To have the Holy Spirit is to let God rather than our having God be our confidence" (I/1, 462–63).

To call redemption "eschatological" does not mean that it is a purely negative, other-worldly, or irrelevant theme; rather, redemption means "above all *final*, i.e. conclusive, definitive, and unsurpassable."[9] Like the Christian idea of "mystery" itself, eschatology wields a two-edged sword against the vagaries of the present moment, both setting limits and offering possibilities. In keeping with the constant interplay we have been exploring between the real and the ideal, the concept of redemption both adds and subtracts something from every theological statement.

What it adds is an energetic sense that human life, through the power of the Holy Spirit, must be oriented toward a goal. Redemption presents us with a true possibility that derives from the reality of grace. It is not a work accomplished through some semidivine minion with no intrinsic connection to God's own being. No, the Spirit of redemption is truly God, and the "presence" of the Spirit in human life, when and where it does occur, is the very "presence" of God. Viewed from God's side of the relationship, the Spirit is God's "freedom to be present to the creature" (I/1, 450).

But this "presence" of the Holy Spirit is something exceedingly peculiar. In chapter eight of the Romans commentary, an encounter with the Holy Spirit means that "we have touched the torpedo-fish, and are benumbed."[10] Or again, in the 1929 lectures on "The Holy Spirit and the Christian Life," the redemptive power of the Holy Spirit is what brings human beings into a "presence" that is strangely not-present. "The Holy Spirit must be present," says Barth, but only "in his total *difference*" (Barth's emphasis).[11] We are speaking, then, of a "presence" that, ironically, is not yet completely "present." This "presence" impinges upon us, but for now it is available only in the mode of "promise." It is always in the mode of a "coming presence" (I/2, 95).

Thus the eschatological interpretation of redemption subtracts something from theology, too. It calls for abandoning the false certainty that this or that theological statement, in and of itself, is ever capable of uttering a final word about God. If redemption does indeed lie in the future, then all present theological statements, however truthful in their own way, still remain provisional. They must be judged in the light cast by the one who *has* come but who is still *to* come.

To sum up, Barth's eschatological interpretation of the Holy Spirit and redemption is a unique combination of boldness and reticence. The boldness lies in his belief that human beings, incredible though it may seem, will one day enjoy the fellowship of life with God. But there is a lingering reticence as well. Whatever the peculiar "presence" of God may be, it displays itself most reliably as "an honest and basic lack" (IV/3.1, 322). Life in the Spirit is "a permanent Advent," a perpetual waiting for a revelation that is yet to be consummated.

If the Spirit is "present" but only in the form of "promise," then being a Christian is a matter of hope rather than of immediate attainment. At the very least, the Christian life is not something to be taken for granted. Barth pictures believers as torn between the two states of being Christian, on the one hand, and non-Christian, on the other. Even though being Christian and non-Christian at the same time seems impossible, nevertheless, unremittingly, that is our condition (IV/3.1, 342). So then, one is never in a position to boast of his or her own status as a Christian. Each new day one must cease to be non-Christian and begin to be Christian; and each new day one must invoke the Holy Spirit for this gift.

For this reason, Barth was forever reluctant to use the adjective "Christian," as in phrases such as "Christian" ethics, or "Christian" families, or "Christian" newspapers, or even "Christian" theology—witness his option for a "Church" rather than a "Christian" dogmatics. For Barth there is no one who can claim to be a Christian in any straightforward sense. Being a Christian means that one's life is "hidden with Christ in God" (Col. 3:3). In his many discussions of the Christian life, Barth quoted this biblical passage repeatedly. Since the hiddenness of the living God carries with it a corresponding hiddenness in the Christian life, one is never a Christian pure and simple but one is always in the process of becoming one (IV/2, 285–87). Thus, for Barth, "everything . . . to be said about the person who receives the Holy Spirit . . . is an eschatological statement." Of God alone can one speak non-eschatologically (I/1, 464).

Barth was reticent to speak directly about the Holy Spirit, because "to say Holy Spirit in preaching or theology is always to say a final word." To speak of the work of the Spirit is to move beyond conceptual analysis to the thing itself (*zur Sache*). For when we speak of redemption in the Spirit "we are always speaking of the event in which God's Word is not only revealed to humanity but believed" (I/1, 182). We are pushing beyond reflection to action, and, as we shall see in the next chapter, beyond theology to ethics.

This circumspection has often been misunderstood. Together with his frequent criticisms of Schleiermacher and his blunt and seemingly undiscerning dismissal of human experience as a norm for theology, Barth's reticence concerning the Spirit has led to the assumption that somehow he was indifferent to the "how" questions of theology. The "how" questions include such things as "how" God acts in human life, or "how" one comes to embrace the Christian faith existentially. For some interpreters of Barth *how* the promise of God is appropriated is not nearly as important as *that* the promise was made.[12]

Yet Barth himself was deeply fascinated with these "how" questions and made them integral to his trinitarian understanding of God. As mentioned in chapter three, for Barth the Holy Spirit *is* the "how" of God's trinitarian being-in-act. The Holy Spirit is none other than the *way* God's purposes come to fruition, the efficacy of God made efficacious in creaturely existence. In the Romans commentary, for example, Barth identified the Spirit with the determination of election itself. "The Spirit means election and in no sense rejection."[13] The Spirit is at work in both the divine and human sides of the transaction, both in the determination of God to be "for" humanity *and* in the human determination to be "for" God. Similarly, in the *CD*, the Spirit constitutes the vital connection between *who* God is primordially, on the one hand, and *what* God is doing in human history through Jesus Christ, on the other (I/1, 295–99). If there is both a "who" and a "what" to God's identity, as embodied in the symbolism of the "Father" and "Son," there is also a "how," or a *means*—the outgoing of God's Spirit—by which God's decision to be "for" human beings primordially, and "with" human beings concretely in Jesus Christ, is made efficacious "in" and "among" them historically.

Some of Barth's critics charge that defining the Spirit as the link between the "Father" and the "Son" renders the Spirit superfluous.[14] The Spirit's "betweenness," they say, is reduced to a mechanical function that is insufficient to establish a unique divine identity. Yet the linkage Barth sees accomplished by the Spirit is much more dynamic and agential than these critics have been willing to see. The linkage achieved by the Spirit is not a static linkage confined to the sublime regions of the inner life of God, the so-called "immanent Trinity." Rather, this linkage constitutes the actual manner in which God's being-in-act comes to fruition. The "actualism" for which Barth is so famous is nothing less than the action of the Spirit.[15]

We learned also in chapter three that the being of God is the being of one who loves in freedom. We must now add that it is the Spirit who constitutes the very expression of that freedom. "The Spirit of God is God in God's freedom to be present to the creature, and therefore to create this [divine-human] relation, and therefore to be the life of the creature" (I/1, 450). If the Spirit constitutes and makes possible the very spiritual life of God's creatures, then the Spirit has a dynamic role indeed.

The Spirit, it would seem then, is the focal point of God's acting, the means by which God's own eternal efficacy is made efficacious in the midst of God's creatures. The Spirit is the unique "mode" of God's being through which creatures actually participate in God's own reality. The Spirit is the "way" in which God relates to the world. When Barth speaks of the Spirit as a type of "going-in-between," or *Zwischentreten* held in common by the Father and the Son, the purpose of this language is not to denigrate the Spirit's unique agency in the economy of salvation but, in fact, to establish and enhance it. The Spirit is not superfluous to God's dynamic being-in-act but forms the summit of God's every act. Every act of God is consummated in the acting of God the Spirit. And every act of God is oriented toward the ultimate goal of redemption.

The raising of "how" questions in the *CD* is one of the ways Barth tacitly raises questions about the Holy Spirit and redemption.[16] Barth defines the key issue in redemption as the question of *how* any human being can have an experience of God, or to put it another way, the question of *how* anyone comes to say that "Jesus is Lord" (I/1, 448). Redemption and reconciliation are differentiated by Barth, though not disconnected. Reconciliation is best conceived as God's present act of judging human beings and fashioning for them a new beginning in Christ. Redemption, by contrast, enables human beings to *become* in actuality what they already *are* in

Christ. Whereas reconciliation points more to the indicative of what human beings now are in Christ, redemption points more to the imperative of what human beings shall become by the power of the Holy Spirit.

The best example of the way redemption, in the form of the question "how," crops up surreptitiously in Barth's theology is found in the waning pages of the fourth volume of the *CD* in its reflections on reconciliation. In those sections Barth finally poses in earnest the question he had raised in a preliminary way at the outset in I/1. As it is framed in volume four, the question is one of *how* the grace that is "for" us primordially in God's own being (*extra nos*) and "with" us concretely in Jesus Christ (*pro nobis*) can somehow become a reality in and among us (*in nobis*) through the work of the Holy Spirit[17] (IV/1, 755; IV/4 (Fragment), 4ff., 17ff.). Consequently, the question toward which each of the three part-volumes on reconciliation pushes is the question of redemption, the question of "how" anyone comes to say that "Jesus is Lord." From one perspective, this only stands to reason, since in volume four Barth was anticipating the theme of the (never-written) fifth and closing volume. But the connection to redemption is not merely anticipatory (though it is that) but also substantive and vital.

In order to demonstrate Barth's ingenious, if mostly obscure, way of weaving redemption into his discussion of reconciliation, we must return to the triadic pattern which will enable us to see something rather surprising. In the triadic pneumatology of the doctrine of reconciliation the doctrine of vocation is made the locus in which the experiential component of Barth's theology, suppressed for so long, finally reaches its summit.

EXPERIENCE AND THE
CENTRALITY OF VOCATION

Barth's indirect way of speaking about the Holy Spirit has led to the assumption that he preferred to remain ensconced in the heady regions of doctrinal analysis and to repudiate any interest in Christian experience. This opinion has been reinforced recently by some "postliberal" theologians who themselves disavow any normative role for religious experience.[18]

Nevertheless, there is an experiential concern that winds its way unobtrusively throughout the *Church Dogmatics*. In the first part-volume of the *CD* Barth affirmed the need for God's Word to become alive in Christian experience, explicitly adopting the broad concept of "experience" (*Erfahrung*) in favor of what he took to be Friedrich Schleiermacher's more restrictive word, "feeling" (*Gefühl*). Barth's stratagem of doing Schleiermacher "one better" as an experiential theologian is deeply ironic. For it was Schleiermacher, of course, who had marked off the playing field of nineteenth- and early twentieth-century experientially-based theologies through his argument that concepts about God should be grounded in an indissoluble relationship between God and humanity.

Barth said he preferred the term "experience" (*Erfahrung*) to Schleiermacher's word "feeling" (*das Gefühl*), since the concept of "experience" embraces a deeper and wider range of the dimensions of life. Barth also objected to Schleiermacher's explanation of religion in terms of a "feeling of absolute dependence." The term "dependence" (*Abhängigkeit*), Barth argued, connotes a certain passivity in the religious life, and thus it tends to eliminate from religious experience the active determination of the self (*Selbstbestimmung*). Barth's point is that people in their own self-determination can also come to be determined by God's Word. If this were not the case, then the experience of God would not be *our* experience. "It is precisely our self-determination," says Barth, "which needs determination by God in order for it to be experience of [God's] Word" (*CD* I/1, 201 rev., *KD*, 210).

Now Barth wanted to refrain from turning this experience into something foundational or "given" within universal human consciousness, while also affirming it as an authentic encounter. To this end, Barth held that humanity has an ability (*Können*) to participate in the event of revelation; but this ability is nothing like an inherent capacity (*Fähigkeit*), nor a predisposition (*Hinordnung*), nor anything of critical-normative significance (*kritisch-normativen Bedeutung*) in the human makeup by which to measure God's Word. Rather, this "experience" is a reconstituted experience of submission before a "center" (*Zentrum*) or "whence" (*Woher*) that, in contrast to Schleiermacher's "whence," is pictured as determining a person from outside the self (*KD*, I/1, §6.3, esp. 207, *CD*, 198–99). With an emphasis on the entire line in the German text, Barth writes, it is "just this determination (*Bestimmung*) of the existence (*Existenz*) of the knowing human being which we name 'experience'" (*KD*, I/1, 206, *CD*, 198). Experience of the Word of God, in short, is "more than experience" (I/1, 208).

Not only does Barth embrace the concept of an "experience" of God's Word, he also gives the concept a technical meaning. Since it was his custom to avoid systematization in theology, the very creation of a term of art in this manner is something to which an interpreter must pay close attention. Barth defined the experience of God's Word as a fundamental "determination" (*Bestimmung*) of human existence. It was a matter of "being determined" (*Bestimmtsein*) at the same time both by God and by one's own authentic action. Thus it conformed to what George Hunsinger has called the "Chalcedonian pattern," whereby divine and human action follow a paradigm of asymmetry, intimacy, and integrity.

This double agency of the divine and human is "asymmetrical" because the priority is placed always on the divine initiative in grace. Thus in defining Christian experience, Barth speaks of it as an "acknowledgement" of God.[19] This double agency is "intimate," because through the agency of the Spirit, divine and human action are thought to perfectly coincide. Yet the two actions have their own "integrity," in the sense that "being determined" is both one hundred percent human and one hundred percent divine.[20]

Now four things about this definition of experience are noteworthy. The first is that Barth believed conceiving experience as a "determination" (*Bestimmung*) would lead to a more encompassing (*Umfassenderes*) concept than Schleiermacher's notion of "being affected" (*Affiziertsein*). It is worth noting, before concluding hastily that the ever-tendentious Barth was playing fast and loose in his reading of Schleiermacher, that one searches Schleiermacher's writings in vain for any serious or sustained use of today's usual German term for experience, *Erfahrung*. This was partly an accident of etymological history, since the term did not become widespread until long after Schleiermacher's groundbreaking work. The early Schleiermacher of the *Speeches* called the focal point of this relationship the "intuition" (*Anschauung*) of the Universe; the later Schleiermacher of *The Christian Faith* called it "the feeling of absolute dependence" (*das Gefühl schlechthinniger Abhängigkeit*), i.e., the sense of "being affected" in one's deepest emotional and affective commitments. Even though this relates perhaps as much to the vagaries of etymology as to anything else, it is still important for interpreting Barth. Is it not ironic that the theologian whom contemporary scholars often take to be the quintessential theologian of experience, namely Schleiermacher, seldom even used that term, whereas the supposedly antiexperiential Barth expressly adopted it?

Barth's stated reason for preferring "experience" to Schleiermacher's term "feeling" is that "experience" is a comprehensive and holistic term, one more capable of embracing life in all its various dimensions. With some mischief, to be sure, Barth is arguing that Schleiermacher is not experiential enough!

Second, conceiving experience as "determination" (*Bestimmung*) should not be misinterpreted as though it meant the ordination of something fixed or predetermined in human experience. Barth's understanding of the relation between God's sovereignty and human freedom would allow for nothing quite so rigid, nor would his view of the work of the Spirit permit of anything so cut and dry. The experience of God's Word in the Spirit is for Barth an upsetting, disorienting, and reorienting reality. It calls into question the fixities of life. This point is well-illustrated by a passage on the Holy Spirit in the Romans commentary in which Barth asks "*Whence* comes this crisis" of theology?[21] Now Schleiermacher had used the term "Whence" (*Woher*) to signal the object of the feeling of absolute dependence, and Barth is here making a deliberate, if veiled, allusion to that usage. Barth frequently complained that Schleiermacher's theology placed too much of a premium upon peaceful repose.[22] In contrast to the relative security of Schleiermacher's feeling of absolute dependence, Barth employs Schleiermacher's same term—with typical cunning—to speak of something disruptive. "With the question of the 'Whence?' comes the insight into our absolute sinfulness and mortality (*schlechthinnigen Sündigkeit und Sterblichkeit*)." As noted earlier, Barth likened this experience to the sting of a torpedo fish. Thus he took Schleiermacher's language of romantic repose and turned it into the electrifying language of postmodern dislocation. The point is this: rather than ignoring experience Barth was seeking to reconfigure what counts in reference to God as experience in the first place.

Third, the "determination" of human existence by God does not eliminate human "self-determination." This posed another reason Barth rejected Schleiermacher's term "dependence" (*Abhängigkeit*); it seemed to connote passivity and the elimination of any active self-determination. "It is precisely our self-determination (*Selbstbestimmung*)," said Barth, "which needs determination by God in order to be experience of [God's] Word" (*KD*, I/1, 210, *CD*, 201). Another way to put this is to say that the experience of God is not the abolition of freedom, but it provides freedom with its very condition of possibility.

This leads to a fourth point that becomes visible if one reads between the lines. Although Barth did not call attention to the fact, the language he used to define Christian experience is the same language, significantly, that Immanuel Kant used to speak of ethical experience in his second critique, the *Critique of Practical Reason*.[23] For Kant, as for Barth, the issue of freedom was paramount. For Kant, one exercises true freedom only when a pure, categorical imperative (that is, an imperative that the actor could wish to be elevated to the status of a universal law) occupies the "determining ground" (*Bestimmungsgrund*) of one's will. The will's determining ground is that which forms its overriding direction and goal. To have a pure imperative as the determining ground of one's action is Kant's definition of true freedom. Stated somewhat differently, being moral is not an activity that constricts our freedom but quite the contrary: being moral actually is constitutive and productive of freedom.

Barth was striving for a similar ideal when he defined Christian ethics as a "freedom for obedience." Barth's choice of "determination" as a term of art for experience was not merely fortuitous. Barth had read and reread Kant's second critique as a young theology student, and he was steeped in the philosophy of neo-Kantianism. By adopting Kantian terminology, Barth was seeking to reconstruct the angle from which Christian experience was conceived. He was searching for a vocabulary by which to speak of Christian experience primarily as a matter of achieving authentic freedom through the Spirit. It will be recalled that freedom in the Spirit was precisely the definition Barth gave to "redemption," the ultimate goal of Christian existence.

Now this accent on the word "experience" in the early pages of the *CD* may seem disingenuous, since it then lies dormant through so much of the rambling course that follows. If use of the term "experience" in the *CD* is lean, however, Barth's use of the word "determination," the specific term of art he adopted for experience, is abundant. It arises in discussions of numerous topics, not least in the case of election and covenant. Election is God's "determination" to be "for" and "with" humanity; and the covenant requires a human "determination" to be "for" God and "with" one another.

Perhaps Barth is not so much downplaying the place of experience in theology as he is seeking to rethink its strategic meaning. Thus, the issue of experience resurfaces in earnest in the waning pages of volume four when Barth turns to the concept of "vocation." George Hunsinger has recently noticed that for Barth "the existential moment of salvation . . . is . . . understood primarily in terms of vocation rather than justification or sanctification."[24] This is true, and it is of critical importance. What is also true is that the particular formulation of experience given in vocation has a more open-ended, tensive, and even fractured quality than most interpreters have heretofore acknowledged.

This tensive quality of Christian experience, which opens the door to a postmodern appropriation of Barth's thought, is expressed through the triadic shape of Barth's treatment of the Christian life. Barth presents the Christian life through the threefold grid of justification (IV/1, §61), sanctification (IV/2, § 66), and vocation (IV/3, § 71), introduced in exactly this sequence. Yet instead of making vocation the apex of Christian living, as most interpreters read him, Barth actually made vocation an intervening mode of suspension between justification, as the event in which the Christian life is inaugurated, and sanctification, which is its ultimate goal (see figure 6.1).

To consider this interpretation more carefully, justification, first, is the divine act by which humanity, which lives in contradiction to God, is reconciled to God and to fellow human beings. Justification is the promise of being made right with God (IV/1, §61). Barth thinks of this in a typically dynamic way. Justification is an inaugurating "event" in the life of a Christian and not merely a static "connection"; it is the commencement of an ongoing drama. It is the living act of God which is the "presupposition" of a person's future (IV/1, 554). As such, justification presupposes the resurrection "Verdict of the Father" by which a "no" was pronounced against sin and death and a "yes" heralded in favor of a new and realized humanity. Just as God in Jesus Christ is "determined" in the decision of election to be "for" humanity, so in justification humanity becomes transformed for the purpose of living "for" God. Justification is the first moment

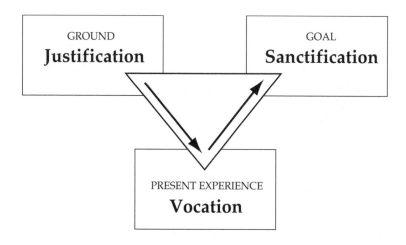

FIGURE 6.1

in fulfilling the covenantal admonition, "you will be my people." Using
the term of art he had delineated for experience in I/1, Barth says that justification "determines" human existence, giving human beings "a very
definite direction" (*eine ganz bestimmte Richtung*) (IV/1, 558). This "direction" initiated by justification as *terminus a quo* spills over, in turn, into
sanctification as *terminus ad quem*.

Sanctification, second, is the divine work that brings humanity's conversion to God to accomplishment (IV/2, §66). If justification lies, so to
speak, behind Christians, sanctification is on the horizon out in front of
them. In contrast to Protestant orthodoxy, for which sanctification was a
subjective work in the believer and justification an objective act of atonement achieved by Jesus Christ, Barth makes sanctification no less objective
than justification (IV/2, §66.2). Relying on 1 Cor. 1:30 ("[God] is the source
of your life in Christ Jesus, who became for us wisdom from God, and
righteousness and sanctification and redemption"), Barth maintains that
a believer's sanctification is in a real sense already accomplished in Jesus
Christ. In grace, Jesus Christ achieved not only his own sanctification but
that of all humanity as well. To be sanctified is to participate in the exaltation of the humanity of Jesus Christ.

Jesus Christ in principle (*de iure*) sanctifies all persons, whether Christian or non-Christian; but in actuality (*de facto*) he sanctifies only those
who are specifically "awakened to conversion" through the work of the
Spirit. Through the Spirit, these "called ones" are introduced to a new

form of existence as the covenant partners of God. Collectively speaking, this new form of existence is the church (IV/1, §62; IV/2, §67; IV/3, §72). The church lives as a provisional representation of what God ultimately intends for all people, that they be made well-pleasing to God and blessed.

If justification gestures to the indicative of the divine-human covenant, "I will be your God"; then sanctification is the realization of the imperative, "You will be my people." Justification and sanctification, therefore, are linked not as two successive activities or discrete stages in the Christian life but as two aspects of the one divine act of reconciliation in Jesus Christ. Following the Chalcedonian pattern, these two moments can neither be confused nor separated, neither transformed into one another nor unduly contrasted.

Before turning to the third aspect of the Christian life, or "vocation," three comments are necessary. First, one may wonder how "experiential" Barth's theology can really be, given the way he objectifies justification and sanctification in the accomplishment of Jesus Christ. This is not so problematic, however, if one recalls that in Barth's theology grace always moves from God to humanity before it then completes the circuit by bringing humanity to an affirmation of God. Justification and sanctification are achieved in Jesus Christ first and are then made real derivatively for others.

Second, in presenting these two concepts of justification and sanctification, Barth repudiated the idea of an *ordo salutis* from Protestant orthodoxy. He would hear nothing of psychologizing justification, sanctification, and vocation, as though they occur in a temporal sequence that must somehow be narrated in the biography of every Christian. Barth had little interest in pinpointing the day and time of salvation.

This then helps to explain, third, why Barth departs from the typical ordering that one might have expected him to follow. If Barth were following the linear progression of Protestant orthodoxy, one might have expected his account of the Christian life to follow the usual development from justification (being made right in a once-and-for-all act) to sanctification (being made holy in an ongoing process) to glorification (finally being made luminous in the eschatological presence of God). Glorification, not vocation, would then have capped off the final stage of salvation.[25] Instead, for Barth vocation embraces the whole of Christian life in the here and now, with justification as presupposition and sanctification as consequence. Although third in the order of presentation, vocation is *not* third either temporally or materially. Rather, vocation provides the crucial experiential bridge that links the clear beginning of the Christian life in justification to its logical climax in sanctification.

Barth's most tightly constructed statement on the relationship between justification and sanctification reads as follows:

> In the *simul* of the one divine will and action justification is first as
> ground and second as presupposition, sanctification first as aim [or
> goal] and second as consequence, and therefore both are superior and
> both subordinate. (IV/2, 508)

This compact and rather cryptic statement is rendered lucid if we interpret it within the dynamic pattern of "presupposition" and "consequence"
we have mentioned several times now.

Justification and sanctification, of necessity in Barth's view, must be
considered from two different angles. In the explanatory text, Barth speaks
of these two angles as a "first" (*Prius*) and a "second" (*Posterius*), though
this is a logical and not a temporal ordering (IV/2, 507). Sanctification is
"first in [divine] intention" even though it is "second in execution" (IV/2,
508). Presumably "execution" means execution in human experience.
Sanctification is what is "intended" in election and what is "executed" in
the course of salvation history. For justification, on the other hand, the order is the reverse. As a matter of divine intention, justification is second,
since it is the means God devised whereby to effectuate reconciliation. Yet
in the order of execution it occupies a primary status as the "presupposition" in the light of which the Christian life unfolds.

In short, there are two ways of perceiving the relationship between justification and sanctification: one as a matter of divine intentionality, the
second as a matter of human experience. Divine intentionality always
moves on a trajectory from God to humanity: "I will be your God." Divine
execution precipitates a reciprocal movement from humanity back to God:
"You will be my people."

The statement quoted above may then be charted as shown in figure
6.2. The statement should then be exegeted as follows. Looked at in the
first way, from the standpoint of divine intentionality, Barth is saying that
justification is the "ground" (*Grund*) and sanctification the "goal" (*Ziel*) of
God's work in humanity's midst. The significance of the language of
"ground" and "goal" is that justification points us backward to the originating work of God the Creator and sanctification forward to the consummate work of God the Redeemer.

Looked at in the second way, from the standpoint of the outworking of
salvation in human experience, justification is considered the presupposition (*Voraussetzung*) of true Christian action and sanctification the consequence (*Folge*). From an experiential point of view, justification is behind
us as what must be taken for granted: being made right in God's sight.
Sanctification emerges in front of us: it is what we are on the way to becoming.

Note that this interpretation is in keeping with Barth's explanatory statement from *Dogmatics in Outline*, which I noted earlier, about the relationship

	JUSTIFICATION (Origination)	SANCTIFICATION (Consummation)
FIRST LEVEL Divine Intentionality	Ground	Aim/Goal
SECOND LEVEL Outworking in Human Experience	Presupposition	Consequence

FIGURE 6.2

between "presupposition" and "consequence." It is also in keeping with Barth's insistence that justification and sanctification cannot be separated according to rigid temporal distinctions, but both must impinge upon human existence considered as a concrete whole. Neither justification nor sanctification, in other words, is straightforwardly "present" to human existence. Instead, their influence exerts itself according to this indirect pattern of presupposition and consequence.

This dialectic of presupposition and consequence functions in a way analogous to the scheme of "anticipation" and "recollection" by which Barth understood the witness of scripture. The Old Testament is an "anticipation" while the New Testament is a "recollection" of the revelatory work of God in Jesus Christ (I/2, §14). The scheme of presupposition-consequence also bears a more remote analogy to the pattern which Barth asserts is always at work in any statement about God's revelation. We are always in a position, he says, of either "not yet" or "no longer" speaking about the revelatory act of God.

This interpretation receives further support from a statement drawn from Barth's final lectures at Basel on "The Ethics of Reconciliation." These lectures were meant to comprise volume IV/4 of the CD but remained unpublished during Barth's lifetime. In an introductory section, Barth sums up his whole understanding of ethics as obedience to the divine command in this way, "The command of God is the event in which God commands. It is the specific command of God in each specific form of [God's] dealings with humanity in each specific time." He then informs us that the command of God is a specific command,

> in relation to the presuppositions [*Voraussetzungen*], the possibilities [*Möglichkeiten*], and the consequences [*Konzequenzen*] of each specific existence of each human being.[26]

Here again, we see the pattern of presupposition and consequence; but we notice now that there is also an intervening moment in between. This moment marks the interval between promise and fulfillment in which we weigh our possibilities.[27] Suffice it to say, Barth is notorious for using language in idiosyncratic ways with precious little explanation of its technical meaning. One will look in vain in Barth's corpus for any sustained explanation of human life as a tensive existence stretched out between conceptual "presuppositions" and experiential "consequences." Yet this is just what his structuring of the Christian life contemplates.

Assuming that this interpretation is correct, then how did Barth characterize the experiential place one must occupy while living out this tensive form of existence? How is the gap between these two moments of presupposition and consequence to be configured? The answer lies in his treatment of Christian vocation.

Even as creation and redemption constitute the grand, thematic beginning and ending of the Christian narrative of God's action, so justification and sanctification mark the beginning and ending points of Christian living. What forms the concentrated midpoint between these two horizons is the concept of vocation. Vocation, like reconciliation itself, comprises the primary sphere in which Christian existence is lived out in the here and now (see figure 6.3).

On the triadic reading I have been advancing, it turns out that vocation emerges as the place where Barth's early endorsement of Christian experience finally comes to fruition. When Barth reached the idea of vocation in IV/3, he was finally ready to make clear what he understood Christian experience to be. Although the hiatus from I/1 to IV/3 may seem a long one, it was necessary in order to reconfigure the way Christian experience had been conceived in the theology Barth had inherited from the nineteenth century.

Nineteenth-century theology influenced by Ritschl had used the metaphor of an "ellipse with two foci," signaling religion on the one side and ethics on the other, divine action in connection with human response.[28] Barth argues, to the contrary, that we must prefer the metaphor of a single, unifying center, one circle of divine and human togetherness-in-act.

In the framework of IV/3 vocation refers to the call addressed to particular individuals to become Christians (§71). Two distinctions will help clarify Barth's meaning. First, in his earlier treatment of creation Barth had also spoken of vocation, but only in the broad sense of pursuing an occupation or a particular form of work (*Beruf*) (III/4, §56). Here in IV/3 the meaning is different. Here vocation (*Berufung*) is more broadly the work of living the Christian life. Vocation is not, in the first instance, the calling to be a monk or a minister but the calling to be a Christian.

Second, by locating the calling to become a Christian concretely in the lived experience of particular persons, Barth was departing in a significant way, once again, from Protestant orthodoxy. Orthodoxy had pinpointed God's choice of particular individuals in the eternal decree of election that occurs before the creation of the world. For orthodoxy, the mystery of who would be chosen and who would not was attributed to the inscrutable will of God. For Barth, by contrast, *all* have been elected for salvation by God in Jesus Christ. Thus, the controlling question was who would end up living out his or her election concretely in the world and who would let the gift of election lie dormant. This was a question located not in the mystery of the being of God but in the mystery of human existence itself.

The mystery of human existence is that only some end up realizing in their own lives the freedom in grace which is boundlessly available for all. Like justification and sanctification, the vocation of an individual to become a Christian is a peculiar moment in the broader event in which all

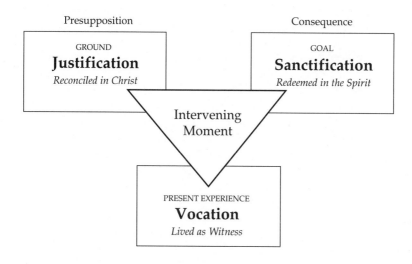

Presupposition   Consequence

GROUND
Justification
Reconciled in Christ

GOAL
Sanctification
Redeemed in the Spirit

Intervening
Moment

PRESENT EXPERIENCE
Vocation
Lived as Witness

FIGURE 6.3

creaturely reality is being transformed. Unlike justification and sanctification, however, vocation is not an event that exists always and from the outset for all people. All are justified and all are sanctified in Christ; but "not all human beings . . . are called as such" (IV/3.2, 483). All are meant for it, but not all are called in any specific, experiential sense to be Christians. To fulfill one's vocation is to have a specifically "determined" Christian experience.

Barth emphasizes that vocation, which responds and corresponds to the prophetic office of Christ, is an event that manifests itself in history, within the temporal sphere of human beings (§71.2). In contrast to justification and sanctification, vocation is not merely a forensic, or arm's length, transaction but the concrete "coming into being of a relationship" (IV/3, 483).

Barth finds some help in conceptualizing this point from Calvin's distinction between election and calling. According to Barth's reading, Calvin thought of election as the "presupposition" (the word is specifically Barth's, not Calvin's) behind every believer's vocation, and of vocation as "the historical fulfillment of election" (IV/3, 484). As we are by now aware, this pattern of presupposition and fulfillment is of pivotal importance. Barth understood election and vocation to fall upon a dynamic continuum, except that at the point of vocation something of an interruption occurs. Amidst the exigencies of history, not all in fact realize their election.

"Many are called, but there will only be few who in following the call will prove worthy of it, and act in accordance with, the fact that as the called of God they are His elect, predestined from all eternity for life with Him and for His service" (IV/3, 485). Here Barth is drawing a distinction between God's eternal election of all people and the specific experiential calling to be a Christian. Who becomes "called" on Barth's scheme is no less mysterious than who is "elected" on Calvin's, but the mystery in Barth's case is located at the level of lived human experience.

This experiential component of vocation becomes even more evident if we recall Barth's earlier use of the word "determination." Barth summed up his understanding of vocation by drawing a distinction between a person's eternal "calling as such" and his or her "determination" (*Bestimmung*) to it (*KD*, IV/3, 566, *CD*, 492). It is only in being *determined* experientially, that is to say, that the benefits of election come concretely into existence.

This determination of one's existence to Christian vocation consists of more than simply being formed in the Christian tradition (§71.4). Contrary to the approach of some postliberal admirers of Barth, Christian vocation is much more than merely coming to own for oneself the cultural-linguistic system of Christianity. Indeed, when he penned this lengthy section on vocation in 1959, Barth was prescient in his awareness that the "Christian West," the society in which being Christian was given automatically with the culture, "no longer exists" (IV/3.2, 525). Vocation is not so much the adoption of a particular cultural-linguistic tradition it is a particular spiritual stance that calls the externalities of tradition and culture constantly into question. But "spiritual" here does not mean other-worldly or transcendental. Vocation, said Barth, should not be abstracted either from its "historical or supra-historical presupposition" nor from its "consequence" in the concrete existence of the community. It is neither subjective nor objective in isolation. "It is neither an isolated humanity nor an isolated God, but God and humanity in their divinely established and effected encounter," in the one, total address of God to humanity in togetherness (IV/3.2, 498).

What is emerging here is a portrait of Christian existence as a peculiar way of living with a particular experiential shape. As surprising as it may be to those who believe Barth had no interest in anthropological or experiential description, he even contends that there is a concrete structure (*Struktur*) to the Christian life of vocation (*KD*, IV/3.2, 638, *CD*, 556). One may certainly be Christian in a multiplicity of forms, and each Christian's vocation consists in a unique and different set of functions and tasks. Yet they all partake of the same "freedom, orientation, and determination" (*Bestimmung*) (IV/3.2, 554).

To arrive at a concept by which to typify this "structure" of Christian life, Barth considers several competing but ill-suited candidates. The first is that time-honored motto that Christians should act as though they lived "in" the world but not "of" the world. But since the dialectic of worldliness and unworldliness cannot be normative for believers, Barth considers the "in but not of" motto to be a distortion of the being of the Christian, who must always maintain an ultimate solidarity with the world. Since all are meant for vocation, even if all do not realize it, Christians must be respectful of all, must address all as morally accountable beings, and must see their own calling as for the sake of all (IV/3.2, 493–96).

A second candidate to be rejected was the idea that Christians must live according to a particular ethic, such as the love of God and love of neighbor. In the next chapter we will consider the important place of ethics in Barth's theology. As attractive as this ethical alternative may be, however, there is still a work of God that is anterior to the particular outworkings of Christian ethics in each concrete situation.

The third erroneous answer was the classical answer of Protestantism, namely that Christians are distinguished from others in their capacity as recipients of grace. But this classical answer is the most problematic of all. For it distorts the unity of the Gospel by subtly encouraging one to live for the benefits of grace over living for the glory of God. It ignores the fact, too, that non-Christians display qualities of grace-filled living. And it leads to egocentricity by making the assurance of salvation the centerpiece of Christian living.

Instead of these false answers, the basic "structure" of Christian existence is defined by the simple task of being God's "witnesses" (§71.4). To be a "witness" is to point to something strictly beyond oneself. In keeping with the classical Reformed tradition, Barth can think of Christian experience using the concept of "union with Christ." But the union with Christ which vocation accomplishes, to Barth's way of thinking, is not something presently visible in believers. Like Christ's own unity with God the Father, the unity of the Christian with Christ remains concealed from us in the here and now (IV/3.2, 540–54). We may speak of an experience of being "in Christ" and of Christ's being "in" the Christian. But, as always for Barth, this "in" is never a simple "presence." It "transcends even though it also includes its local signification" (IV/3.2, 547).

The work of Christ in the Christian is not statically present but dynamic, for Christ does not exist "concentrically" but "ec-centrically" (IV/3.2, 548). This means that the center of Christ's work was never simply to focus people on his own person for his own sake, but to realize and actualize the existence and freedom of others. Similarly, the life of the Christian in Christ is to display a parallel dynamic. The Christian never exists to realize some static "union with Christ" for the Christian's own benefit, but the Christian lives dynamically "from out of the center," or "ec-centrically." As we shall explore in more detail in the following chapter, union with Christ is not an end in itself but a dynamic calling towards the other.

The primary argument for conceiving Christian vocation as a witness, therefore, is that the call of Christ consists not in achieving a special status but in undertaking a particular task and service. Union with Christ is, first, a union with Christ's mission. Second, it is a union with Christ's work in the community, a fellowship of action (*Tatgemeinschaft*) that is "determined" (*bestimmt*) by the order of relationship between Christ and the Christian (*KD*, IV/3.2, 685, *CD*, 597). The fellowship of life, in other words, realizes itself in a corresponding fellowship of action. Third, union with Christ is a participation in the wide context of the unfolding reign of God in the world. Although the Christian is by no means divine, the Christian is still veritably an actor, a legitimate player in the ongoing drama of the work of Christ. Fourth, vocation means to live as a "sign" of God's action on behalf of all people. Christ lives in both Christians and non-Christians, according to Barth, but what distinguishes the Christian is that she recognizes this and bears prophetic witness to it in her own being.

The experience of vocation leads both to affliction and to liberation. In 1922 the Christian affliction (*Bedrängnis*) that most plagued Barth, as noted in the Introduction, was the conflict between the divinely-given obligation to speak about God and the all-too-human and profoundly-felt inability to do so. Toward the end of his career, as he reflected on the Christian's obligation to speak about God, the word "affliction" came readily to Barth's mind once again. The experience of "affliction" in Christian vocation is not the suffering that all flesh is heir to, but it is the unique strife that comes specifically from being a Christian. The witness of being a Christian brings one into inevitable tension and outright hostility, even oppression, with the exigencies of the "world." To the extent that the Christian fails to experience such tension, Barth believes, she should question the genuineness of her Christianity. In the same way that the "little lights" of the world reflect the truth of the one who is the "Light of the World," so also the "little passion" of individual Christians exercising their vocation reflects the supreme passion of the cross.

But despite the fractured quality of the experience of vocation, it leads the Christian toward personal fulfillment. This fulfillment, or at least a foretaste of it, is real in human experience. A Christ without the Christian leads to dead orthodoxy just as surely as a Christian without the Christ is but a sterile mysticism. For even though the gospel is real, whether or not it has any witnesses, God in Christ does not desire to tread the road of reconciliation without the human companion, and not without working for the concrete realization of reconciliation in human experience. Vocation is an existential determination (*existentielle Bestimmung*) of one's life that leads one into freedom. It is an endowing and equipping, an alteration of one's being, an urging to consider both God and the neighbor (IV/3.2, 649–53).

Barth adopts the term *Befreiung* rather than *Freiheit* to indicate, yet again, that vocation is a dynamic occurrence of "liberation" rather than the static possession of "freedom" (*KD*, IV/3.2, 760, *CD*, 663). Poised triadically as it is between promise and fulfillment, the liberation wrought by Christian vocation is, first of all, an ongoing event that is only just now commencing; but it is also, in the second place, a movement of exemplary significance that anticipates not only its own completion but that of all things. Third, this liberation, this unfettering, is not so much the content of ministry as it is the indispensable condition of possibility of ministry. Using the terminology we have now seen him adopt so often, Barth speaks of the personal liberation of the Christian as a "presupposition" to ministry.

Barth then concludes, fourthly, with the question whether this liberation has really become consequential for believers. The answer to this question lies not in whether the Christian holds a particular experience as her own possession, but in whether the Christian herself is possessed by an experience that is compelling and inescapable. Has the Word of the gospel provoked a crisis in my experience to which I must answer "yes" or "no"?

Just as justification is the work of the Spirit behind us that offers us the "presupposition of our future" (IV/1, 554), and just as sanctification signals the goal, the consequence, and the completion of our life in Christ through the Spirit's work out in front of us, so also vocation is the Spirit's "movement in between" (*Dazwischentreten*) in the tensive moment of the present, inviting us to make the dynamic movement of God's being-in-act the determining ground of our own transient action.

Whatever the deficiencies in Barth's way of treating the Holy Spirit and redemption, it is scarcely credible to regard his thought as "modalistic" or "binitarian." Instead, we must regard it as a highly complex and creative attempt to reconfigure the angle from which redemption and the experience of the Spirit should be conceived.

In the contemporary language of postmodernity, it is "nonfoundationalist" in its deepest intentions, because of its open-ended reluctance to treat the Christian life as any sort of "given." Instead the Christian life is a thoroughly problematic task. Its fulfillment comes only through being "determined" in the freedom for obedience by which Barth conceived the moral life of the Christian. It is to this open-endedness of the Christian moral life that we now turn.

PART THREE

THE MYSTERY OF THE OTHER

A theology which insists on the use of *certain particular* words and phrases, and outlaws others, does not make anything clearer (Karl Barth). It gesticulates with words, as one might say, because it wants to say something and does not know how to express it. *Practice [die praxis]* gives the words their sense.

Ludwig Wittgenstein, Culture and Value, 85

The problem of ethics reminds us of the Truth of God, which is never actually present or actually apprehended in our act of thinking however sublime.

Karl Barth, The Epistle to the Romans, 426

Being in encounter is a being in the openness of the one to the other.

Karl Barth, CD, III/2, 250–51

7

AN OPEN-ENDED
ETHICS OF OTHERNESS

It is by no means self-evident that we may count on the Christian life's being a reality. There thus arises the question of its foundation.
Karl Barth, *The Christian Life*, 45

Throughout this study, I have been seeking to uncover a more open-ended side to Barth's theology, a side that accents the need for ongoing questioning and exploration, the need, in respect to every theological issue, to "begin again at the beginning." The point of Barth's theology is not to repristinate an ancient tradition but to hear the unheard of "new thing" God is enabling and requiring of human beings in the present moment. That "new thing" is not a new gospel—there can be no such thing for Barth—but the new and life-changing implications of a gospel already revealed but still working itself out in the unfolding of human history. Since God's reign is in God's act, this act "is always and everywhere a new and free reality, [God's] own reality that cannot be domesticated."[1]

Although our attention so far has been devoted to Barth's conceptual reconstructions of traditional doctrines, he himself was convinced that conceptual reflection alone is not enough. Barth was more concerned, to put it in the language of Emmanuel Levinas, with the continual "Saying" of theology than with the already "Said."[2] What counts most in theological inquiry is not what the apostles or prophets said but what we must now be saying in the light of that earlier word. This "saying" implies and includes a "doing." Being must be understood squarely in reference to act. Since both God and human beings have their being in activity, theological reflection is only worthwhile when pursued as a prelude to action. Who we are, our identity as Christians, Barth would say, is validated in reference to our own love in freedom.[3]

Thus it is ethics that stands at the pinnacle of theological inquiry. Accordingly, each of the four divisions of the *CD*—God, Creation, Reconciliation, and Redemption—was to have reached its summit with a treatment of theological ethics. Unfortunately, Barth completed only the first two projected volumes, "The Command of God" (II/1) and "The Command of God the Creator" (III/4). He started and almost finished the projected third volume, "The Command of God the Reconciler," but left it incomplete.[4] Moreover, death intervened before Barth could even set his pen to the ethics of Redemption, although the Redemption theme itself was frequently anticipated throughout the *CD*.[5]

Barth has often been criticized for the vague and episodic nature of his ethics. He conceived ethics as the human response to the unique command given by God in every new situation. This approach, so the critics charge, reduces ethics to an enigmatic "occasionalism," an arbitrary response to unfathomable fiat that provides no basis for moral consistency from one occasion to the next. Yet this sort of criticism fails to appreciate the irreducibly nonfoundationalist intention that inhabits so much of Barth's theology. Anyone looking to Barth for detailed ethical admonitions will surely be disappointed. For if God is a God of hiddenness and mystery, then ethics and the Christian life, too, must remain—in significant part—a matter of concealment.

Failure to grasp Barth at this point will lead to failure at every other point. To put it plainly, the very open-endedness, provisionality, and inclusiveness of Barth's deliberations count, from a nonfoundationalist point of view, not as weaknesses but as strengths. The truly ethical, that which God commands, cannot be equated—certainly not in any straightforward fashion—with the acceptable canons of self-interested and ideologically-grounded human reason. God is ultimate mystery, and so what God requires of us surpasses and sometimes even shatters all our ordinary conceptual structures. To conceive of theological ethics as a ready-made system would constitute an infringement upon the freedom of God.

In and of itself theological ethics is incapable of dispensing direct answers to moral questions. Instead, Barth views ethical inquiry primarily as a process of continually putting one's own preconceived notions of the moral life into question. Ethical reflection poses myriad "points to be considered" designed to prepare one to hear God's disrupting yet empowering command for this particular situation. Since the very will of God is the content of morality, the discipline of theological ethics cannot render its subject matter immediately through its own power. Whereas God, in the power of the Holy Spirit, confers upon human beings a particular "wisdom" or "direction" (*Weisung*) for life, theological ethics performs the derivative task of offering ongoing "counsel" or "instruction" (*Unterweisung*).[6] Ethics is the discipline of "instructional preparation" (*unterweisende Vorbereitung*) for the ethical event itself (*KD*, III/4, 18–19, *CD*, 18). In short, the will of God forms the content of ethics, but that content can never be grasped in advance of an immediate context. Barth's ethics is radically contextual: one can know the will of God only in the very act of obedience in a given situation.

What can we make of a theological ethics conceived in this way? What, if anything, does it contribute to the postmodern possibilities of theology? To the extent it insists on the primacy of God's will, it may seem to support John Webster's contention that Barth's ethics offers "one of the most powerfully anti-modern statements by a Christian theologian since the Enlightenment."[7] Yet Barth's challenge to modernity is not merely "anti-modern," and even less is it naively "premodern," but it points to a possibility that may be designated genuinely "postmodern." It is not that he wishes to turn back the hands of time to an age that had yet to strive for the Enlightenment ideals of freedom and tolerance. It is, rather, that he wished to reorient modernity according to a theologically enriched understanding of its own high-minded goals.

Modernity, for the most part, has repudiated the ethics of divine command in favor of moral theories that exalt human autonomy and our own definitions of the good life.[8] Barth challenges this modern preoccupation with autonomy but does so not in order to negate it but to sublate it, to give it its proper orientation. True freedom is the freedom for obedience, and true obedience is freedom for the "other." True humanity, as noted in chapter four, is a "being in encounter." To truly be oneself is to be "for" and "with" the other. It is a "being in the openness of the one to the other with a view to and on behalf of the other" (*KD*, III/2, 300, *CD*, 250–51).

Barth's validation of theology through the prism of ethics contributes to a shift away from the ontology-based approach of premodernity, and from the epistemology-based approach of modernity, and toward an ethically-based openness that is postmodern. Openness to the other provides the confirmation of theology. Theological claims about what *is* must be judged ethically in reference to what *ought* to be. Being is validated in act; theology comes to fruition in ethics.

In this way, the "identity" issues that dominate so much of Barth's *Church Dogmatics* must be assimilated, in the end, to "praxis" issues. Just as God is identified as the one who is "for" and "with" us in Jesus Christ, so one's human identity is grounded not in neutral separation or sameness but in concrete, engaged openness to the "other."

Barth's formulation of this unique human identity could not be more radical: human action must be analogous to divine action. Just as God's action is hidden in the humanity of Jesus Christ, so also, in a secondary way, is the human imperative hidden in the humanity of one's neighbor. Being confronted by the neighbor presents us with the problem of enabling human life to be truly human.[9] Indeed, "the existence of our fellow human beings presents us with the problem of the hidden God."[10] Because the humanity of Jesus Christ is the sacrament of the living God, all human life takes on a sacramental quality (I/2, 436).

One of the most promising things about Barth's approach to ethics is the potential it has to overturn the usual stereotypes about his narrow confessionalism. The interplay Barth envisions between theology and ethics opens up an implicit possibility (and perhaps obligation) for the theologian to test theological claims pragmatically. The proof of one's theology, that is to say, must be made in the living. And this validation must be pursued through an engagement with information derived from all manner of human phenomena. The obligation to embody the purposes of God, as we shall soon see, necessitates an investigation into the whole range of human existence and not just Christian existence narrowly conceived.

This last claim may surprise those who have too readily accepted the old stereotypes of neo-orthodoxy. It may startle some to learn that, despite Barth's confessional starting point, he conceived ethical inquiry as demanding an open engagement with the full range of human experience, including data derived from nontheological and even non-Christian sources. When it comes to ethical inquiry, a theology guided by Barthian lights must be willing to adopt a more open standpoint toward the ambiguous multiplicity of the world. Ethics provides the pivotal tool by which to pry Barth's otherwise narrowly confessional theology open.

To test this thesis, let us conclude our reflections with a sketch in Part Three of Barth's theological ethics. The spotlight will fall on the nonfoundationalist dimensions of his method and, in particular, on Barth's view that ethics marks the sphere in which theology itself must be critiqued and validated. By no means is the purpose here to present an exhaustive account of Barth's ethics, and still less to launch a detailed consideration of the many pronouncements he made about specific moral issues. As was the case in considering his theology, I am more interested in the possibilities Barth's ethical reflections open up for us today than in uncovering his own opinion on this or that topic.

ETHICS AS THEOLOGICAL VERIFICATION

Consider Barth's rather dramatic statement, "As thunder follows lightning, that is the way humanity recognizes God" (KD, III/2, 210, CD, 176, rev.). This comment bespeaks the awesome character of the mystery that surrounds the knowledge of God. Just as there is no second-guessing when or where a lightning bolt will strike, so too there is no fathoming how the being and life of God are made efficacious in our midst. Despite the electrifying peremptoriness suggested by Barth's statement, God's self-identification in Jesus Christ is an event that prompts a definite reverberation in human experience. Whenever the lightning strikes, inevitably the thunder follows. To know God is to be changed. To hear God's Word is to obey. Theological presupposition must give rise to ethical consequence.

We have noted in previous chapters how Barth's mature theology lies suspended between "presupposition" and "consequence," between that which lies, so to speak, behind us and that which still awaits fulfillment out in front of us. Similarly, Christian ethics attends to the specific command of God as it relates to "the presuppositions [*Voraussetzungen*], the possibilities [*Möglichkeiten*], and the consequences [*Konzequenzen*] of each specific existence of each human being."[11] It is within the "suspended" moment of one's present "possibilities," resting on the cusp of this gaping "mean time" between who we are and who we ought to be, that the ethical question, in all its ambiguity, first rises to the surface. It is in this ambiguous space that our theological presuppositions must find their verification in action.

What is the relationship between theological presupposition and ethical consequence? In *Romans* Barth had maintained that no "action" of any type occurs without implicit presuppositions—those concepts that are formulated and nurtured in "thought."[12] Similarly, no presupposition is complete in itself (*an sich*), since thought must make itself known in action. Thus the relationship between "presupposition" and "action" runs in two directions. Not only does "action" serve to verify our "presuppositions," but our "presuppositions" themselves either explicitly or implicitly inform our "actions." Still it is "action" that provides the driving force that tests our thinking. Ironically, then, genuine thought will always be "broken" thought, as Walter Lowe observes, or thought that allows itself to be interrupted by the in-breaking authority of the ethical imperative.[13]

The disturbance precipitated by the ethical problem is especially acute when it comes to God. The presupposition that "God is God" is the only presupposition that really counts for a theologically-informed ethics. "All ethical stances (*Setzungen*) are only ethical as expositions of this presupposition (*Voraussetzung*) that is not something already known."[14] This is the uncoercible presupposition which cannot be fully fathomed or fully possessed. It is the presupposition par excellence, the grand thought "which wishes to make itself known" in the world.[15]

But how can this presupposition, "God," be known? According to Barth, it becomes luminous only *in act*. It is only in action, only in obedience to the ethical command, that God becomes known:

> [B]reak off your thinking that it may be a thinking of God; break off your dialectic that it may be indeed dialectic; break off your knowledge of God, that it may be what, in fact, it is, the wholesome disturbance and interruption which God in Christ prepares, in order that He may call human beings home to the peace of His Kingdom.[16]

Thus, the ethical imperative dislocates our theology precisely in order to authenticate it. It "disturbs our conversation about God, in order to remind it of its proper theme; sublates it [*aufheben*], in order to give it its proper relationship; kills it, in order to make it alive."[17] It is the demand of ethics, in short, that puts our theological thinking to its most profound and rigorous test.

In the light of this, all the theology we have explored up to now, indeed all the theology that was crafted with such laborious detail throughout the

CD, serves as but a prelude or "presupposition" to action. If it does not come to completion in ethics, theology is nothing more than a "narrowed and emptied" intellectualism (I/2, 787). Only by attending to ethics does theology reach its pinnacle. Or, to put it another way, theological "being" can only be construed in reference to ethical "act."

Recall that the terms "presupposition" and "action" in Barth's technical vocabulary are construed according to a Kantian meaning. In the *Critique of Practical Reason,* Kant had argued that moral action is able to furnish practical verification of certain beliefs that are otherwise unverifiable.[18] "Theoretical" reason (the concern of the *Critique of Pure Reason*) can neither prove nor disprove such things as the existence of God or the reality of human freedom; but these beliefs can be validated, argued Kant, as necessary "postulates" (or, in Barth's terminology, "presuppositions") of practical reason. For Kant such postulates (presuppositions) are, in fact, "necessary" in that they provide the precondition for rendering moral action intelligible. To engage in moral action, at least on one way of reading Kant, is to place an implicit wager upon the truthfulness of one's presuppositions. To act morally, for instance, is to presuppose freedom. To believe in a moral universe, still more, is to presuppose some notion of God.

In Barth's case, similarly, morality is the realm where theological presuppositions work themselves out and are validated. Through morality, life is rendered "determinate," "actual," "concrete"—with all the rich meaning Barth garnered to these terms as explored in the preceding chapters. In contrast to Kant, however, Barth refused to separate theoretical and practical reason, and even less to simply reduce theology (theory) to ethics (practice). He thus refused to emulate theologians such as Ritschl, Herrmann, and Troeltsch who, in keeping with Kant, posited a special, independent (*selbständige*) ethics that was somehow supposed to be separate from theology. To bifurcate reality into such a duality was unacceptable to Barth. The Ritschlian metaphor of the "ellipse with two foci"—positing religion as one focus of the ellipse and ethics as the other—was rejected, as we have seen, in favor of Schleiermacher's image of the "circle" with a "single center," that center being configured by the divine-human relationship enacted in Jesus Christ. Schleiermacher understood well the need for a unity of theology and ethics; his mistake, argued Barth, was to seek that unity of "knowing" and "doing" in a description of the pious Christian life that he naively believed to be already "given" in advance of theological reflection. This naivete is what generates the real problem with Schleiermacher. For the Christian life is not itself a "given" but a task (I/2, 785–86).

Noting this similarity—and difference—between Barth and Kant on theology and ethics places us in a position to understand the earlier claim in *CD* I/1 that God cannot be known except through the prism of action. In an analogy to Kant, Barth claimed that theological beliefs are validated in ethics, though he did not wish to reduce theology to ethics. It is only through "act" that our theological presuppositions come to fruition. This connection between theology and ethics may be illustrated through the linkage between election and the divine command.

Election, as we saw in chapter three, is the divine self-determination to be "for" and "with" humanity in Jesus Christ. The divine command, in turn, is the reverse side of this divine election (II/2, §36). Just as the electing God says, "I will be your God," the commanding God says, "You will be my people." Election as divine self-determination elicits obedience to the divine command as a human self-determination. To be obedient is to complete the covenant, to be "for" and "with" God and "for" and "with" one another. True Christian action lies on a trajectory of consistent obedience to the divine command.

Does grounding ethics in the divine command mean that there is a "foundation" to the Christian life after all? Does the command of God constitute something that is "given" and ready-made to ethical existence? As we shall see momentarily, Barth does assert that the Christian life rests on a "foundation" which he specifically denominates as such, namely the event of "baptism in the Holy Spirit." But this "foundational" event still remains to be fully actualized and made concrete in human existence. One is always in the situation of "not yet" being a Christian but of remaining caught up in the process of still becoming one. Thus, it is a "foundation" that, to the extent it rests in the mystery of God, remains in a peculiar way "nonfoundational." It has not yet been fully realized in human experience.

We spoke in previous chapters of the "foundationally nonfoundational" character to Barth's theology. The same is true of his ethics. Ethics is not a "given" but a "task." There is thus a reiteratation in ethics of the perpetual interplay (noted in previous chapters) between the real and the ideal.[19] On the one hand, the command of God is a reality. To the extent it impinges upon us, to the extent it confronts us in the interstices between "what is" and "what ought to be," it is real and, in that specific sense, foundational. Its reality is grounded in God's election to be "for" and "with" humanity in Christ. But this "reality" is by no means something that is straightforwardly "given" to the world as it is. As yet, its content is neither rationally known nor empirically realized. As long as our theological reach exceeds our ethical grasp, as long as the divine command levels a question mark against the whole of life "as it is," then all talk of ethical "foundations" that are fixed and accessible remains problematic.

The question of ethical foundations was raised in classical form by Plato in the *Euthyphro*. Is a thing good, Socrates asked, because divinity commands it, or does divinity command a thing because it is already good? In the first case, the good seems to be the subject of divine caprice—in which case, it would seem, God can do whatever God wishes. In the latter case, the good seems to form a prior foundation that places constraints upon the action of divinity—but then in that case how can God be God?

From Barth's point of view, this Socratic query, by means of its implicit separation between God and the good, insinuates a false dilemma. For Barth, God alone is good, and goodness is identical with who God is and what God is doing. On the one hand, the good is defined by God; but, on the other hand, God's definition is not arbitrary. For what God does is always circumscribed by God's overarching election to be "for" and "with" humanity in Jesus Christ. Thus, God's commands are always in accordance with the good which is already inherent in God's character. Yet what this good is in a given situation cannot be known apart from the immediate context. This means that while God alone is the "foundation" of the good, we are speaking of a "foundation" that, strangely, has neither made itself fully available to reason, nor yet established itself empirically in the world. For the command of God has yet to be enacted *by us;* the Reign of God has yet to become fully present *in us.*

This "foundationally nonfoundational" character of the divine command bears a striking similarity, once again, to Immanuel Kant's notion of a categorical imperative. Kant conceived the categorical imperative as the pure "ought" that bears down upon us in any given situation. At one level, it is a purely formal principle calling upon the agent to act in such a way, first, that the maxim or policy behind one's action could be applied as a universal law; second, that all persons affected by one's actions be treated as "ends in themselves" and never merely as "means"; third, that one treat oneself as an autonomous, self-legislating agent; and, fourth, that in performing one's ethical duty one must take account of the integrity of the moral community, or what Kant termed the "kingdom of ends."[20] To obey the categorical imperative, in other words, would be to follow a pure ethics of duty; to act freely and irrespective of personal merit, reward, or the extrinsic good to be produced; and to consider the concrete good of the "other" in the moral community as a matter of utmost importance. Thus, categorical imperatives are to be contrasted with "hypothetical" imperatives, those imperatives that arise from mere prudence, from hope of reward, or from merely self-interested or utilitarian designs.

As the level of metaethical theory, Kant's categorical imperative is best understood as performing a purely formal and heuristic function. Kant labors to describe the conditions that make morality possible but then leaves it up to free human beings to enact that possibility in practice. Kant elucidates the formal features of the imperative in great detail, while only seldom illustrating its actual application. One of his best-known and most notorious illustrations of how to apply the imperative was his judgment that one should never tell a lie under any circumstances, even if to do so might prevent a murder.[21] This has always seemed to many a strange result. Moreover, Kant was convinced that the content of the command was always and everywhere the same and that it was accessible by the powers of reason. At this level, of course, Barth and Kant part ways.

Barth's ethics is not universal and rational but contextual. Yet it still bears an affinity to Kant. It is conceivable that one could accept Kant's formulation of the categorical imperative as a formal metaethical "ought" and disagree with the way Kant applies that "ought." One might apply the categorical imperative in a different way than he did. For example, one might agree that the imperative requires truthfulness but disagree over what "truthfulness" in any given situation really means. In short, one could envision the imperative requiring different obligations in diverse contexts.

Thus, one might interpret the categorical imperative as merely a heuristic device that is empty of content. As a merely formal construct it transcends individual contexts even as it gathers new content in diverse situations through the years and across geographical boundaries. Thus, to posit the categorical imperative formally, as Kant does, is not (in and of itself) to assert that anyone has ever managed to obey it materially. One can "think" the categorical imperative as a formal rule without being able to live up to it morally; one can conceive it without being sure one has ever seen an example of its actual accomplishment. Nor is the categorical imperative (in itself) able to tell us the moral thing to do in any given case. All it can provide, one might argue, is an inventory of what counts as truly moral in making decisions, namely universalizability, freedom, respect for the "other," and the priority of ethical community. As a purely formal law, void of content, it still must yield in every case to a contextual, empirical analysis of the relevant facts arising in each new situation.

Something similar to these last remarks is at work in Barth's theological ethics. Unlike Kant, Barth has no interest in generating universal norms. Nor does he believe that ethical obligation can be discerned through an act of pure reason. Barth is a radically contextual ethicist. His understanding of moral obligation is much more similar to H. Richard Niebuhr's "responsible self" than to either its purely deontological or consequentialist competitors.[22] Nevertheless, Barth's divine command theory, like the formalist ethics of Kant, is "categorical" in that it does impose a radical and purely formal regard for the "other."

To say that the *ethics* of divine command is purely formal does not mean that the divine command *itself* is devoid of content. Rather, for Barth, the particular obligation revealed by God in each new situation is precisely what furnishes the content one needs in order to act. Thus, the command of God is more than a merely rational formality. The command of God is only a command of *God,* if it expresses the concrete content of *who* God is. Thus, just as God is "for" and "with" human beings, so too human beings must be fundamentally "for" and "with" their neighbors.

This injunction to be radically "for" the other, when stated in this way, remains a purely formal imperative. It does not indicate what being "for" the other might mean in any given situation. Knowing what one must do in any given situation requires one to attend to all the material circumstances at hand. Theological ethics "has to listen to all other ethics in so far as it has to receive *from them* at every point *the material* for its own deliberations. To that extent its attitude to every other ethics is not negative but comprehensive" (II/2, 527). To heed the ever-new and unheard-of divine command requires a fundamental openness to everything that is going on in the world.

But therein lies the enigma. For how can *this* content—a content that is never given in advance but that must emerge in the concrete moment of action—be considered a "foundation" made present and ready to hand? Walter Lowe, in *Theology and Difference*, has argued that Kant's approach to the categorical imperative is not foundationalist, because it did not reify its concepts of the transcendent and because it refused to reduce the requirements of morality to the prudential calculus of the world "as it is."[23] Kant's rationally conceived imperative has no material content and thus no "foundation" in empirical reality as such. With this formal and heuristic nature of Kant's categorical imperative in mind Barth remarks, "the categorical imperative as such will never be a command" (II/2, 666–67). This is because a true "command," if it comes from God, must be much more than a heuristic rule of reason. The divine command, Barth clearly states, is not merely an "idea" or a "principle" that can be grasped cognitively; instead it is a concrete "event" to be realized practically (II/2, 548). "The will of God is always concrete or else it is not the will of *God*" (III/4, 15).

To understand the meaning of "concreteness" here, recall the earlier discussion from chapter three, and in particular, the illustration of the motion picture. To consider something in the concrete, I suggested, is not to abstract it from the multiplicity of its relationships, the way one might "freeze frame" a film while it is still in motion. It is not possible to understand the "whole" from the standpoint of the one, individually frozen frame. We are in no position to consider the movie "concretely" until it reaches its end and we have considered it "whole."

This way of thinking leads to a remarkable way of conceiving the command of God. To speak as though "there is" a command of God, declares Barth, is a mistake! Whatever "there is" in the world, or whatever we refer to ostensively is by definition *not* the command of God (II/2, 548). For the command is not something already "there" or "present" to the world as it is, but it is an unsettling impingement, a crisis that provokes us to embrace the world as it ought to be.

Recall that to think about God and humanity in the concrete means avoiding all talk of divinity or humanity "in itself." To consider anything "in itself" is to abstract it from the context of its relationships. In the same way, when it comes to ethics, "there is no divine claim in itself. There are only concrete divine claims" which are particular instances of the one divine command directed to the eventful particulars of each new situation (II/2, 566). The command of God is something vital and emerging and not something already statically "given" or "there."

Thus, "we never at any point know the divine command in itself and as such, but only in its relationships" (II/2, 550). This means we only know it in the concrete—i.e., holistic, relational, actualizing—event of ethical action itself. It is not as if we could first hear the command and then obey; but we truly hear it only *as* we obey. We know God only in the prism of our act.

In short, the divine command is the foundation of ethics, but is not a foundation that is simply ready to hand. For an example of this "foundationally nonfoundational" quality of the divine command let us turn to Barth's treatment of the ethics of creation in *CD* III/4 published in 1951. In an earlier set of ethics lectures delivered at Münster in the 1928–29 academic year, Barth had employed favorably the concept of the "orders of creation." The "orders" are those fixed and foundational structures of human existence, such as marriage, family, and the state. Prevalent in Lutheran ethics, the theology of the "orders" conceived the roles and structures of life as established universally by God for all time. Yet in *CD* III/4, Barth explicitly abandoned this thoroughly foundationalist concept. Why do you suppose he did so? What was at stake in Barth's rejection of the theology of the "orders"?

Similar to the dangers he perceived in "natural theology," the danger of continuing a concept of divine "orders" was that it tended toward the kind of conservatism that simply equates God's purposes with the powers that be, as though the present order of the world were already suitable for all time. This danger was vividly brought home to Barth by the way the "German Christians" appealed to the "orders" in the 1930s to promote the ideological claims of National Socialism. To baptize our present concepts of what is "natural" or "orderly" is to risk elevating the tyranny of our own prejudices to the level of God's own truth.

Accordingly, Barth stipulated three reasons for rejecting the doctrine of the "orders" (III/4, 37–39). First, the doctrine tended to construe the world in abstraction from the concreteness of God's Word. Again, it is a cardinal mistake to conceive any reality as though it could be disconnected from its relations to the continuing act of God. Second, the doctrine isolated its gaze on the supposed fixtures that comprise creation per se in separation from the ultimate transformation of these created features in redemption. Since the present world is not yet what it shall be, the given order of things cannot reflect the apodictic will of God. Third, advocates of the doctrine were overly impressed with the "obscure witness of so-called 'reality' " rather than looking more concretely to the dynamic relationship between the Creator and the creature, a relationship that is still realizing itself in the world.

Rather than craft the ethics of creation on a foundation of immutable "orders," Barth organized the topic around the theme of human freedom: freedom for God, for one's fellow human beings, for life itself, and freedom within the limits of life (CD, §§53–56). That the ethics of creation is principally an ethics of freedom is itself revealing. It means that the concept of creation, at the very outset, points us forward to the redeemed world that God desires human beings to enjoy and to help bring into being. Creation as a theme, then, is not about life "as it is" but about life "as it ought to be" in the exercise of freedom.

A similar questioning of the "orders" is evident in Barth's teaching concerning the state.[24] From one point of view, his teaching might be interpreted as a flat endorsement of the existing order of things.[25] But we must remember that this is the same author who penned the 1934 *Barmen Declaration* proclaiming the lordship of Jesus Christ above the overbearing claims of the Nazi state under Adolf Hitler.[26] So too, in his last lectures on ethics the petition, "Thy kingdom come . . . " requires the Christian to embrace a revolutionary protest against the "lordless powers" that rule this present world.[27] For their part, political institutions are mere "human inventions" possessing only mundane, relative, and not absolute authority.[28] For its part, God's kingdom "is God . . . in the act of normalizing human existence," and, as such, says Barth (resurrecting language from the Romans commentary), it comes "straight down from above" (*senkrecht von oben*).[29] It contemplates a remaking of existing orders. To be sure, this "revolt against disorder" presupposes a higher "order" that is normative. But it is God's eschatological order Barth has in mind, an order that has yet to achieve its actualization. It is the order of "obedient life . . . in fellowship with God" which includes the guarantee of "human right, freedom, and peace."[30] All protests on behalf of this order, in keeping with his ethics of otherness, are directed against institutions and not against people; and, by the same token, it is people who are championed and not ideological causes. Ideology is in play whenever ideas and commitments are reduced to "isms," slogans, and propaganda. "Ideas are systematized as idealism . . . reality as realism. . . . History gives us historicism and existence existentialism. Freedom . . . becomes liberalism, society . . . socialism or communism, private ownership . . . capitalism," and so on. Even recognition of Christ is reduced to "christocentrism."[31]

A significant dimension of Barth's theology, then, includes a relativizing of all social and political orders. I mentioned earlier, however, that Barth did not always live up to his own best lights. A glaring illustration of this is Barth's approach to gender questions. For example, when writing on the roles of "Man and Woman," Barth counseled that "we cannot and may not prejudge the issue with an abstract definition" of male and female (III/4, 150). But then he transgressed against his own insight by simply accepting the patriarchal world as it presented itself. How do we explain this? Is it consistent or at odds with the trajectory we have been tracing?

From the standpoint of the more open-ended ethics we have been pursuing, some of Barth's initial comments on the subject look promising. Male and female in their relation to one another, he says, are an expression of the co-humanity to which God calls all people. There is no man or woman in the abstract but only man and woman in concrete relationship to what God is doing in the world. Even to speak of *this* individual man or *this* individual woman is "to point to something which cannot be expressed, to the mystery in which humanity stands revealed to God and to [God] alone." That our humanity presents itself as ultimate mystery is significant; for "it is at the point where [humanity] is indefinable that [humanity] is sought and found by the divine command" (III/4, 150). And the divine command, you will recall, may enjoin fresh ways of thinking and acting in each new situation.

With this sort of beginning, one might expect a treatment that avoided the rigidity that has infected so many traditional construals of human gender and sexuality. Regarding the status of women, Barth was innovative enough to suggest that the question of gender roles "ought certainly to be posed in each particular case as it arises, not in the light of traditional preconceptions, honestly in relation to what is aimed at in the future" (III/4, 155). Unfortunately, Barth was not content to leave it at that. He went on to construe the relationship between man and woman as a hierarchy formed between a superordinate "A" (the male) and a subordinate "B" (the female). This hierarchy is marked, he claims, by a definite order that is irreversible (III/4, 168). The existence of this hierarchal conception is mitigated only slightly by the fact that the man must transform his own superordination into a "primacy of service," while the woman herself gains a certain "primacy," because the subordination she undergoes is a participation in Jesus Christ's very own subordination.

This last rationale, of course, could be used to justify all manner of oppression in the name of following the example of Jesus. Aside from that, and more to the point, Barth's acceptance of a traditional gender hierarchy amounts to the very legitimation of the "orders" that his methodological principles should have led him to reject, or at the very least to seriously call into question. Regarding the relationship of male and female, Barth sinks to baptizing the given order of the world as it is and thus fails to live up to his own best theological lights.

Throughout this study I have been focusing on a certain "nonfoundationalist" trajectory in Barth's thought. I have made no claim that Barth succeeded in following this trajectory at every turn. By his own account, he failed at several critical junctures to achieve what a nonfoundationalist program required. Consider the need he felt early on to thoroughly renovate the *Romans* commentary, and then later the prolegomena to the aborted *Christian Dogmatics*, in order to eliminate from them all vestiges of an anthropological foundation left over from his days as a "liberal" theologian. This suggests that Barth's whole career was an experiment to find a way not to reduce God to the foundations of the world as it is. Faithfulness to the mystery of who God is required Barth to rethink and to reshape his theology constantly to the very end.

One such rethinking and reshaping occurred in Barth's last lectures on ethics. I am speaking of Barth's reflections concerning baptism. In the final fragment of the CD published in 1967, Barth rejected the traditional belief that these Christian rites can legitimately count as "sacraments." Although this rejection has perplexed many of his interpreters, I want to suggest that it becomes understandable once one considers it in connection to Barth's overall nonfoundationalist intention. His teaching on baptism, I will argue, becomes intelligible when considered in connection to the overall nonfoundationalist trajectory in his theology.

ETHICS, FOUNDATIONS, AND SACRAMENT

Barth came to consider the two traditional Reformed sacraments of baptism and the Lord's Supper not as "sacraments" at all, but as our own human, ethical response to God's grace. How do we account for this shift? I propose we view it as a consistent working out of the belief, accented throughout this study, that God is never simply "given" or straightforwardly "present" to humanity. Although many have been puzzled by this particular turn in Barth's theology, one cannot invoke the mantle of Barth without accounting for this peculiar aspect of his teaching.[32]

Earlier, in *The Teaching of the Church Regarding Baptism*, published in 1943, Barth had rejected the traditional Roman Catholic idea that baptism serves to "convey" grace.[33] Grace is not a "thing" to be dispensed but the free and personal activity of God. Barth also repudiated the ancient practice of infant baptism as being contrary to the New Testament. Where is there any biblical indication, he queried, that the baptized person was to be a passive recipient? No, declared Barth, she must submit herself for baptism affirmatively as a response to God's grace.

One of the key distinctions Barth made in 1943 was between the causative and the cognitive theories of the significance of baptism. Barth rejected the causative view, namely the Roman Catholic position that baptism actually mediates salvation, embracing instead the cognitive view essentially as it had been espoused by John Calvin. On this latter view, the sacrament does not convey grace on its own power but it does help bring one to a knowledge of grace.

In his last lectures on baptism, however, Barth found he must also reject even this second, cognitive meaning in favor of a third rationale that is predominantly ethical in orientation. Baptism does not convey grace either causatively or cognitively, he concluded, but represents an ethical response to the prior initiative of God. The rite of baptism represents "the human action that corresponds to the divine action" (IV/4, 105). As such, it is to be received by professing adults and not by infants.

This nonsacramental, ethical view became crystallized for Barth after reading his son Markus's 1951 rejection (on New Testament grounds) of baptism as a sacrament. From this exegetical basis, Barth drew his own (theological) conclusion that in and of themselves, the "sacraments" of baptism and the Lord's Supper cannot be considered as "means" of grace at all, not even in the cognitive sense he had previously retrieved from Calvin. He found instead that he had to abandon his long-held Calvinist sacramental theology in favor of a view that he admitted could be labeled "Neo-Zwinglian." The great Swiss reformer, Huldrych Zwingli, was correct to repudiate traditional sacramentalism, he argued, even though Zwingli's positive teaching remained unsatisfactory. Barth mourned what he considered Zwingli's "sterile" focus on the communal meaning of baptism. Barth's own reformulated sacramental teaching was championed as a way to "understand Zwingli better than he understood himself" (IV/4, 128–30).

What was this reformulated teaching? Agreeing with Zwingli while also pushing beyond him, Barth rejected the idea that baptism and the Lord's Supper are themselves "mysteries" (sacraments) in the New Testament sense. Instead, the mystery of God is mediated chiefly in the concrete history of Jesus Christ. In a similar way Martin Luther had opined in the *Babylonian Captivity of the Church* that there is really only one sacrament, Jesus Christ, with three sacramental signs: baptism, penance, and the Lord's Supper.[34] Barth does not mention Luther, but he moves in a direction even more radical. He says there is only one true sacrament, Jesus Christ, and one true sacramental sign, baptism in the Holy Spirit. The traditional liturgical rites are something other than sacraments.

In the first place, the humanity of Jesus Christ qualifies as this one true "mystery," or "sacrament," the one divine-human point of contact that personifies the grace of the living God. In the second place, baptism in the Holy Spirit is the one true sacramental deed. This is the baptism that only God can accomplish, a baptism from on high that must be sharply distinguished from the human act of baptism with water.

The event of baptism in the Holy Spirit depends, moreover, on two "presuppositions" that are intrinsically connected: the resurrection of Jesus Christ from the dead and the fact that the Holy Spirit actually is at work in the lives of human beings. The resurrection, first of all, is part of a history "which, because it happened once-for-all, is present to all later times and indeed to all earlier times, cosmically effective and significant history" (IV/4, 24). Resurrection inaugurates the beginning of a process by which what Jesus Christ did "there and then" becomes manifest "here and now." The ongoing work of the Holy Spirit, second of all, effectuates this new beginning in the lives of believers. The presupposition of resurrection focuses on the power "from above," while that of the Holy Spirit's ongoing work considers the power effective in believers "from below." As we have seen previously, the mention of the Holy Spirit raises the question of *how* there can be a real experience of grace.

How can the history of Jesus—a history that occurred apart from us (*extra nos*)—become an effective history "in" and "among" us (*in nobis*)? How does the story of Jesus Christ become the believer's own story? Two answers are to be avoided. We must reject both the "christomonistic" answer that attributes everything to Jesus, as well as the "anthropomonistic" solution that attributes everything to human effort. Recalling the Chalecedonian pattern, the answer is that the Christian life is the concurrence of a dual agency that is both one hundred percent human and one hundred percent divine.

The main thing to note here is that the "beginning" of the Christian life, as set in motion by the Spirit, is neither perfect nor complete but is still moving toward that goal which "is not yet present." As something that is still coming into existence, the Christian life remains, so to speak, "one long Advent season" (IV/4, 31–40, 24).

It is often charged that the rejection of traditional sacramental theory in IV/4 marked a decisive shift away from Barth's earlier teaching. It is also alleged that by declaring Jesus Christ the only "real" sacrament and questioning the sacramentality of baptism and the Lord's Supper, Barth was also eliminating all talk of sacramental reality whatsoever, aside from the particular humanity of Jesus. Both of these suppositions need to be significantly qualified.

The sacramental centrality of Jesus' humanity was by no means an innovation of the baptism fragment of IV/4. Nor had Barth ever ceded to baptism and the Lord's Supper a "primary" status as sacraments. As noted in chapter three, Barth had long maintained that the humanity of Jesus is the true sacramental focal point of revelation. Jesus' humanity, he said early on, is the "first sacrament" (II/1, 53–54). It subsists with other "signs," such as the existence of the Jews, of the church, of the scriptures, and, especially, of the humanity of other human beings. Long before he reached volume four of the *CD*, then, Barth had held that all these subordinate signs draw their significance from the primacy of what God did in Jesus Christ.

The question is, does the repudiation of the sacramental character of baptism and the Lord's Supper in CD volume four also undercut all that Barth said previously about the sacramental or sign-bearing character of certain realities other than the humanity of Jesus? Barth does not answer this question directly. CD volume four does, of course, speak of Jesus' humanity as the "one" sacrament that works by its own power, *ex opere operato* (IV/4, 65, 82, 102ff., 129f., 172); but it is the one sacrament to which the signs of baptism and the Lord's Supper are "subordinate," to which they give "testimony," and to which they still "correspond" (IV/4, 102, 105).[35] Baptism and the Lord's Supper thus retain a functional connection to Jesus as the primary sacrament. The teaching of IV/4 is that baptism and the Lord's Supper do not "in themselves" constitute an "event," and thus they possess no real efficacy independent of the history of Jesus Christ. Apart from the history of Jesus—the "event" par excellence—these rites are merely abstract and not "concrete."

What should we make of this correspondence, subordination, and attestation between the humanity of Jesus and the various signs that bear witness to it? The best interpretation is that even though the "sacramental continuity" between them is set aside in CD IV/4, there still persists what we might call a "symbolic continuity" or a "continuity of attestation."[36] The denial of sacramental continuity does not entail the elimination of all continuity per se. The humanity of Jesus Christ "is the one *mysterium,* the one sacrament, and the one existential fact before and beside and after which there is no room for any other *of the same rank*" (IV/1, 296, emphasis added). Note the language "of the same rank." Whatever character we may attribute to these other signs bearing witness to Jesus Christ, they are not "of the same rank" as the humanity of Jesus itself.

Recall our earlier discussion that Barth in I/2 had already subordinated the sacramental function to the function of sign-giving (I/2, 228–32). There is no need to believe that Barth meant in IV/4 to eliminate this sign-giving function of attesting to the significance of the true humanity of Jesus Christ. Even if sacramental continuity has been eliminated, symbolic continuity persists. Baptism and the Lord's Supper still "belong to something that God has permitted and entrusted and commanded to Christians, namely the answering, attesting, and proclaiming of the one act of revelation of salvation that has taken place in the one Mediator between God and humanity (1 Tim. 2:5) who himself directly actualizes and presents and activates and declares himself in the power of the Holy Spirit."[37]

Barth's stark rejection of traditional sacramental teaching, a rejection that so many of his interpreters have simply dismissed as unintelligible, can only serve to buttress the line of interpretation I have been following throughout this study. Is it not strange that interpreters who otherwise agree with Barth's theology have almost universally declined to follow him in this repudiation of the traditional view of sacraments? Instead, they prefer to believe that Barth's theology somehow jumped the track on this issue and, inexplicably, in the waning days of his career, spun wildly out of control.

I want to argue, instead, that Barth's ethically-focused, non-sacramental view of baptism and the Lord's Supper is a consistent working out of his previous theological assumptions. It makes sense when seen as a bringing to completion of his basic nonfoundationalist theological intention. To put it bluntly, how else can we make sense of Barth's renunciation of the traditional claim that there is a "real presence" of God in these sacramental rites? Aside from the exegetical arguments, is he not bringing to bear on this issue of the sacraments the consequences of his more primary convictions about the unsublatable mystery of God? Barth's revision of traditional sacramental theology reflects his primary conviction that God is not simply "given" or "present" to human disposal, otherwise than in the hiddenness of the human life of Jesus Christ. If there is an incoherence in his later sacramental theology, it has less to do with the repudiation of "real presence" and more to do with the overly-individualistic implications of his disavowal of infant baptism. Aside from the exegetical arguments (which are debatable), there is no reason infant baptism need be rejected in principle. Although I do not intend to do so here, one could follow Barth's reasoning about "real presence" but still retain the practice of infant baptism by developing a more community-oriented understanding of these rites as ethical response.

To sum up, the life of Jesus Christ as imparted in the baptism of the Holy Spirit forms the "foundation" of Christian experience. It is a "foundation," however, that always remains God's possibility and not humanity's. The way God operates in the Christian life remains hidden. In order for it to become a concrete reality requires human beings to adopt God's purposes as their own when they perceive the divine "command" in given situations.

ETHICS AND DIVINE COMMAND

What does it mean to obey the command of God? One cannot specify an answer in the abstract, apart from a particular situation. For God's command "is always an individual command for the conduct of this human being, at this moment and in this situation" (III/4, 11). Yet the divine command is not simply episodic. "Each of our decisions and responsibilities as such is an anticipation in miniature of the total responsibility which, with our whole life, we fulfill before God" (II/2, 642). To follow God's command is to be led consistently along a particular "way," a road whose twists and turns mark the unique history of each of God's followers.[38] For example, the Christian who knows herself to be God's creature orients her life in accordance with the sabbath, with confession, and with prayer (III/4, §53). The same one who knows herself to be reconciled in Christ lives out the Christian virtues of faith, hope, and love, a point to which we shall return in the next chapter (IV/1, §63; IV/3, §73; IV/2, §68).

The "way" of Christian obedience unfolds with pretemporal, supratemporal, and posttemporal trinitarian significance. God precedes us, accompanies us, and follows after us upon this way. The command of God the Creator, the Reconciler, and the Redeemer is still one command, but a single command with multiple significance for diverse circumstances. This "way," to push further, must be fitting or suitable (*ist gemäss*) to the being of God itself (II/2, 559). The Christian life, in other words, should assume a particular shape that echoes the character of God. God's character as being "for" and "with" us in Christ must now be reflected "in" and "among" us in an ethical life shaped by the power of the Spirit. We too must be "for" and "with" others, although Barth is resigned that "no Christian has demonstrated and presented himself in a life that simply follows a consistent course from his election and vocation."[39] In the person of Jesus Christ this imperative of the "for" and the "with," has for once been successfully enacted—it is a reality. For once in human history, in the person and work of Jesus Christ, the will of God has been done "on earth as it is in heaven." That same reality of obedience now lies before us to be realized as the only true and proven possibility. That the divine command still lies before us means that it is still pressing into being, still awaiting our enactment. It is a "reality," that is to say, that retains a certain "ideality." The Christian life is always an unfolding story and never a fixed "state" of being (III/2, 157–64). It is a history moving toward a goal. Once again, "everything that is to be said about the human being who receives the Holy Spirit . . . is an eschatological statement" (I/1, 464).

In the previous chapter we saw that pursuing one's "vocation" (*Berufung*) as a reconciled human being means to be poised between promise and fulfillment, to be stretched out between creation and redemption. When we turn to the ethics of reconciliation we discover that, in keeping with this tensive conception of the Christian life, Barth selected "invocation" (*Anrufung*) as the concept best able to capture the ethical significance of reconciled existence.[40] After considering a number of other options (e.g., "decision," "freedom," "faith," "thanksgiving," "conversion," "faithfulness"), Barth concluded that the term "invocation" was sufficient to incorporate them all.[41] The one who is "called upon" by God to a particular vocation (*Berufung*) must also "call upon" God in invocation (*Anrufung*).

To "call upon" or "invoke" God is to invite all the theological reflections concerning who God is to form the basis of one's concrete action in the world. By itself, invoking God does not tell one what to do; nor does it imply that God has already determined the outcome. By posing this vocative to God, the point is to acknowledge the priority of God's purposes in all things while also undertaking a constructive response of one's own.[42] In the vocabulary of our earlier discussions, to "invoke" God is to entreat God as the "presupposition" for our every action.

"Invocation" is not merely aloof, disinterested, or neutral. In contrast to the dispassionate ethics of Kant, Barth connects "invocation" with an inescapable "passion." This is especially interesting, since Barth is so often accused of disavowing the role of experience or feeling. Invocation of God flows, in part, from a suffering or an unfulfilled longing which seeks satisfaction. Barth names this passion the "zeal for the honor of God."[43] Devoid of this passion, Barth declares, one would either be "not yet" or "no longer" a Christian. To have this passion, on the other hand, is to seek to give God, the Word of God, and the divine command a certain "precedence" in human life.[44]

Barth admits that speaking of the "precedence" of the Word of God may seem "a fairly restrained expression."[45] Although the Word of God constitutes a definite "factor" in the Christian's life, it forms only one factor competing among many others in the struggle for existence.[46] The Christian is not without God in the world; but neither is the Christian capable of perfect sainthood. "The Christian cannot be a saint, a person who, again in intention and result, can be determined only by his knowledge of God."[47] Barth has no doubt that the ambiguity this competition between various proximate values injects into human life will not soon be lifted. Therefore, one must be "determined," amid the always undiminished exigencies of life, to give priority to God.

As we noted in reference to the freedom of God in chapter three, to be "determined" is not quite the same thing as deliberating and making a "choice." From Barth's standpoint, having to deliberate is not a sign of freedom at all but of contradiction and bondage. We err in believing that freedom is equivalent to neutral choice. Does a parent deliberate whether to run into the road to save the endangered child? Should we deliberate whether to steal someone's wallet? To be free is to perceive what is right and good in a given situation and to do it. The freedom to be arbitrary or to opt out of responsibility is not true freedom at all. True freedom, whether divine or human, is always a freedom for obedience. Motivated by this passion or zeal for the honor of God, one invokes God not merely for one's own private needs and concerns; instead one longs for the manifestation of the Word of God. One awaits the embodiment of the purposes of God in a world of unrelieved ambiguity.[48]

Some may object that orienting one's ethics by the rubric "invocation" is overly passive. Are we to merely stand by and wait for God? Do we leave it up to God to do that which we ourselves should be doing but have failed to do? Such passivity is not what Barth is advocating. As Nigel Biggar observes, Barth's ethics calls for a "hastening that waits."[49] The Christian is not passive but active in her openness to what God is doing in the world. This openness is reflected in the way that theological ethics as a discipline is supposed to respond to the full range of human problems. So crucial is ethics to Barth's project that he can say it poses "*the* theological problem" (*KD*, I/2, 884, *CD*, 790). Ethics is not merely an afterthought, a minor component added on to all the others, but it represents the final expression of dogmatic content. His theology strives to be an ethical theology.[50]

What is this problem which ethics uncovers? It is the same problem that confronted Barth in so much of his theology, that of how to be truly human. Ethics is the pivotal issue in addressing this problem, because it forms the dimension in which the total "existential problem of humanity is revealed." Indeed, we must treat ethics as a "general human problem" and not merely a "church problem." To the extent that theology embraces the concerns of ethics, it shares with all human beings the far-ranging philosophical, political, and pedagogical question, What ought we to do? (II/2, 535, 645–61).

Consequently, Barth advises the theologian as ethicist to cast a wider net than was true of the theologian as dogmatician. The theologian as dogmatician takes her cue from scripture and tradition, even though, as we have seen in the preceding chapters, neither scripture nor tradition should function as a foundationalist "given." When the theologian turns her gaze toward the realm of action, however, she must look beyond the words of scripture and tradition to consider the way the human problem presents itself in all the diverse arenas of life. Theological inquiry that is also ethical must remain "absolutely open to all that it can learn from general human ethical inquiry and reply" (II/2, 524). Through this openness, ethical inquiry potentially serves to contextualize theology. It requires the theologian to take account of the full range of information that may bear upon any particular human problem. This accords with the theocentric belief that God is at work in all ages and in all places. As a corollary, Barth avows that the will of God is often better fulfilled outside church than within it (II/2, 569).

Furthermore, Barth specifically acknowledges a type of ethical inquiry that may be implicitly theological, and thus offer a true witness to the divine reality, even though it happens to lie outside the scope of theology per se. One may discover "traces," he says, of this "more or less inexplicit knowledge of the Word of God" reflected "indirectly" in certain nontheological sources. These traces may be found lurking, for example, in the thoughts of certain novelists, in the ideas of certain "philosophical moralists," and more generally "in certain old and new political and social conceptions" (II/2, 540–42). Unfortunately, Barth merely points to this intriguing possibility without developing it or showing what it would look like in a fully-developed theology. To put it another way, he fails to show us what it would look like to craft a theology that was not only "dogmatic" but "practical" as well. Although he invites theologians to explore the whole range of human knowledge as it pertains to ethics, he nevertheless remains strangely content to confine his own ethical reflections to the staid and sometimes stodgy analysis of Christian concepts. As with "secular parables of truth," so with nontheological ethics, he leaves it to others to incorporate these nonconfessional insights into theology.

Let it be noted and underscored, however, that such a wide-ranging type of exploration is held out as a legitimate option by Barth himself. It was an option, regrettably, he chose to neglect, preferring instead to concentrate on what must always remain for the theologian the most salient factor. He was determined not to avert his attention from the being and activity of God.

Barth's ethics, in short, requires an openness to all the enigmatic ambiguity of life. According to *Romans*, ethics confronts us as a great and disturbing problem. For in speaking of ethics, we speak of a subject matter (*Gegenstand*) possessing no objectivity (*Objektivität*) in human terms.[51] The goal of theological ethics, accordingly, cannot be to generate foolproof rationally-grounded answers to the questions of life but to ponder life's very questionability itself, and in the midst of that pondering, to render oneself receptive to the challenge of the divine command. According to the Barth of *Romans*, grace calls the Christian to obedience; yet it also dissolves (*aufhebt*) the parameters by which ethical decisions would ordinarily be made. To this extent, ethical inquiry must remain perpetually in motion, never resting upon foundations that are fixed in human experience. This is not to say Barth's ethics revels in being cryptic or that it glories in the irrational. For the goal is to be sensitive to the God who is the true foundation of all that is good and right.

But this, in turn, places ethical life within a pervasive tension. On the one hand, what matters in ethics is the pure act of God, apart from all the ambiguities and fragmentation that afflict human existence; on the other hand, openness to God's direction—the God who is "with" us—requires one to affirm and immerse oneself in those very same ambiguities. We too must be fundamentally "with" the other. Indeed, every human being, says Barth, is a "parable" of the oneness of humanity with God.[52] For "the existence of our fellow human beings presents us with the problem of the hidden God."[53]

Barth professes an ethics of radical and hopeful openness to the "other," both God and neighbor. "The discovery of the One in the other can occur only as each single individual is confronted by particular concrete others."[54] It is an openness to the "other" who, though never simply present to us, nevertheless, at the same time, claims our whole allegiance. Ethical action is "an unconditional, genuine preference" for the "other," an *election* of the other, if you will, that echoes God's own election of us. It is a determination for the "other" which in love and freedom "expects nothing in return."[55]

This unconditional—and, from a human point of view, impossible—quality to the ethical command helps explain why "invocation" became the operative center of ethics for Barth. Invocation is the recognition, which should accompany every action, that God is the one before whom all human action will be judged to be either good or bad. In placing the term "invocation" at the center of ethical activity, Barth underscored that the Christian life is never a possession but a hope. This virtue of hope, as we shall see in chapter 8, forms the core of the Christian's openness to what God is doing in the world.

8

EC-CENTRIC EXISTENCE
AND THE CENTRALITY OF HOPE

> Christ . . . does not exist merely for himself and to that extent Con-
> centrically, but . . . he also exists Ec-centrically, i.e. in and with the real-
> ization of the existence of these human beings. . . .
>
> CD, IV/3.2, 548 (rev.)

Each of the three sections of *CD* volume IV (IV/1, IV/2, IV/3) concludes with a treatment of one of the traditional theological virtues: faith, love, and hope. In each of these sections, Barth returns once again to his ever-present metaphor of the "center," this time to describe the mystery of transformation wrought in human experience by the Spirit of God.

Barth conceived the history of creation and redemption as a circle that departs from God and reverts to God, thus reiterating the ancient pattern of *exitus* and *reditus* found in Neo-Platonic philosophy, in Thomas Aquinas, and elsewhere throughout the Christian tradition. This same pattern con-figures the existence of individual Christians in history. Apart from the Spirit, declares Barth, human beings would live in their own "closed cir-cle"; whereas, when they abide in the Spirit, they are opened up to an "Ec-centric" (*Ekzentrisch*) existence.

The German word Barth selects to sum up the Spirit-led life, "*Ekzen-trisch*," means "from the center." The standard English edition of the *CD* translates it simply, "eccentric," which is misleading. Barth is not trying to say that the Christian life is idiosyncratic or bizarre, though in some in-stances it may be that. Rather, he is saying that true Christian existence is not self-centered but God-centered. Lest there be any mistake, the German word usually employed to translate the English adjective, "eccentric," would be "*Exzentrisch*." No doubt Barth's use of the term, *Ekzentrisch* is in-tended to allude to the other word, *Exzentrisch*—he is, after all, convinced of the "wholly alien character of Christianity in relation to the world around" (IV/2, 735). But he coins this word *Ekzentrisch* with the goal of de-liberately carving out a different (though perhaps related) meaning. The Christian life may seem "eccentric" by ordinary standards, but this is be-cause it takes an "Ec-centric" shape, living "from" the divine center that calls all other centers into question.

By the *Ekzentrisch,* or "Ec-centric," then, Barth is referring to an exis-tence in which Christians live "from" or "out of" the divine "center" and thus have a center "outside themselves" (*KD*, IV/1, 830, *CD*, 743; *KD*, IV/2, 893–94, *CD*, 788; *KD*, IV/3.2, 629–30, 631, *CD*, 548, 549).[1] Perhaps a closer English equivalent would be "ecstatic," although this word some-times has connotations of the nonrational that are far removed from what Barth wishes to convey.

Barth's use of this term has hardly been noticed by his English-speaking interpreters.[2] Given the reflections of the preceding chapters, we may expect that an "Ec-centric" mode of living will not be one of straightforward peace and repose. Christians live "outside themselves" because in the humanity of Jesus they have been elevated into fellowship with God, an elevation that is not merely a mystical knowing (*Wissen*) or contemplation (*Betrachtung*) but a recognition (*Erkenntnis*) of new identity, a recognition that must come to fruition in the self-denying ethical act (*Tat*).

As noted in chapter 4, Barth spoke of a similar mode of existence in his discussion of "real" humanity (III/2, 176–202). It is nothing less than a human being's own active participation (*aktive Beteiligung*) in the trinitarian movement of the divine self-identification which comes from God and returns to God (*an der von Gott herkommenden und zu Gott zurückkehrenden Erkenntnisbewegung*) (*KD*, III/2, 214, *CD*, 179). To become caught up in this divine and human history is to become "detached" from oneself. It is to live so as to "become to oneself as another" (III/2, 250–51).

Living the "Ec-centric" life is what it means to be in union with Christ. The belief that "Christ is in the Christian" signifies that Christ, as our forerunner, lives ec-centrically for the other. The belief that "the Christian is in Christ," similarly, means that the Christian no longer lives for himself but is awakened to a genuine humanity for the "other" (*KD*, IV/3.2, 629–30, *CD*, 547–48). Barth conceives this not as a theo- or christo- or pneumato-monism but as a relationship of free encounter in which the human being finally comes into its own as a free "subject."[3] Through this encounter the Christian recognizes the true identity of God and also of oneself in God (*KD* III/2, 214, *CD*, 180; *KD* IV/1, 837–46, *CD*, 749–57).

The virtues of faith, hope, and love set the pattern for this Ec-centric existence. These virtues, which come to be exhibited on the human side, correspond to the salvific work of justification (IV/1, §61), vocation (IV/3, §71), and sanctification (IV/2, §66) on the divine side. The virtues come to expression in the lives of Christian individuals; however, for Barth the witness of the faithful, hopeful, and loving individual is always subordinate to the primary witness of the justified, called, and sanctified community (IV/1, §§62, 63; IV/3, §§70, 71; IV/2, §§67, 68).

It was argued in preceding chapters that the material covered in *CD* IV/1 marks the logical beginning of Christian life and IV/2 the logical conclusion. The material in IV/3 forms the connecting link between the first two. In keeping with that argument, the virtue, hope, which brings *CD* IV/3.2 to a completion is the virtue that, so to speak, lies suspended between faith as source and love as goal (see figure 8.1).

As we saw in chapters five and six, more is at stake in this triadic interpretation than the trivialities of geometric design in the *CD*. Barth is saying something important here about the Christian life. Who is in a

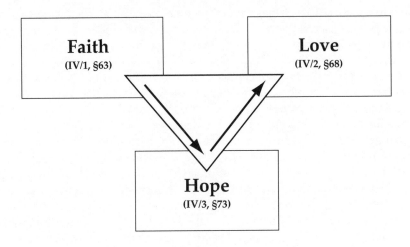

FIGURE 8.1

position to declare herself a Christian? Who can claim actually to have embodied the purposes of God? The Christian life, far from providing an unclouded fixed point or foundation for theology, instead remains thoroughly problematic. Who really lives the Christian life? Configured by the centrality of hope, the Christian life must be awaited and anticipated as a gift rather than presumed in advance as a given. Let us then conclude our reflections on Barth's ethics with a discussion of these three Christian virtues.

FAITH

The first virtue, faith, stands at the logical beginning of one's entry into the Christian life. Faith is the virtue, as set forth in *CD* IV/1, that corresponds to God's gracious act of justification on behalf of human beings (see chapter six). In a certain sense, then, faith lies behind us. This is a logical priority and not simply temporal, for faith determines our future as well as our past (IV/1, 744). We move from God's faithfulness (ἐκ πίστεως) into our own continual journey of faith (εἰς πίστιν) (Rom. 1:17).

Faith arises as a particular human response, nurtured in the gathered community of the church (IV/1, §62), to God's self-humbling and risk-taking deed to procure human beings' justification (IV/1, §61) in the humiliation of the "Lord" as "Servant" (IV/1, §59). So important is this response of faith, observes Barth, that many modern theologies have constructed a massive dogmatic structure upon the concept of faith as a foundation. This is the procedure followed by Schleiermacher and Troeltsch, the procedure known as *Glaubenslehre*.[4] In contrast to the method of *Glaubenslehre*, however, faith for Barth is not a foundation but a result. True faith can have no foundation or "object" in itself but must arise from the divine act of being baptized in the Holy Spirit. Faith's true object is Jesus Christ, to whom it is oriented, from whom it originates, and in whom it is constituted (IV/1, 740–57).

In the act of faith, a new human being emerges, the new human being made possible by justification (IV/4, §63.2). The drama of justification, Barth argues, cannot be conceived or experienced in some sort of static or extrinsic way but must be known in the living. On the one hand, it is the *archē* of the Christian life, having concrete consequences in human experience, striking a division between one's yesterday and one's tomorrow, and marking a transition in one's "real today." On the other hand, it is an *archē* that eludes being located in a straightforward fashion, as though one could say "Lo, here," or "Lo, there." "For although that removing and putting to death has come to me, it has not taken place in me" (IV/1, 771). Instead it lies as a presupposition behind us, and it is experienced only by perceiving that it occurred "for" us and is still operative in the ongoing history of Jesus Christ himself. In Jesus Christ the old human being is passing away and the new is coming.

Thus faith occurs dynamically *as* one actually believes. In correlation with the foregoing discussion of ethics, one becomes a Christian subject only "in act." To enact faith is, first, to acknowledge (*anerkennen*), second, to recognize (*erkennen*), and third, to confess (*bekennen*) the "Lord" who was humbled to become a servant. One acknowledges not a doctrine but Jesus Christ himself. One recognizes this Lord through the witness of scripture, which, by means of the diversity of its witnesses, leaves open many possibilities of seeing and understanding the significance of Jesus (IV/1, 757–99). In faith, through baptism, one confesses this Lord publicly before a world that does not comprehend, even though it too is included in the divine act to which baptism bears symbolic witness.

Since God is the ultimate reality around which human life is to be focused, Barth considers the absence of faith to count as an ontological impossibility. Faith is the only "real" or "actualized" possibility there is; it is what makes one a Christian (IV/1, 740ff.). Grounded in justification by grace, faith cannot be located in either the empirical or ideal aspects of the self but only in the active work of God who is the Lord of this contrast. The Christian belief in being dead and then alive, in being lost and then found, does not look to a datum or foundation within subjective experience; rather it finds its orientation in a work that is continually transforming experience.

In short, faith is an active and forward-looking receptivity, the logical beginning of the Christian life, which, as such, looks to a goal beyond and outside itself. That goal is embodied in the second theological virtue, which is love.

LOVE

Through the virtue of love, the "real" humanity discussed in chapter four is exhibited most luminously. I noted in that chapter that humanity lives in a present situation of "reciprocity" one to the other. On its own, however, humanity is not capable of genuine fellowship (*Gemeinschaft*). The "electing," "purifying" and "creative" love of the triune God (IV/2, 766–83) is "with" and "for" humanity; but human beings, while they are "with" one another, are thwarted by sin from being truly "for" one another. Yet this possibility of being genuinely "for" one another is opened up to humanity through the reconciling activity of God. Justification, or forgiveness, is not all that happens in reconciliation; it also includes the positive and forward-moving "direction" given in sanctification. This "direction" of the Holy Spirit is grounded in the elevation of humanity, an elevation accomplished in Jesus' exaltation as royal human being (IV/2, §66). Since Barth posits justification and sanctification as two sides of one and the same reality, faith is not faith if it does not spring to action in love. Love is the human self-giving, nurtured by the "upbuilding" of the Christian community (IV/2, §67), that God's own love poured out in Jesus Christ elicits.

The Christian life is conceived as a dynamic movement from faith as origin to love as fulfillment. Faith, at the climax of IV/1, is the Christian virtue that coincides with God's downward movement "for" and "with" us in the humiliation of the "Son" (IV/1, §59). Forming the climax of IV/2, on the other hand, love is the virtue that concurs in God's upward movement in elevating the "Servant" as "Lord" (IV/2, §64). Just as faith resonates with God's gracious act of justification, love is the experiential corollary of God's salvific work of sanctification (IV/2, §66).

True love is without contradiction. It is "a pure and total self-giving and surrender" corresponding to the free grace received through faith (IV/4, 730). On the triadic interpretation of reconciliation, love marks the climax or *telos* of the Christian life. Love must confirm what is received in faith, since the two are but distinguishable moments of the one vital history which is Christian existence. To put it succinctly, there is no other faith but that which works in love.

Love is the *telos*, but it is a *telos* that remains difficult to discuss. Alone among the virtues Barth speaks of love as a "problem" (IV/4, §68.1). Why is this? It is because love is the consummate virtue; it sets the definition of what humanity ought to be. It is humanity in Augustine's state of being unable to sin (*non posse peccare*). It poses a "problem," because God is the only one who loves in perfect freedom. God not only loves, but God *is* love. God is the only one for whom being and act are in concert (II/1, §28). Thus, to speak of human existence as love presents a problem. Love is the one virtue, much more so than faith or hope, that is eschatological in its connotations. It is the virtue toward which one is summoned in faith and hope.

The perfected quality of Christian love, for instance, is evident in Barth's distinction between *eros*, or possessive self-love, and *agape*, or gracious self-giving love. Barth conceives these two as totally opposed. *Agape* love is alien to the unredeemed love that inhabits the world as it is. *Agape* is a pure act that corresponds to the conviction that one's being comes from God and returns to God. *Eros*, by comparison, is the adulterated act in which one contradicts the true direction of one's being (*KD* IV/2, §68, 844, *CD*, 743). Neither *agape* nor *eros* is a part of humanity's "essence." This is clearer in the case of *eros*, for how can it be humanity's "essence" to deny God? But neither is *agape* part of humanity's "essence" either. *Agape* and *eros* are two different sorts of historical determination of that essence; each in a different way expresses it. Through *agape* human beings accept God as humanity's eternal counterpart and respect their fellow human beings in I-Thou encounter. Whereas the self-aggrandizement of *eros* is a denial of true co-humanity, *agape* is a correspondence of humanity's true nature in Jesus Christ.[5]

The "basis" of this love is the fact that one has been incorporated into the love of the triune God. Human love must correspond to that great movement of love in which God is dynamically engaged. Love's "basis" corresponds to faith's "object" (IV/2, §68.2). Barth rejects Luther's view that the Christian stands somehow between God and the neighbor as God's "instrument." This denies love as a free human action. So how can one talk about the "ground" of this free act, since it is not groundless? The answer: the Christian loves *as* and *because* God loves. The Christian's life subsists in a secondary analogy to the primary movement in which God is preeminently engaged. God's act is a dynamic summons to action from which human love arises as secondary initiative.

The Christian's act of love itself, then, is a genuine human response, a turning away from oneself in order to center on the other. We love, says the apostle John, because God first loved us. The person who has been claimed by God in the *exitus* of divine love turned towards humanity must return that love in the *reditus* that finds its completion in God.

The "act" of love itself embraces being both "for" God and "for" the neighbor (IV/2, §68.3). Such a love is oriented both to God and to the neighbor for their own sakes (IV/2, 784–85, 790, 793, 803–05). Love of God demands love for the neighbor, though Barth is dubious about claiming a

vague and abstract "love for all humanity." Love requires concrete proximity; and it is only in such proximity that love of neighbors and enemies
arises. The only real love is that which is directed concretely toward the
other.

Setting up a priority that is typical of his theology, Barth accents love
as a reality within the Christian community. One's first obligation is to the
neighbor near at hand, though there is also an obligation to the distant
neighbor (III/4, §54.3). Accordingly, one should remain constantly open
to the demands of love which confront one from beyond one's own ordinary community of relationships. It is only such an ever-widening embodiment of love which properly reflects the ever-widening circle of grace
which orbits the center of God's covenantal love for all humanity.

HOPE

This leads us to the virtue that crowns volume IV/3, the virtue of hope
(§73). According to the triadic interpretation, the virtue of hope is an in-
terim or in-between posture between the beginning of the Christian life in
faith and its consummation in love. As I have emphasized throughout this
study, Barth sees only one act, complete in itself, that includes faith, hope,
and love; but it is an act that is *still moving toward its fulfillment* (KD
IV/3.2, 1036; CD, 903) (emphasis Barth's). Even though Christian life is
positively determined (*bestimmt*) by that which Jesus Christ already is, the
Christian lives an enigmatic existence underneath the "not yet" of the here
and now, always faced with the "sinister possibility" that she or he might
become a liar against the truth.

Hope is necessary because this life is not yet what it shall be; it still
awaits eschatological fulfillment. One's faith and love are nourished in the
particularity of Jesus Christ, but what springs from this experience is hope.
This hope is not focused inward but outward: it is a hope that embraces all
people. Hope arises in the community that is "sent" by the Holy Spirit
(IV/3, §72). In hope, the Christian perceives that God has still to utter a last
Word, because God "has not yet spoken universally" (IV/3.2, 902).

Despite this hope for universality, Barth asserted that Western Christians
in an increasingly post-Christian age would see themselves as part of a dis-
appearing minority, a group living in self-contradiction, with the only certainty being their own hastening toward death (IV/3.1, 18–38). But this is
not the end of the story. The content of Christian hope removes the twilight
of ambivalence, replacing it with the light in which there is no shadow. Yet
this consummation has not yet taken place, and so Christian hope cannot be
anything other than hope, even as it is fortified by faith and presses towards
love. Whereas previous theologies of Christian hope often focused on indi-

vidual salvation, hope in Barth's mind is directed beyond the individual toward what God is bringing into being. If love is the goal of a certain manner of living flowing out of faith, then hope is faith directed toward its ultimate goal. Since hope centers on the universal God and God's reign, it is not merely individual and private but corporate and public.

Christian hope is clear and certain even as it is threatened. This is because the future it awaits is not obscure: it is the coming-again of Jesus Christ in consummate form. Yet this hope is not focused upon some pie in the sky denouement that eclipses one's interest in the here and now. Instead the situation should be like this: "expecting the ultimate each new day and in each new situation in which the day may set him, [the Christian] expects in each new day and every situation before him intimations of the ultimate . . . in . . . the penultimate." Because one places one's hopes in the great light, one is also permitted to hope, albeit with a provisional joy, in the promise held forth in the "little lights" (IV/3.2, 937–38).

This mention of the "little lights" at the end of IV/3.2 alludes to Barth's earlier discussion in IV/3.1 of secular parables of truth. As we noted in chapter two, Barth expects to see lights on the periphery of Christian meaning that are nonetheless authentic expressions of the Christian "center." This is altogether fitting for a theologian who understands salvation to be an as yet unfinished drama.

To sum up, it is through action that one comes to know God truly. Action is the nodal point of embracing and responding to who God is. Faith marks the origin of Christian action, love its goal, and hope its primary way of being. The priority given to action signals that no one yet exists in a "state" (*Zustand*) of already being a Christian but each one hopes in the dynamic "event" (*Ereignis*) of becoming Christian. To live with hope amidst the ambiguities of life is appropriate to a theology that does not believe the Christian life comes ready-made, a theology that understands reconciliation in Christ and salvation in the Spirit as still an unfinished drama.

The way in which Barth makes hope the centerpiece among the Christian virtues is congruent with his "foundationally nonfoundational" approach to Christian ethics. In making ethics the summit of theology, in insisting that one's being must always be validated in act, Barth invites every Christian to test his or her theology in the living. Only such an open-ended approach to theology and ethics is able to sustain faith, hope, and love in a postmodern age.

CONCLUSION

Karl Barth and the Postmodern
Foundations of Theology

The 'post-' indicates something like a conversion: a new direction
from the previous one.

Jean François Lyotard[1]

The theology of Karl Barth with its emphasis on God as ultimate mystery raises in a provocative way the question of the postmodern foundations of theology. No doubt the term "postmodern" is coined in such a vague and imprecise fashion today and applied in so many diverse and even conflicting contexts that it is at profound risk of becoming merely an ideological slogan. Still, this term is fast becoming a place holder for the many new ways of approaching intellectual work in our time, and it is coming to be used by a growing number who perceive in Barth the harbinger of a new postmodern theological possibility.[2] With increasing frequency, one hears the suggestion that Karl Barth was the first "postmodern" or "postliberal" theologian. I have taken the risk, then, of applying the term "postmodern" to Barth out of the dual conviction that theology in a postmodern age is worth doing and that the theology of Karl Barth has much to contribute to that venture.

A major feature of postmodern theology is its nonfoundationalism. A truly nonfoundational approach will seek to abandon all appeals to presumed self-evident, non-inferential, or incorrigible grounds for its intellectual claims. This does not mean that one must simply give up on questions of truth and rationality, nor that one must put aside all one's Christian presuppositions. But it does mean that presuppositions are just that: they are starting points that must remain subject to ongoing criticism and revision.

In thinking through this task of criticism and revision, many philosophers and theologians have become fond of describing postmodern nonfoundationalism using the metaphor of a leaky boat in constant need of repair. In the dire situation of postmodernity, the emergency repairs to this hapless vessel must all be made while the craft is still at sea with no chance to take it in to harbor.[3] The situation must be salvaged with no dry dock for a "foundation" and nothing but the raging sea beneath one's feet.

The nonfoundationalism of a theologian such as Barth, however, is rather different than this metaphor of the leaky boat would suggest. For Barth theology need not—indeed cannot—abandon its ancient moorings altogether. Christian theology does have a "center" or "foundation" it wishes to know and to proclaim, for it believes in the living God. Nevertheless, this God cannot be reduced to a foundation located in human experience or tradition or anywhere else. In one sense God alone is the foundation of theology; but God is never reducible to a simple "given" or "presence." Rather than proclaiming the absence of a "center," therefore, Barthian theology insists that it is the divine center *itself* that infuses the postmodern intellectual task with all its instability and risk.

Perhaps a better nautical metaphor to describe the theologian's dilemma is that of an offshore oil rig.[4] Massive drilling rigs must drill for oil in deep water often under extreme conditions. In order to drill in such conditions it is critical for the rig to stay directly over its "center," the well head on the bottom of the ocean floor. Yet keeping the rig stable against the force of a turbulent sea is an inherently impossible task. No anchor is sufficient to accomplish this feat, for wind and wave keep the equipment constantly off balance. To meet the challenge of keeping the rig solidly focused requires a technology called "dynamic positioning." Mounted on the hull of modern drilling rigs are an array of powerful thrusters that work continually to reposition the equipment over the ever-elusive target. Able to swivel, if need be, a full 360 degrees, these thrusters are there to respond, should currents change or winds shift, to meet the changing conditions of an untamed sea.

To be true to its task, theology today must meet the novel conditions of a changing sea. As Barth says, theology must be willing to begin again perennially at the beginning. Theologians are indeed to "center" on the reality of God, but knowing all the while that this divine reality remains forever beyond possessing and beyond fathoming. The "center" of theology is not the Christian cultural-linguistic system itself, as it is for Troeltschian as well as for many contemporary postliberal theologies. Rather, the "center" of theology for Barth is God in dynamic relationship to humanity through Jesus Christ by the power of the Spirit. Like the open hole at the core of a forever rotating wagon wheel, Barth reflected, this is a "center" that "decenters" all the theologian's efforts to contain it.

It decenters scripture, for scripture is not identical with the "Word of God" but is a "sign" that seeks to bear witness to who God is. It decenters the human self, for our "real" humanity, made visible in Jesus Christ, exists out in front of us as a task still waiting to be performed. And yes, it decenters our reflections about Jesus Christ too. On the one hand, it will not do to think about God apart from Jesus Christ. The humanity of Jesus Christ is the sacrament of the living God. *God is as Jesus Christ is; God does as Jesus Christ does.* This affirmation represents Barth's celebrated "christocentrism." Yet on the other hand, neither will it do to think about God as though God's reality were exhausted in what happened in Jesus Christ. The humanity of Jesus Christ points beyond itself to God and to God's continual activity in the world. Because Jesus Christ is the mystery of *God*, inevitably there are manifold ways of speaking of how Jesus Christ embodies that mystery. There are myriad ways of understanding who

Jesus Christ is as the image and Word of God, no one of which can exhaust the wonder of who God is in Jesus Christ. There must always remain an openness at the "center" of the wheel.

The openness of this "center" is captured in the dynamic way Barth constructs his theology of creation, reconciliation, and redemption. On the one hand, this scheme presents a comprehensive vision of promise and fulfillment. God's gracious action in being "for" and "with" human beings in Jesus Christ is also being brought to fruition "in" and "among" human beings by the power of the Holy Spirit. In reaffirming this ancient meta-narrative, Barth's theology deviates decisively from those streams of post-modernity that drift in directions that are skeptical or merely apathetic. On the other hand, Barth consistently deferred any final attainment of this theological vision from the standpoint of human rationality. For one thing, "redemption" lies on an eschatological horizon. Redemption is the "not yet" that emerges from the "no longer" of creation. Between these two horizons—the protological and the eschatological—reconciliation is working itself out as an ongoing reality, a work that is stretched out between an *archē* that is beyond proving and an outlying *telos* that is knowable only in the prism of continual and obedient action.

To posit a complete apprehension of God's will and purpose would contradict Barth's fundamental tenet that the accomplishment of God's purposes depends on God's own ongoing activity. The *being* of God is not known "in itself" but only in the outworking of God's *act*. God is made known in what God achieves in the midst of human beings. So then, there is more to God than what one can learn through "freeze-framing" the action of this ongoing redemptive drama. There is always much more about God that still remains to be said.

Both what has been said and what remains to be said are brought into focus for Barth through an interaction between the "center" and the "periphery." To know God as ultimate mystery is something that cannot be achieved at the "center" but only from the "periphery" of the peculiar "wheel" that is theology. For the theologian who would be Christian, the "periphery" must begin with the historic confession of the church's creed. The theologian starts here, reclaiming the themes and concepts of Christian doctrine, and does so not to repristinate an ancient dogma but because, pragmatically speaking, one can only begin with the language and concepts of one's own community. Still, there is also the need to plumb "how far" and "to what extent" these ancient formulations are true. God's mystery and our human fallibility are such that "we do not know what we are saying" when we recite these tenets from our creedal past. Our faith must seek understanding, and this can occur only by means of ongoing theological construction.

In considering this ongoing constructive work, we uncovered texts from Barth that—in contrast to the old stereotypes—opened the door to non-Christian and even nonreligious voices. Barth expects to encounter "secular parables" that speak persuasively of the truth of God. He recognizes, moreover, that a whole array of non-Christian sources is able to speak persuasively about the "phenomena" of the human, even though "real" humanity remains forever focused in Jesus Christ. More broadly still, Barth envisions a range of information derived from all the disciplines of human life being taken up and sifted every time we engage in ethical action. All these sources from the periphery—that is, from the open-ended penumbra of the wagon wheel's "rim"—have the potential to add new perspective to the mystery of the "center."

In relationship to this "center" Barth believes we are always either "not yet" or "no longer" where we need to be. Our every "now" disappears into the "no longer" of prior revelatory moments even as that same "now" awaits the "not yet" of anticipated future meaning and insight. Only the Word of God itself is beyond this dialectic of the "not yet" and the "no longer" (I/2, 52). Yet this side of redemption, the Word of God is never simply a "presence" in the Derridean sense. Instead we know the Word of God, if at all, only in the modes of "anticipation" or "recollection" (I/1, §§7.1; I/2, 14). Or as noted in the previous chapter, the Christian life, which begins in faith and aims toward love, is always configured in the open-ended mode of hope.

Barth's focus upon hope as the pivotal theological virtue offers a promising suggestion about how to reconfigure theology in the postmodern age. As Paul Ricoeur has put it, theology or philosophy conducted in the mode of hope resists finality. It "breaks the closure of the system; it is a way of reopening what was unduly closed."[5] Before the unfolding mystery of God, construed in the mode of hope, there can be no point of premature closure. Construed in the light of mystery, theology is a thoroughly fallible enterprise, a ceaseless activity with neither resting place nor any fixed point of unerring certainty. Most fascinating and most holy, the mystery of God presents an enigma ever exceeding the theologian's grasp. Divine mystery calls into question all our preconceived foundations.

Some may counter that theology ought to set about the task of shoring up the foundations of tradition rather than calling them into question. Should not religion, after all, speak a word of clarity within a world of fragility, brokenness, and unrelieved ambiguity? There is a measure of truth in this objection, for religion should be more than the baptism of the world as it is. But then, this is precisely Barth's point. What Barth's theology calls us to is not to accept the world as it is but to embrace the world as it ought to be. If we are to embrace this world, however, we must enter into its fragility and brokenness. That is the good news of the God who is "for" us and "with" us in Jesus Christ, the very God who embraces our condition of fragmentation and despair. In the face of radical evil, the only God who can inspire our worship is one whose *action* is also an incarnate *passion*. As observed in chapter

4, the menacing persistence of evil poses a considerable challenge to theology. To those who suffer under the absurdities of this world's cruelty, for those whose very humanity stands under threat, what Barth calls "the Nihil," or "Nothingness," is not nothing. It is that to which God says "no" and to which we too must say "no." It calls us not simply to be in some vague way "for" the other but to be concretely "with" the other who suffers and to be engaged "among" the others gathering and building up a community of faith, hope, and love. How theology negotiates the shaking of the foundations precipitated by the massive evils of our time will in significant measure determine its prospects of speaking an intelligible word in a postmodern world.

While this does not mean that one should simply jettison the prima facie pertinence of traditional Christian beliefs, it does mean that traditional claims must be subjected to continual sifting and faithful reconstruction. How far can this sifting legitimately be pursued? Throughout this study I have presented Barth's theology, in both its methodological commitments and its substantive proposals, as an effort *not* to settle either upon a straightforward realism or a completely open and arbitrary constructivism, nor to devise a synthetic hybrid between them, but to keep the demands of realism and constructivism in ceaseless interplay. Barth reaffirmed divine reality: God is the Creator, Reconciler, Redeemer. Yet in professing this ancient story anew he also problematized it, reconstructed it, and opened it up to continual new meaning.

Perhaps it is this interplay between the real and the problematic, between the call for confession and the need for ongoing construction, that has caused some interpreters to see a permanent instability in Barth's theology. According to Hans Frei, for example, the excessive emphasis on divine hiddenness and human fallibility in Barth's early writings—including not only the Romans commentary but also the early volumes of the CD itself—drove a wedge between the givenness of God's revelation and the problematic features of human language. Frei saw a way out of this instability, however, augured in the CD's later part-volumes on reconciliation. In these later volumes Frei believed he discerned a heightened emphasis on the biblical narrative and a new approach to theology as an exercise in "conceptual redescription." The mature Barth sought to depict the conceptual world of the Bible as a thoroughly realistic narrative that "means what it says."[6] According to this reading, the literary "what" of Christianity takes a priority over the experiential "how."[7] Theology becomes a self-descriptive rendering of the biblical story designed to lead modern readers back into a world long forgotten.

It is true that Barth sought to reclaim the biblical story; but it is not true that the biblical story forms a theological resting place or "given." If there is an "instability" in Barth's theology, it is there for a reason. "The truth," Barth said, "demands complete openness. From the standpoint of the truth itself, thoroughgoing conservatives are as useless as thoroughgoing modernists" (II/2, 648). To focus one-sidedly on the "narrative" or the "rules" camouflages the inexorable problem of divine mystery, and it eclipses the way Barth set about to reconstruct the "rules" and to restate the "narrative" according to the exigencies of his own situation.

Neither is it true that Barth minimized the "how" questions in theology. Although the priority of divine mystery would not permit him to turn God into a "given," Barth's focus on true humanity would not allow him to give up on the question of the "how." Instead, as we have seen, both the emphasis on mystery and the question of the "how" persist even into the final pages of the *Church Dogmatics.*

The apparent instability that Barth maintains between realism and constructivism, ironically, is actually meant to provide a stability of a certain sort. The interplay between the real and the problematic, which is ceaseless, assures that we will neither deny the mystery of God nor presume to reduce that mystery to our own fallible constructions. In the first place, the category of "mystery" is not an abstraction void of content, as though mystery signaled a blank ignorance of God, but it represents a concrete Christian conviction. Against the sort of untethered constructivism that would dissever the task of theology from its nexus in Christian meaning, the mystery is that God is "for" us and "with" us in Jesus Christ, and the grace of God is mediated "in" and "among" us by the power of the Spirit. This divine reality, and Barth's hopeful conviction about that reality, guide all his theological construction and represent the crux of what he believed a Christian needs to say about God. The "entirety" of who God is may be summarized in this "for" and this "with."

In the second place, there always remains more about God that needs to be said. The grace of God is "for" us; but there is always more to learn about the depths of that claim. The grace of God is "with" us; but *how* does this grace become a reality "in" and "among" us? No human construal of these questions is ever adequate to the mystery of who God is. Rather, every statement about God must be left open-ended and subject to ongoing inquiry and construction. Theology, on Barth's view, is not so much a way of "corresponding" to reality but a set of presuppositions by which we live.

I have presented Barth's theology as a complex project that reaches its summit in praxis. The God of decentering mystery (Part 1), who is "for" us, "with" us, and at work "in" and "among" us (Part 2), calls us to the act of faithful, hopeful, and loving obedience (Part 3). If theology is to be based on Christian "presuppositions," these convictions must reach their "consequence" in action. Just as God's being is in act, so it is in act that we both know God truly and become what God has truly meant for us to be. For this reason, an ethics of otherness serves as the validation of Barth's theology. This does not mean that the mystery of God is reduced to human action; but it does mean that human action is the arena in which God's identity is being made known. "We can and must *act* as those who know. But we must not claim to *be* those who know." For "those who really know will always find and confess that they do not know" (IV/2, 124–25, emphasis supplied).

In short, the voluminous pages of conceptual analysis that make up the *Church Dogmatics* are not intended as an end in themselves. Instead they attempt to state a set of presuppositions to action. In light of the "new thing" God is forever doing, Barth's decentering theology remains an "in-between activity." It is an inquiry (*Forschung*), a reflection (*Nachdenken*), or a meditation (*meditatio*), that stands poised between the explication of sources from the past and the practical engagement with the demands of the present. It situates itself between the explication (*explicatio*) and application (*applicatio*) of the Word (I/2, §22). That is to say, it plumbs the claims of traditional Christian witness in order to ask what "new thing" God may be doing in our midst today. It "does not ask what the apostles and prophets said but what we must say on the basis of the apostles and prophets" (I/1, 16).

Barth's highly conceptual mode of theology, to put it another way, can be pushed in the opposite direction from a repristinating traditionalism. One should read it more like a constitution than a statute. Like a constitution, Barth's theology of God, the Creator, Reconciler, Redeemer, creates a framework for further interpretation. Rather than setting narrow limits on the type of discourse to be permitted, it opens up possibilities for an expansion of discourse. To treat the words he wrote as though they were frozen in time and to refrain from exploring the constructive implications of his message reminds one of the reactionary strict constructionists in constitutional jurisprudence. They wish to construe the American constitution as though it were a statute or code book rather than as a living document. As a living framework, theology is suggestive, provocative, and capable of producing new meaning.

Barth himself knew that interpretation is a delicate art. So in the preface to the third edition of his Romans commentary, he advocated "loyalty" as one of the best preconditions for correct interpretation. Barth stood with loyalty before the text of the apostle Paul, straining to peer over Paul's shoulder and catch a glimpse of what Paul saw. In listening to Paul, he was mindful that no human word, not even the words of Paul, can convey absolute truth. Every text is riddled with ambiguities, and these ambiguities themselves are productive and make possible an enlargement of meaning. Proper interpretation, said Barth, will try to disclose these ambiguities, and in so doing, learn to "see beyond Paul."

In the same way, I have labored in these pages to be loyal to Barth by attempting to see what Barth saw, and in that way to "see beyond Barth." What I have tried to present in this study is a "useable" Barth, a more "open-ended" Barth who may still speak with power to a postmodern age.

Whether his theology can still speak in this way depends on the "consequences" its principal "presuppositions" continue to open up. It remains to be seen whether the presuppositions of Barth's theology will still continue to carry freight in the postmodern age. One can think of theological approaches today that are much more radical than Barth's, theologies that consider the ethical demands of the present situation to call for a much more fundamental rethinking of traditional theological claims. It would be a mistake, however, for these new approaches to turn a deaf ear to Barth. What if, for instance, one were to read the argument of the present study in the opposite direction? What if one were to begin with Barth's claims about ethics (Part 3) in order to rethink the question of divine identity (Part 2) with the goal of further rethinking the traditional claims of Christian conviction (Part 1)? What might be learned from such an experiment? Only time will tell. One thing is for sure from the standpoint of Barth. All theological proposals, whether old or new, with whatever light they may shed on the human predicament, must draw their inspiration from the "great light" that has dawned in Jesus Christ. Faithfulness to what God is doing in Jesus Christ is measured not by adherence to dogmatic formulae, but it tests itself in the living. Obedient human action, the place where meanings that are otherwise invisible and beyond proving finally come into focus, is where the aesthetic and highly formal nature of a theology such as Barth's ceases to be a "mere" aesthetic and transforms itself into testimony as faith, hope, and love. The test comes not in establishing assured foundations but in the invitation to "come and see" (cf. John 1:39, 46).

NOTES

INTRODUCTION

1. Karl Barth, *Die Kirchliche Dogmatik,* I/1–IV/4 (Zurich: TVZ, 1932–1970) (hereafter abbreviated *"KD"*); ET: *Church Dogmatics,* ed. G. W. Bromiley and T. F. Torrance (Edinburgh: T. & T. Clark, 1936–77) (hereafter abbreviated *"CD"*). Citations within the body of the text are made to the English edition unless otherwise indicated. Where the English translation has been revised, this is indicated by the abbreviation "rev."

2. A "theocentric" theology seeks to uphold the priority of God in all things. Christocentric theology, in turn, seeks to understand God in light of God's revelation in Jesus Christ. In Christian, trinitarian perspective, the terms theocentric and christocentric need not be seen as opposites. See William Stacy Johnson, "God the Center of Theology: A Reinterpretation of Karl Barth" (Ph.D. dissertation, Harvard University, 1992). The terms "christocentric" and "theocentric" have been used rather loosely in modern theology. See Jean Milet, *God or Christ? The Excesses of Christocentricity* (New York: Crossroad, 1981). One of the earliest usages of the term "theocentric" (*theocentrisk*) of which I am aware occurs in Kierkegaard. Søren Kierkegaard, *Concluding Unscientific Postscript,* trans. David F. Swenson and Walter F. Lowrie (Princeton: Princeton University Press, 1941), 19. Later the term was often applied to the theology of John Calvin and his heirs, among whom, of course, would be numbered Karl Barth. Emile Doumergue, *La pensée religieuse de Calvin,* vol. 4 of *Jean Calvin: Les hommes et les choses de son temps* (Lausanne: Georges Bridel, 1910), 37, 428–30. But Barth usually avoided the term "theocentric," because it had been coopted by a contemporary, Erich Schaeder, whom Barth interpreted as too much influenced by Schleiermacher, despite Schaeder's criticisms of Schleiermacher. See Erich Schaeder, *Theozentrische Theologie: Eine Untersuchung zur dogmatischen Prinzipienlehre,* 2 vols. (Leipzig: Scholl, 1909, 1914). In his later years, Barth seemed to prefer the term "theanthropocentric" (e.g., *CD,* III/2, 13).

3. Karl Barth, *Das Wort Gottes und die Theologie,* Gesammelte Vorträge, Band 1 (Munich: Chr. Kaiser Verlag, 1925), 158; cf. *The Word of God and the Word of Man,* trans. Douglas Horton (Grand Rapids, 1935), 186.

4. Karl Barth, *Wolfgang Amadeus Mozart,* trans. Clarence K. Pott, foreword by John Updike (Grand Rapids: Wm. B. Eerdmans Publishing Co., 1986), 55.

5. "Neo-orthodoxy," when used pejoratively, usually connotes a theology that resorts to the dogmatic reassertion of biblical revelation with little regard for cultural context. As a twentieth-century theological movement, it was marked by a

radical rethinking of the heritage of nineteenth-century liberalism. Representative figures, united more by a sharing of overlapping themes than by real consensus, included such diverse theologians as Karl Barth, Eduard Thurneysen, Friedrich Gogarten, Rudolf Bultmann, Emil Brunner, Paul Tillich, Reinhold Niebuhr, and H. Richard Niebuhr. See Alasdair I. C. Heron, *A Century of Protestant Theology* (Philadelphia: Westminster Press, 1980); James C. Livingston, *Modern Christian Thought: From the Enlightenment to Vatican II* (New York: Macmillan Publishing Co., 1971), ch. 11.

6. For a survey of the relevant issues, see John E. Thiel, *Nonfoundationalism*, Guides to Theological Inquiry (Minneapolis: Fortress Press, 1994).

7. Francis Schüssler Fiorenza, *Foundational Theology: Jesus and the Church* (New York: Crossroad, 1986), 287.

8. Karl Barth, *Der Römerbrief*, Zweite Fassung, 1922 (Zurich: TVZ, 1989), 11; *The Epistle to the Romans*, trans. Edwyn C. Hoskyns (Oxford, 1935), 35.

9. See Gordon D. Kaufman, *In Face of Mystery: A Constructive Theology* (Cambridge: Harvard University Press, 1993), ch. 2.

10. Cf. George A. Lindbeck, *The Nature of Doctrine: Religion and Theology in a Postliberal Age* (Philadelphia: Westminster Press, 1984).

11. See Karl Rahner, *Foundations of Christian Faith*, trans. William V. Dych (New York: Crossroad, 1978); Paul Tillich, *Systematic Theology*, 3 vols. (Chicago: University of Chicago Press, 1951–1963); David Tracy, *Blessed Rage for Order: The New Pluralism in Theology* (Minneapolis: Seabury Press, 1975); idem, *The Analogical Imagination: Christian Theology and the New Culture of Pluralism* (New York: Crossroad, 1981). For a critique of correlational theology as inappropriately "foundationalist," see Francis Schüssler Fiorenza, *Foundational Theology: Jesus and the Church* (New York: Crossroad, 1986), 276–84.

12. An example of the type of postmodern theology that we should not follow is the brilliant but unacceptable proposal of Mark C. Taylor, *Erring: A Postmodern A/theology* (Chicago: University of Chicago Press, 1984).

13. Jean-François Lyotard, *The Postmodern Condition: A Report on Knowledge*, trans. Geoff Bennington and Brian Massumi (Minneapolis: University of Minnesota Press, 1984), xxiv.

14. Karl Barth, "Der Christ in der Gesellschaft," in idem, *Das Wort Gottes und die Theologie*, 33–69, 40; ET: "The Christian in Society," in *Word of God and Word of Man*, 272–327, 282; idem, *The Epistle to the Romans*, 184; idem, *Evangelical Theology: An Introduction*, trans. Grover Foley (Grand Rapids: Wm. B. Eerdmans Publishing Co., 1963, 1979), 10. Cf. Barth's objection to Hans Urs von Balthasar that one cannot reduce his method to a guiding "thought form" (*Denkform*), but rather his method employs a dynamic "movement of thought" (*Denkbewegung*). Karl Barth, *Fides Quaerens Intellectum: Anselms Beweis der Existenz Gottes im Zusammenhang seines theologischen Programms* (1931), ed. Eberhard Jüngel and Ingolf U. Dalferth, Gesamtausgabe II. Akademische Werke, 1931 (Zurich: TVZ, 1981), 6 (ET: *Anselm: Fides Quaerens Intellectum*, trans. Ian W. Robertson [Cleveland and New York: World Publishing Co., Meridian Books, 1960], 11).

15. The present study differs considerably from the essay by S. W. Sykes, "Barth on the Centre of Theology," in *Karl Barth: Studies of His Theological Method*, ed. S. W. Sykes (Oxford: Clarendon Press, 1979), 17–54. Sykes unjustly accuses Barth of being a conservative who simultaneously reduces the "center" to a christological core and effectuates an apotheosis of the so-called "inwardness" tradition for which the

essence of Christianity is achieved at a "critical distance from the tradition in all its external forms." See idem, *The Identity of Christianity: Theologians and the Essence of Christianity from Schleiermacher to Barth* (Philadelphia: Fortress Press, 1984), 200.

16. The distinction between the "early" Barth and the "mature" Barth does not signal any intention on my part to provide a genetic account of the origins or development of Barth's thought, nor does it imply any sharp distinction between the basic theological position represented in Barth's early and later work. As to Barth's development and the overriding continuity of his theological vision, the perspective of this study presupposes the groundbreaking historical work of Bruce L. McCormack, *Karl Barth's Critically Realistic Dialectical Theology: Its Genesis and Development 1909–1936* (Oxford: Clarendon Press, 1995).

17. Something similar is suggested by Gotthard Oblau, *Gottzeit und Menschenzeit: Eschatologie in der Kirchlichen Dogmatik von Karl Barth* (Neukirchen: Neukirchener Verlag, 1988). According to Oblau, the Christian hope for redemption is effectuated in one event realized in Jesus Christ. For Oblau it is the resurrection which in Barth forms the pivotal moment that looks backward to the cross of reconciliation and forward to the eschatological future of redemption. In chapter 5, I shall argue that it is Pentecost that forms this pivotal moment in that it looks backward to the resurrection and forward to the "Second Coming."

18. Charles Sanders Peirce, "How to Make Our Ideas Clear," in *Collected Papers of Charles Sanders Peirce*, ed. C. Hartshorne, P. Weiss, and A. Burks, 6 vols. (Cambridge: Harvard University Press, 1935–1958) 5:388–410.

CHAPTER 1:
IN QUEST OF THE GOD OF THEOLOGY

1. Karl Barth, *Vorträge und kleinere Arbeiten, 1922–1925*, ed. Holger Finze, Gesamtausgabe III (Zurich: TVZ, 1990), 167; *Das Wort Gottes und die Theologie*, Gesammelte Vorträge, Band 1 (Munich: Chr. Kaiser Verlag, 1925), 171–73; cf. *The Word of God and the Word of Man*, trans. Douglas Horton (Grand Rapids: Wm. B. Eerdmans Publishing Co., 1935), 206–7.

2. *"Unterricht in der christlichen Religion," Erster Band, Die Lehre von Gott/Die Lehre vom Menschen*, ed. Hinrich Stoevesandt, Gesamtausgabe II, Akademische Werke, 1924/1925 (Zurich: TVZ, 1990), 1:147; ET: *The Göttingen Dogmatics: Instruction in the Christian Religion*, trans. Geoffrey W. Bromiley (Grand Rapids: Wm. B. Eerdmans Publishing Co., 1991), 1:120.

3. Friedrich Schleiermacher, *Der christliche Glaube nach den Grundsätzen der evangelischen Kirche im Zusammenhange dargestellt*, 7th ed., based on the 2d ed. of 1830–31, ed. Martin Redeker, 2 vols. (Berlin: de Gruyter, 1960), §§3–5, esp. pp. 28, 30. The German ed. is hereafter cited as *Glaubenslehre*. Reference is also made to the English translation of the 3d ed.: *The Christian Faith*, trans. H. R. Mackintosh and J. S. Stewart (Edinburgh: T. & T. Clark, 1928). Regarding divine givenness, Schleiermacher was resolute in denying that God is ever "given" to "sensible self-consciousness" through the objects of the mundane world. "Sensible self-consciousness" is the determination of consciousness in relation to the world of nature. Divinity cannot be reduced to the givenness of one of the mundane objects of the natural world (*gegebenden Gegenstandes*), for then God would be subject to human manipulation and counterinflu-

ence. Still, even though there can be no "fusion" (*Verschmelzen*) between the "feeling of absolute dependence" and the "sensible self-consciousness," there is nonetheless a "coexistence" (*Zugleichsein*) between them. Ibid., 35, ET, 21. To this extent, God *does* constitute a "presence" in human experience. Indeed, for Schleiermacher "God is given to us in feeling in an original way" (ibid., 30; ET, 17).

4. Karl Barth, *Der Römerbrief* (zweite Fassung) 1922, foreword by Hinrich Stoevesandt (Zurich: Theologischer Verlag, 1989), 257 (original 1922 ed., 236); *The Epistle to the Romans*, trans. Edwyn C. Hoskyns (London: Oxford University Press, 1933), 254 (Barth's emphasis). Hereafter triple citations are given to the recent Stoevesandt edition, to the 1922 original, and to the standard English version of the Romans commentary.

5. On Barth's background as a Herrmannian liberal, see Bruce McCormack, *Karl Barth's Critically Realistic Dialectical Theology*, 31–77; and see generally, Simon Fischer, *Revelatory Positivism? Barth's Earliest Theology and the Marburg School* (Oxford: Oxford University Press, 1988).

6. On the relation between Barth and Troeltsch, see Wilfried Groll, *Ernst Troeltsch und Karl Barth—Kontinuität im Widerspruch*, Beiträge zur evangelischen Theologie, Band 72 (Munich: Chr. Kaiser Verlag, 1976); and Thomas W. Ogletree, *Christian Faith and History: A Critical Comparison of Ernst Troeltsch and Karl Barth* (New York and Nashville: Abingdon Press, 1965).

7. Brian Gerrish, *Continuing the Reformation: Essays on Modern Religious Thought* (Chicago: University of Chicago Press, 1993), 153.

8. Friedrich Schleiermacher, *Kurze Darstellung des theologischen Studiums*, ed. Heinrich Scholz (Leipzig, 1910), ET: *Brief Outline of the Study of Theology*, trans. Terrence N. Tice (Richmond: John Knox Press, 1966).

9. Schleiermacher, *Glaubenslehre*, §10, 71–72; ET, 50.

10. See Ernst Troeltsch, *Die Bedeutung des Protestantismus für die Entstehung der Modernen Welt* (Berlin: 1911) (ET: *Protestantism and Progress: The Significance of Protestantism for the Rise of the Modern World*, trans. W. Montgomery [1912; Philadelphia: Fortress Press, 1986]), esp. ch. 1. On Christianity's genesis in history, cf. "[Christianity] . . . is not an event arising fortuitously in our culture, but the ripened fruit of all past developments of the Mediterranean peoples . . . the ideology which is bound inseparably with the whole ongoing life and work of our culture." "Logos und Mythos in Theologie und Religionsphilosophie," in *GS*, 2:814 (ET, "Logos and Mythos in the Philosophy of Religion," in *Religion and History*, trans. James Luther Adams and Walter F. Bense, Fortress Texts in Modern Theology [Minneapolis: Fortress, 1991], 53).

11. On the importance of "*Weltanschauung*," see "Moderne Geschichtsphilosophie" (1904), in *GS*, 2:673–728 (ET: "Modern Philosophy of History," in *Religion in History*, 272–320).

12. See K. A. Apfelbacher, *Frömmigkeit und Wissenschaft: Ernst Troeltsch und sein theologisches Programm* (Munich: Paderborn, 1978); John P. Clayton, *Ernst Troeltsch and the Future of Theology* (Cambridge: Cambridge University Press, 1976); Sarah Coakley, *Christ without Absolutes: A Study of the Christology of Ernst Troeltsch* (Oxford: Oxford University Press, 1988); Wendell S. Dietrich, *Cohen and Troeltsch: Ethical Monotheistic Religion and Theory of Culture*, Brown Judaic Studies, no. 120 (Atlanta: Scholars Press, 1986); Peter C. Hodgson, *God in History: Shape of Freedom* (Nashville: Abingdon Press, 1989); Robert Morgan, "Introduction: Ernst Troeltsch on Theology and Religion," "Troeltsch and Christian Theology," and Michael Pye, "Troeltsch and the Science of Religion," in Morgan and Pye, eds., *Ernst Troeltsch: Writings on Theology and Religion*

(Atlanta: John Knox Press, 1977); Trutz Rendtorff and Friedrich Wilhelm Graf, "Ernst Troeltsch," in Ninian Smart et al., eds., *Nineteenth-Century Religious Thought in the West* (Cambridge: Cambridge University Press, 1985); Walter E. Wyman, Jr., *The Concept of Glaubenslehre: Ernst Troeltsch and the Theological Heritage of Schleiermacher*, AAR Academy Series 44 (Chico, Calif.: Scholars Press, 1983); Toshimasa Yasukata, *Ernst Troeltsch: Systematic Theologian of Radical Historicality* (Decatur, Ga.: Scholars Press, 1987).

13. This is seen most clearly in "Das Wesen der Religion und der Religionsgeschichte" (1906), in *GS*, 2:452–99 (ET: "Religion and the Science of Religion," in Morgan and Pye, *Ernst Troeltsch: Writings*, 82–123). Troeltsch's comparison of his own understanding to that of Hegel is instructive. Troeltsch interpreted Hegel's system as a deductive metaphysics of the Absolute, whereby philosophy tracks the career of the Absolute Spirit through the various "determinate" religions of the world in which the implicit union between the infinite and the finite is becoming manifest. Ultimately it has become manifest in Christianity as the "absolute" religion. (See G.W.F. Hegel, *Lectures on the Philosophy of Religion*, ed. Peter C. Hodgson, 3 vols. [Berkeley and Los Angeles: University of California Press, 1985].) Troeltsch, by contrast, understood universal history as a metaphysics of a posteriori conclusions in which the answers flow out of the facts themselves and thus cannot be known in advance.

14. Troeltsch speaks of "forging a new synthesis of the gains of the past and the living present" through value construction arising out of historical analysis. "Moderne Geschichtsphilosophie" (1904), in *GS*, 4:166–91 (ET: "Modern Philosophy of History," in *Religion and History*, 303).

15. The following is informed by "Über historische und dogmatische Methode in der Theologie" (1898), in *GS*, 2:29–53 (ET: "Historical and Dogmatic Method in Theology," in *Religion in History*, 11–32).

16. William James, *The Varieties of Religious Experience* (Cambridge, Mass.: Harvard University Press, 1985).

17. For a constructive proposal that takes seriously the issue of historicism, see Richard R. Niebuhr, *Resurrection and Historical Reason: A Study of Theological Method* (New York: Charles Scribner's Sons, 1957).

18. Whether Troeltsch was consistent in applying his early insights is debatable. See the account of Troeltsch's development in Sarah Coakley, *Christ without Absolutes: A Study of the Christology of Ernst Troeltsch* (Oxford: Oxford University Press, 1988).

19. "Was heisst 'Wesen des Christentums'?" (1903, 1913), in *GS*, 2:386–451 (ET: "What Does 'Essence of Christianity' Mean?" in Morgan and Pye, *Ernst Troeltsch: Writings*, 124–79). For an analysis of this issue in modern theology, see Stephen Sykes, *The Identity of Christianity: Theologians and the Essence of Christianity from Schleiermacher to Barth* (ch. 7 covers Troeltsch).

20. See Peter C. Hodgson, *God in History: Shapes of Freedom* (Nashville: Abingdon Press, 1989), ch. 3; William Dean, *History Making History: The New Historicism in American Religious Thought* (Albany, N.Y.: State University of New York Press, 1988).

21. See E. Troeltsch, "Rückblick auf ein halbes Jahrhundert der theologischen Wissenschaft," in *GS*, 2:193–226 (ET: "Half a Century of Theology: A Review," in *Theology and Religion*, ed. Morgan and Pye, 53–81).

22. See especially E. Troeltsch, "Zur Frage des religiösen Apriori" (1909), and "*Logos* und *Mythos* in Theologie und Religionsphilosophie" (1913), in *GS*, 2:754–68, 805–36; and *Die Absolutheit des Christentums und die Religionsgeschichte* (Tübingen, 1902; 2d ed., 1912) (ET: *The Absoluteness of Christianity and the History of Religions*, trans. David Reid [Richmond: John Knox Press, 1971]).

23. This is most clearly evidenced in Ernst Troeltsch, "Empiricism and Platonism in the Philosophy of Religion: To the Memory of William James," in *Harvard Theological Review* 5 (1912): 401–22.

24. "[E]ach moment has at the same time an immediate, individual significance of its own, a direct relationship to God which belongs only to it." "*Logos* und *Mythos,*" 831; ET, 67.

25. Ernst Troeltsch, *Glaubenslehre,* Nach Heidelberger Vorlesungen aus den Jahren 1911 und 1912, ed. Gertrud von Le Fort (Berlin: Scientia Verlag Aalen, 1981), §11, 129 (emphasis added).

26. Barth, *Die Protestantische Theologie im 19. Jahrhundert: Ihre Vorgeschichte und ihre Geschichte,* zweite verbesserte Auflage (Zurich: EVZ, 1952), 384. I cite to the German edition throughout. Cf. ET: *Protestant Theology in the Nineteenth Century: Its Background and History,* trans. Brian Cozens, John W. Bowden, et al. (London: SCM Press, 1976).

27. On Barth and socialism, see Friedrich-Wilhelm Marquardt, *Theologie und Sozialismus: Das Beispiel Karl Barths* (Munich: Chr. Kaiser Verlag, 1972); Helmut Gollwitzer, *Reich Gottes und Sozialismus bei Karl Barth* (Munich: Chr. Kaiser Verlag, 1972); George Hunsinger, ed., *Karl Barth and Radical Politics,* (Philadelphia: Westminster Press, 1976); Ingrid Jacobsen, ed., *War Barth Sozialist? Ein Streitgespräch um Theologie und Sozialismus bei Karl Barth,* Radikal Mitte, Band 13, Schriftenfolge für christliche Erziehung und Kultur (Berlin and Schleswig-Holstein: Verlag Die Spur, 1975).

28. E.g., "Der Christ in der Gesellschaft" (delivered in Tambach, September 25, 1919), in *Das Wort Gottes und die Theologie,* 33–69.

29. Karl Barth, "Die dogmatische Prinzipienlehre bei Wilhelm Herrmann," in *Vorträge und kleinere Arbeiten, 1922–1925,* ed. Holger Finze, Gesamtausgabe, III (Zurich: TVZ, 1990), 597–98; *Die Theologie und die Kirche,* Gesammelte Vorträge, Band 2 (Munich: Chr. Kaiser Verlag, 1928), 279 (cf. ET: *Theology and Church: Shorter Writings 1920–1928,* trans. Louise Pettibone Smith [London: SCM Press, 1962], 267).

30. *Vorträge und Kleinere Arbeiten,* 587; *Die Theologie und die Kirche,* 268; cf. *Theology and Church,* 259.

31. On this point, see Bruce McCormack, *Karl Barth's Critically Realistic Dialectical Theology,* ch. 6.

32. For a groundbreaking inquiry into the origins and development of Barth's early thought, see Bruce L. McCormack, *Karl Barth's Critically Realistic Dialectical Theology: Its Genesis and Development 1909–1936* (Oxford: Clarendon Press, 1995).

33. *Der Römerbrief,* 16 [15], cf. ET, 39–40. See McCormack, *Karl Barth's Critically Realistic Dialectical Theology,* ch. 6, 241–290.

34. *Vorträge und Kleinere Arbeiten,* 588; *Die Theologie und die Kirche,* 269; cf. *Theology and Church,* 260.

35. *Der Römerbrief,* 35 [32], ET, 57. Elsewhere Barth elaborates: "Nothing human remains which desires to be anything more than an empty space (*Hohlraum*), a privation, a possibility, a sign-post (*Hinweis*), anything more than the most imperceptible thing (*unscheinbarste*) among the phenomena (*Erscheinungen*) of the world . . . " (ibid., 92 [84]; ET, 110).

36. Ronald F. Thiemann, *Revelation and Theology,* 42–43.

37. *The Oxford English Dictionary,* 2d ed., ed. J. A. Simpson, 20 vols. (Oxford: Clarendon Press, 1989), 4:613.

38. On this point see Garrett Green, *Imagining God: Theology and the Religious Imagination,* chs. 2 and 3.

39. Karl Barth, "Nein! Anwort an Emil Brunner," in *Theologische Existenz heute,*

Heft 14 (Munich: Chr. Kaiser Verlag, 1934); ET: "No! Answer to Emil Brunner," in *Natural Theology: Comprising "Nature and Grace" by Professor Dr. Emil Brunner and the reply "No!" by Dr. Karl Barth,* trans. Peter Fraenkel (London: Geoffrey Bles, 1946), 65–128.

40. Barth, *Unterricht in der christlichen Religion,* 1:110–12; ET, 91–92.

41. Cf. Jean-Luc Marion, *God without Being: Hors Texte,* trans. Thomas A. Carlson, foreword by David Tracy (Chicago and London: University of Chicago Press, 1991).

42. Eberhard Jüngel, *God as the Mystery of the World: On the Foundation of the Theology of the Crucified One in the Dispute between Theism and Atheism,* trans. Darrell L. Guder (Grand Rapids: Wm. B. Eerdmans Publishing Co., 1983), 182.

43. For a treatment of Jüngel's handling of this issue, see J. B. Webster, *Eberhard Jüngel: An Introduction to His Theology* (Cambridge: Cambridge University Press, 1986), ch. 6.

44. Walter Lowe, *Theology and Difference: The Wound of Reason* (Bloomington and Indianapolis, Ind.: Indiana University Press, 1993). Barth is treated in chapters 2 and 6. Chapter 2 first appeared as "Barth as Critic of Dualism: Re-reading the *Römerbrief,*" in *Scottish Journal of Theology* 41 (1988): 377–95.

45. For example, Graham Ward goes too far in claiming that Barth somehow anticipates Derrida in valorizing the absence of God. Graham Ward, *Barth, Derrida and the Language of Theology* (Cambridge: Cambridge University Press, 1995), chs. 1, 11.

46. "Translator's Introduction," in Jacques Derrida, *Writing and Difference,* trans. Alan Bass (Chicago: University of Chicago Press, 1978), xviii.

47. See Terence Hawkes, *Structuralism and Semiotics* (Berkeley and Los Angeles: University of California Press, 1977).

48. Jacques Derrida, *Of Grammatology,* trans. Gayatri Chakravorty Spivak (Baltimore and London: Johns Hopkins University Press, 1976).

49. Lowe, *Theology and Difference,* 13–16.

50. Lowe, *Theology and Difference,* 13.

51. John Ellis, *Against Deconstruction* (Princeton: Princeton University Press, 1989), 41.

52. Jacques Derrida, "Structure, Sign, and Play in the Discourse of the Human Sciences" (1966), in Jacques Derrida, *Writing and Difference,* trans. Alan Bass (Chicago: University of Chicago Press, 1978), 293.

53. Jacques Derrida, "Ellipsis" (1967), in *Writing and Difference,* 297.

54. For further reflections on this, see Jacques Derrida, *The Gift of Death,* trans. David Wills (Chicago and London: University of Chicago Press, 1995).

55. *Theology and Difference,* 41, citing Karl Barth, *The Epistle to the Romans,* 29–31.

56. *Theology and Difference,* 41, citing Karl Barth, *The Epistle to the Romans,* 29.

57. *Der Römerbrief,* 22–23 [21]; ET, 45–46.

58. Karl Barth, *Unterricht in der christlichen Religion,* 1:164; ET, 1:134.

59. *Der Römerbrief,* 11–12 [11], cf. ET, 35.

60. *Der Römerbrief,* 55 [50].

61. I believe this judgment is in accord with the thesis of Bruce McCormack's exhaustive study into the development of the early Barth. See McCormack, *Karl Barth's Critically Realistic Dialectical Theology.*

62. "Schicksal und Idee in Theologie," in *Zwischen den Zeiten* 7 (1920): 309–48; reprinted in Karl Barth, *Theologische Fragen und Antworten,* Gesammelte Vorträge, Band 3 (Zurich, EVZ, 1957), 54–92; (ET: "Fate and Idea in Theology," in *The Way of*

Theology in Karl Barth, ed. Martin Rumscheidt, 25–62 [hereafter "Fate and Idea"]). The one commentator who appreciated the significance of "Fate and Idea" years ago is T. F. Torrance. He interprets the essay incorrectly, however, as tipping the balance between realism and idealism in favor of an objectifying realism. Thomas F. Torrance, *Karl Barth: An Introduction to His Early Theology, 1910–1931,* (London: SCM Press, 1962), 149–80. Says Torrance, "The dialectic between realism and idealism has undoubtedly helped [Barth] to grasp more profoundly the objectivity of the Word, and contributed to his movement into *a fundamentally realist theology,* but it has also shown him that, unless a realist theology has a real dash of idealism, its professed realism may only be the obverse of a fatal idealism." Ibid., 171. For a similar criticism of Torrance's overly objectivist reading of Barth, see George Hunsinger, *How to Read Karl Barth: The Shape of His Theology* (New York and Oxford: Oxford University Press, 1991), 7–9. Barth's own point, in contrast, is that the interplay between realism and idealism is relentless and unresolvable. To consider the one leads to a fresh consideration of the other, and one is incapable of resolving the tension in favor of a higher synthesis.

63. Barth has in mind the version of *analogia entis* advanced by his Roman Catholic friend, Erich Przywara. See McCormack, *Karl Barth's Critically Realistic Dialectical Theology,* 384–91.

64. "Fate and Idea," *Theologische Frage und Antworten,* 52; ET, 25.

65. The pertinent phrase reads: "dass Gott aus dem Gegebenen (nicht anderswoher und aus dem Gegebenen notwendig!)." *Theologische Frage und Antworten,* 62.

66. Ibid., 64–65; ET, 35.

67. Ibid., 68; ET, 38.

68. Ibid., 72–73; ET, 42–43.

69. Ibid., 70; ET, 40.

70. Ibid., 70; ET, 40, rev.

71. Ibid., 77; ET, 47.

72. Ibid.

73. Ibid., 77; ET, 47.

74. Ibid., 83; ET, 52.

75. Said Barth, Hegel had interpreted the idealism-realism split as one "between the eternal truths of reason and the accidental truths of history, *between fate and idea.* . . . " Barth, *Die Protestantische Theologie,* 350–51 (emphasis added).

CHAPTER 2:
IN QUEST OF A THEOLOGY OF GOD

1. Karl Barth, *Die Protestantische Theologie im 19. Jahrhundert,* 411–12.

2. Hans Frei, *Types of Christian Theology,* ed. George Hunsinger and William C. Placher (New Haven and London: Yale University Press, 1992), 19–27, 38–46, 147–63.

3. Karl Barth, *Fides Quaerens Intellectum,* 43 n.8, (ET, 43 n.3).

4. Ibid., 42; ET, 42–43.

5. McCormack, *Karl Barth's Critically Realistic Dialectical Theology,* 431–33.

6. *Fides Quaerens Intellectum,* 70; ET, 70.

7. Cf. *CD*, I/2, 838. The term *"Repristination"* occurs in the German.

8. Karl Barth, "Philosophie und Theologie," in *Philosophie und christliche Existenz: Festschrift für Heinrich Barth*, ed. Gerhard Huber (Basel: Verlag Helbing und Lichtenhahn, 1960), 93 (ET: "Philosophy and Theology," in H. M. Rumscheidt, ed., *The Way of Theology in Karl Barth*, 79).

9. *The Epistle to the Romans*, 321 (rev., emphasis supplied).

10. Karl Barth, *Evangelical Theology: An Introduction*, trans. Grover Foley (Grand Rapids: Wm. B. Eerdmans Publishing Co., 1963, 1977), 37.

11. Barth, *Die Protestantische Theologie*, 3.

12. Ibid., 5–6.

13. Ibid., 60.

14. *Die Protestantische Theologie*, 3, 5–6, 15, 60, passim.

15. See G.W.F. Hegel, *Vorlesung über die Philosophie der Religion*, ed. Walter Jaeschke, 3 vols. (Hamburg: Felix Meiner Verlag, 1984); (ET: *Lectures on the Philosophy of Religion*, ed. Peter C. Hodgson, 3 vols. [Berkeley and Los Angeles: University of California Press, 1985]).

16. For a recent exposition of this section see George Hunsinger, *How to Read Karl Barth*, 234–80.

17. Cf. James M. Gustafson, *Ethics from a Theocentric Perspective*, 2 vols. (Chicago: University of Chicago Press, 1981, 1984).

18. Robert P. Scharlemann, *The Reason of Following: Christology and the Ecstatic I* (Chicago and London: University of Chicago Press, 1991), 203.

19. Karl Barth, "Unerledigte Anfragen an die heutige Theologie," in idem, *Theologie und Kirche*, (Munich: Chr. Kaiser Verlag, 1928), 1–25; ET: "Unsettled Questions for Theology Today," in *Theology and Church*, trans. Louise Pettibone Smith (London: SCM Press, 1962).

20. See George Lindbeck, *The Nature of Doctrine: Religion and Theology in a Postliberal Age*, ch. 6.

CHAPTER 3:
THE MYSTERY OF THE TRIUNE GOD

1. Karl Rahner, *The Trinity* (New York: Herder & Herder, 1970), 21.

2. For the definitive exposition of this concept in Barth's theology, see Eberhard Jüngel, *Gottes Sein ist im Werden: Verantwortliche Rede vom Sein Gottes bei Karl Barth; Eine Paraphrase* (Tübingen: J.C.B. Mohr [Paul Siebeck], 1964); ET: *The Doctrine of the Trinity: God's Being Is in Becoming* (Edinburgh: Scottish Academic Press, 1976).

3. This is a peculiar version of what Immanuel Kant called a "transcendental" argument (Immanuel Kant, *Critique of Pure Reason*, trans. Norman Kemp Smith [New York: St. Martin's Press, 1965], 59, passim). Transcendental arguments provide "conditions of possibility." They state those transcendental conditions that we cannot prove to be true but that *must* be true in order to render possible that which we already know to be true in the first place. If we take it as gospel, in other words, that God is really personified in Jesus Christ, then God *must* be a God capable of just this sort of dynamic activity.

4. This is made clear in the chapter, "Jesus Christ," in Karl Barth, *Dogmatics in Outline*, trans. G. T. Thompson (New York: Harper & Brothers, 1959), ch. 10.

5. Barth, *Unterricht in der christlichen Religion*, 1:11; ET: *The Göttingen Dogmatics: Instruction in the Christian Religion*, 1:9.

6. Eberhard Jüngel, *Gottes Sein ist im Werden: Verantwortliche Rede vom Sein Gottes bei Karl Barth; Eine Paraphrase* (Tübingen: J.C.B. Mohr, 1964; 2d ed., 1966) (ET: *The Doctrine of the Trinity: God's Being Is in Becoming* [Edinburgh: Scottish Academic Press, 1976]).

7. Jean-François Lyotard, *The Postmodern Condition: A Report on Knowledge*, xxiv.

8. See Ronald F. Thiemann, *Revelation and Theology: The Gospel as Narrated Promise* (Notre Dame, Ind.: University of Notre Dame Press, 1985); Hans Frei, *The Identity of Jesus Christ: The Hermeneutical Basis of Dogmatic Theology* (Philadelphia: Fortress Press, 1975).

9. See Robert W. Jenson, *The Triune Identity: God according to the Gospel* (Philadelphia: Fortress Press, 1982).

10. John Calvin, *Institutes of the Christian Religion*, trans. Ford Lewis Battles, ed. John T. McNeill, Library of Christian Classics (Philadelphia: Westminster Press, 1960), book I, ch. 2; book III, ch. 2.

11. Thus it is a mistake to follow Ronald Thiemann in construing theology as if it were merely a matter of "description." See Ronald F. Thiemann, *Revelation and Theology*.

12. The *locus classicus* of Western trinitarian thought is Augustine, *De trinitate* (ET: *The Trinity*, in *Augustine: Later Works*, ed. John Burnaby, Library of Christian Classics [Philadelphia: Westminster Press, 1955]). For a recent critique of Western trinitarianism, see Catharine Mowry LaCugna, *God For Us: The Trinity and Christian Life* (San Francisco: HarperCollins, 1991).

13. See Gregory of Nyssa, *To Ablabius: On "Not Three Gods,"* in W. G. Rusch, *The Trinitarian Controversy* (Philadelphia: Fortress Press, 1980). John of Damascus, *Exposition of the Orthodox Faith*, book I, chs. 5–8 in *Nicene and Post-Nicene Fathers*, 2d series, ed. Philip Schaff (Grand Rapids: Wm. B. Eerdmans Publishing Co., 1983), vol. 9.

14. Jürgen Moltmann, *The Trinity and the Kingdom: The Doctrine of God*, trans. Margaret Kohl (New York: Harper & Row, 1964).

15. Robert W. Jenson, *The Triune Identity: God according to the Gospel* (Philadelphia: Fortress Press, 1982).

16. E.g., Jürgen Moltmann, *The Trinity and the Kingdom: The Doctrine of God*, trans. Margaret Kohl (London: SCM Press, 1981), 139–44.

17. For an able defense of social trinitarianism that, nonetheless, fails to take adequate account of this problem of reification, see Cornelius Plantinga, Jr., "Social Trinity and Tritheism," in *Trinity, Incarnation, and Atonement: Philosophical and Theological Essays*, ed. Ronald J. Feenstra and Cornelius Plantinga, Jr. (Notre Dame, Ind.: Notre Dame University Press, 1989), 21–47.

18. Cf. John E. Smith, *Experience and God* (New York: Oxford University Press, 1968), 52.

19. See Karl Barth, "Extra nos—pro nobis—in nobis," in *Hören und Handeln: Festschrift für Ernst Wolf zum 60. Geburtstag*, ed. Helmut Gollwitzer and Hellmut Traub (Munich: Chr. Kaiser Verlag, 1962).

20. This is sometimes phrased in terms of analysis and synthesis. See Ted Peters, *God as Trinity: Relationality and Temporality in the Divine Life* (Louisville, Ky.: Westminster/John Knox Press, 1993). The distinction between analytical and

synthetic judgments comes from Immanuel Kant. Analytical judgments are based on a formal "analysis" of the meaning of concepts, as, for example, the concept of God. Synthetic judgments are either built up from knowledge derived from experience or they are based on conditions that are necessary before experience can even come into being (Immanuel Kant, "Introduction" to *Critique of Pure Reason,* 41–62).

21. See Karl Barth, *The Humanity of God,* trans. John Newton Thomas and Thomas Weiser (Richmond: John Knox Press, 1960).

22. See Thies Gundlach, *Selbstbegrenzung Gottes und die Autonomie des Menschen: Karl Barths Kirchliche Dogmatik als Modernisierungsschrift evangelischer Theologie* (Frankfurt am Main: Peter Lang, 1992).

23. See Burghard Krause, *Leiden Gottes—Leiden des Menschen: Eine Untersuchung zur Kirchlichen Dogmatik Karl Barths* (Stuttgart: Calwer Verlag, 1980).

CHAPTER 4:
GOD "FOR" US

1. Karl Barth, *Dogmatik im Grundriss* (Zollikon-Zurich: Evangelischer Verlag, 1947), 92; ET: *Dogmatics in Outline,* trans. G. T. Thomson (New York: Harper & Row, 1959), 71.

2. *Die Protestantische Theologie,* 247; ET, 161.

3. Barth, *Dogmatics in Outline,* 70.

4. Lowe, *Theology and Difference,* ch. 1.

5. Lowe, *Theology and Difference,* ch. 6.

6. Schleiermacher, *Glaubenslehre,* §§46–49. See also Langdon Gilkey, *Reaping the Whirlwind: A Christian Interpretation of History* (New York: Seabury Press, 1976), Part III, esp. ch. 9.

7. Barth, *Dogmatics in Outline,* 60.

8. The literature on this subject is voluminous. For one of the groundbreaking studies, see Thomas S. Kuhn, *The Structure of Scientific Revolutions,* 2d ed., enlarged (Chicago: University of Chicago Press, 1962, 1970). For an introduction to the current discussion, see Richard J. Bernstein, *Beyond Objectivism and Relativism: Science, Hermeneutics, and Praxis* (Philadelphia: University of Pennsylvania Press, 1988).

9. Karl Barth, *Dogmatics in Outline,* 59–61.

10. See Hans Frei, "Ad Hoc Correlation," in *Types of Christian Theology,* ch. 6.

11. This possibility has been pursued within Barth's overall framework by T. F. Torrance. See Torrance, *Transformation & Convergence in the Frame of Knowledge: Explorations in the Interrelations of Scientific and Theological Enterprise* (Grand Rapids: Wm. B. Eerdmans Publishing Co., 1984); idem, *Reality and Evangelical Theology* (Philadelphia: Westminster Press, 1982); idem, *God and Rationality* (New York: Oxford University Press, 1971); idem, *Theological Science* (New York: Oxford University Press, 1969).

12. See, e.g., Jürgen Moltmann, *The Trinity and the Kingdom;* Eberhard Jüngel, *God as the Mystery of the World;* Wolfhart Pannenberg, *Systematic Theology,* 3 vols. (Grand Rapids: Wm. B. Eerdmans Publishing Co., 1991–), vol. 1.

13. William James, "The Moral Philosopher and the Moral Life," and "On Some Hegelisms," in *The Will to Believe, and Other Essays* (New York: Longmans, Green & Co., 1907), 184–214, 263–98. James believed in a history that presented an

uncertain future; a history that pushed back when pushed against; a history with "real" winners and "real" losers in which evil is not rationalized away but in which one attends with utmost seriousness to "the cries of the wounded." James, "The Moral Philosopher and the Moral Life," ibid., 210.

14. See Ted Peters, *God as Trinity: Relationality and Temporality in Divine Life* (Louisville, Ky.: Westminster/John Knox Press, 1993), 34–37.

15. Martin Luther, *Werke* (Weimar Edition), vol. 7, 337; *Works of Martin Luther*, vol. 3, 31.

16. Immanuel Kant, *Critique of Pure Reason*, B157.

17. E.g., Herbert Hartwell, *The Theology of Karl Barth*, 130–31. This misinterpretation has been spread principally through Emil Brunner's allegation that Barth in *CD*, vol. III had finally come around to Brunner's own position. See Emil Brunner, "Der neue Barth: Bemerkungen zu Karl Barths Lehre von Menschen," *Zeitschrift für Theologie und Kirche* 48 (1951): 89–100; idem, *The Christian Doctrine of Creation and Redemption*, trans. Olive Wyon, *Dogmatics*, vol. 2 (London: Lutterworth Press, 1952), 42–45.

18. The best example is Barth's reference to Brunner and the Reformation tradition in *KD*, I/1, 251–53, *CD*, 238–40. There Barth rejected, as he always did, the image understood as a "capacity" or as a "possibility which is proper to humanity *qua* creature" or as a supposed moral uprightness (*rectitudio*). Nevertheless, the image does remain objectively for Barth as humanity's *recta natura*, or proper nature (*KD*, 251, *CD* 238). There had even been some vague adumbration of this in *Romans*, where Barth stated that "also within the perverted relationship to God there is still a remnant of 'clear vision,' a last warning presentiment of the secret of God which withstands the arrogance of religion" (*Der Römerbrief*, 30 [28], ET, 53).

19. *Unterricht in der christlichen Religion*, 2:367.

20. *Unterricht in der christlichen Religion*, 2:373. Now that we have the posthumously published Göttingen lectures on theology (1924–25) we can see that what many have interpreted as innovations in Barth's teaching on the image in *KD*, vol. III were already being taught by Barth in 1924. See *Unterricht in der christlichen Religion*, §23. At Göttingen Barth characteristically rejected all notions of the image as a "faculty," "capacity," or "neutral condition."

21. Augustine, *A Treatise on the Spirit and the Letter*, Nicene and Post-Nicene Fathers, ed. Philip Schaff, vol. V, Saint Augustin: Anti-Pelagian Writings, trans. Benjamin B. Warfield (Grand Rapids: Wm. B. Eerdmans Publishing Co., 1971), 80–114.

22. Jürgen Moltmann, *God in Creation: A New Theology of Creation and the Spirit of God*, trans. Margaret Kohl (London: SCM Press, 1985).

23. See Heinzpeter Hempelmann, *Unaufhebbare Subjektivität Gottes? Probleme einer Lehre vom concursus divinus dargestellt an Hand von Karl Barths Kirchlicher Dogmatik* (Zurich: R. Brockhaus Verlag, 1992); Michael Plathow, *Das Problem des concursus divinus: Das Zusammenwirken von göttlichen Schöpferwirken und geschöpflichen Eigenwirken in K. Barths "Kirchlicher Dogmatik"* (Göttingen: Vandenhoeck & Ruprecht, 1976).

24. Numerous examples could be given; one of the most prominent is: François Turretin, *Institutio theologiae elencticae*, Locus 6, questions 5–7 (Geneva, 1688).

25. For a criticism of Barth from this perspective, see John Hick, *Evil and the God of Love* (San Francisco: Harper & Row, 1966, rev. ed, 1977), 126–44. This still remains the best introductory discussion of the theodicy problem.

26. Note that the nuances concerning *"Nichtigkeit"* are absent from the ET.

CHAPTER 5:
GOD "WITH" US

1. See Karl Barth, "Extra nos—pro nobis—in nobis," in *Hören und Handeln: Festschrift für Ernst Wolf zum 60. Geburtstag* (Munich: Chr. Kaiser Verlag, 1962).

2. "Christomonism" is the position that makes Jesus Christ the sole subject of salvation and human appropriation of salvation a mere appendage to Christ's primary work. "Anthropomonism" makes the equal and opposite mistake, turning the work of Christ into a mere cipher of something that emanates primarily from humanity. Christomonism eliminates the work of a liberated humanity, while anthropomonism eliminates the work of the liberating God; the one is a subjectivism from above, the other a subjectivism from below. A prominent critic of Barth as overly christomonistic is G. C. Berkouwer, *The Triumph of Grace in the Theology of Karl Barth,* trans. Harry R. Boer (Grand Rapids: Wm. B. Eerdmans Publishing Co., 1956), which was written before *KD,* IV/2 and beyond. For Barth's response see *KD,* IV/3.1, 198–206, *CD,* 173–80.

3. Barth employed several technical distinctions from Protestant orthodoxy in order to make explicit the non-givenness of deity in Jesus Christ. First, Barth embraced the so-called "extra" dimension of Calvinist christology. Widespread in pre-sixteenth-century Catholicism, the position was labelled the *"extra calvinisticum"* by Lutherans in the 1620s (E. David Willis, *Calvin's Catholic Christology: The Function of the So-Called Extra Calvinisticum in Calvin's Theology* [Leiden: E. J. Brill, 1966]; Heiko A. Oberman, "The 'Extra' Dimension in the Theology of Calvin," *Journal of Ecclesiastical History* 21 [1970]: 43–64). According to the Calvinist "extra," God the "Son," as the second mode of being the triune God, continues a presence and activity "outside" the humanity of Jesus (I/2, 168f.; IV/1, 180–81). The incarnation, that is to say, does not exhaust the reality of the divine Logos.

Second, Barth used the conceptuality of the *"anhypostasis-enhypostasis"* of Jesus Christ to signify the unity of Jesus' personhood and to avoid a bifurcated notion of a divine and human "double existence" in him (I/2, 163–65; IV/2, 49f., 91f.). (See Bruce McCormack, *Karl Barth's Critically Realistic Dialectical Theology,* Part III.) Negatively, the personhood of Jesus is *"anhypostatic"* in that Jesus does not become who he is from any inherent power he possesses in himself, but he draws his life wholly from God. This rebuts any "adoptionistic" understanding, whereby the Word or Logos "raided" or "took over" an already existing human being. Jesus "becomes" human only by the power of God. This negative point leads, in turn, to a positive point. The personhood of Jesus is *"enhypostatic,"* meaning that it comes into being in unity with the agency and action of God the "Son." From the first moment of Jesus' existence, God was an acting subject in him. The will of God and the will of Jesus are working in concert from the start.

In short, Jesus (negatively) is not who he is by his own power, but he is who he is (positively) through the power of God. This is another instance of how neither divinity nor humanity have their existence "in themselves" but only concretely in relationship to one another. For Barth this divine and human togetherness did not result in the divinization of Jesus' humanity but in its proper exaltation *as* human—a point to which we shall return momentarily. The claim against Barth that the *anhypostasis-enhypostasis* distinction undermines Jesus' humanity misses the point that Barth's use of the doctrine is in keeping with its historical origins in Leontius of Byzantium as a way of combatting a Monophysite ("one nature") interpretation of the Chalcedonian definition. (For an example of this erroneous interpretation, see Charles Waltrop, *Karl Barth's Christology: Its Basic Alexandrian Character* [Berlin: Mouton Publishers, 1984], chs. 3 and 5. For the historical origins of the distinction, see Edward Roche Hardy and Cyril C. Richardson, *Christology of the Later Fathers*, LCC [Philadelphia: Westminster Press, 1954], 375–77.) In keeping with classical orthodoxy, Jesus is in two natures, and his person embodies the coincidence of two wills.

The third and parallel scholastic distinction is that between the Logos *asarkos* and the Logos *ensarkos* (IV/1, 52f., 181f.). Some Reformed theologians emphasized that the Logos has its own reality and integrity separate and apart from Jesus' flesh. Thus one could imagine the Logos subsisting apart from Jesus' flesh, *a-sarkos*. Barth objected to this idea, however, that it is a mere abstraction to consider the identity or being of the Logos apart from the action of the Logos in Jesus Christ. Remember that for Barth one always has one's being in act. God the "Son" must be conceived as both *asarkos* and *ensarkos* at the same time. The Logos must be conceived in its "togetherness at a distance" with Jesus' humanity. The two are distinguishable but not separable. The point, as we have discovered before, is that the transcendence of God is a concrete transcendence in Jesus Christ. In Christ the transcendent God is freely yoked to our tragic human cause—and this despite our own perduring inability to be yoked to the purposes of God or to live our lives "for" one another.

4. This is the first major point Barth makes in the discussion of §59, and it comes immediately after a physical break in the German text that indicates the end of his introductory remarks and the commencement of the subject itself (*zur Sache*) (*KD* IV/1, 174).

5. Karl Barth, *The Humanity of God,* trans. John Newton Thomas and Thomas Wieser (Richmond: John Knox Press, 1960), 49.

6. Barth's accent on Jesus' fidelity to his vocation as providing a clue to the meaning of his death continues an insight gleaned from Schleiermacher and first given prominence by Albrecht Ritschl. The point is not that Jesus is just another exemplary hero but that Jesus' being and act have brought about fundamentally transformative consequences both for humanity and for God. On this point, see Wolfhart Pannenberg, *Systematic Theology*, vol. 2, trans. Geoffrey W. Bromiley (Grand Rapids: Wm. B. Eerdmans Publishing Co., 1994), 338, citing Friedrich Schleiermacher, *The Christian Faith*, §101.4, and Albrecht Ritschl, *The Christian Doctrine of Justification and Reconciliation* (Clifton, N.J.: 1966), §48, 442–52.

7. Barth, *The Epistle to the Romans,* 275, 288, 289, 290, 294, and passim.

8. Barth, *Der Römerbrief,* 458 [420–21]; ET, 434–35.

9. Ibid., 477 [438]; ET, 453.

10. Jürgen Moltmann, *The Crucified God: The Cross of Christ as the Foundation and Criticism of Christian Theology,* trans. R. A. Wilson and John Bowden (London: SCM Press, 1974).

11. Jürgen Moltmann, *The Way of Jesus Christ: Christology in Messianic Dimensions,* trans. Margaret Kohl (San Francisco: Harper & Row, 1990), 166.

12. Jürgen Moltmann, *The Crucified God: The Cross of Christ as the Foundation and Criticism of Christian Theology.*

13. Eberhard Jüngel, *God as the Mystery of the World;* idem, "Vom Tod des lebendigen Gottes: Ein Plakat," *Zeitschrift für Theologie und Kirche* 65 (1968): 93–116.

14. See Johannes Cocceius, "De pacto Dei Patris," Caput V, *Summa Doctrinae de Foedere et Testamento Dei* (1648), 60–71. See also Gottlob Schrenk, *Gottesreich und*

Bund im ältern Protestantismus, vornehmlich bei Johannes Coccejus: Ein Beitrag zur Geschichte des Pietismus und der heilsgeschichtlichen Theologie (Gütersloh, 1923; reprint, Giessen: Brunnen Verlag, 1985).

15. Barth specifically objects to G. C. Berkouwer's claim that, because of his concept of evil as an "impossible possibility," he turns Christianity into a "triumphant affair" (IV/3.1, 174).

16. Robert W. Jenson, "You Wonder Where the Spirit Went," *Pro Ecclesia: A Journal of Catholic and Evangelical Theology* 2/3 (summer 1993): 296–304.

17. On this point, see Gotthard Oblau, *Gottzeit und Menschenzeit: Eschatologie in der Kirchlichen Dogmatik von Karl Barth* (Neukirchen: Neukirchener Verlag, 1988).

18. See George Hunsinger, "The Lord and Giver of Life: Karl Barth's Doctrine of the Holy Spirit," An Address Given to the Karl Barth Society, November 1991, *Scottish Journal of Theology*, forthcoming.

19. See *Ethik II: Vorlesung Münster Wintersemester 1928/29, wiederholt in Bonn, Wintersemester 1930/31*, ed. Dietrich Braun, Gesamtausgabe, II, Akademische Werke, 1929/31 (Zurich: TVZ, 1978), § 16; ET: *Ethics*, trans. Geoffrey W. Bromiley (Grand Rapids: Wm. B. Eerdmans Publishing Co., 1981), §16.

CHAPTER 6:
GOD "IN" AND "AMONG" US

1. See F. Schleiermacher, *Glaubenslehre*, §11, in which the essence of Christianity is that everything in it "is related to the redemption accomplished in Jesus of Nazareth."

2. Athanasius, "De Incarnatione" 54.10, *Contra Gentes and De Incarnatione* (Oxford: Clarendon Press, 1971), 268–69.

3. John Calvin, *Institutes*, II.13.2, 477.

4. Karl Barth, *The Christian Life*, trans. Geoffrey W. Bromiley (Grand Rapids: Wm. B. Eerdmans Publishing Co., 1981), 168.

5. *The Christian Life*, 168.

6. Ibid.

7. Barth, *Ethics*; idem, *The Holy Spirit and the Christian Life* (Louisville, Ky.: Westminster John Knox Press, 1993).

8. *Der Römerbrief*, 325 [298]; ET, 314.

9. *Ethics*, 464.

10. *Romans*, 271.

11. *The Holy Spirit and the Christian Life*, 74.

12. See Ronald Thiemann, *Revelation and Theology*.

13. *Der Römerbrief*, 290 [266]; ET, 283.

14. Most prominently, Robert W. Jenson, "You Wonder Where the Spirit Went," *Pro Ecclesia: A Journal of Catholic and Evangelical Theology* 2/3 (summer 1993): 296–304.

15. On Barth's "actualism," see George Hunsinger, *How to Read Karl Barth: The Shape of His Theology* (New York: Oxford University Press, 1991), 4, 30–32, 67–70.

16. This was not a new question for Barth. He had been preoccupied with precisely this question while still under the influence of Wilhelm Herrmann and Marburg liberalism. How was one to conceive the "mode" of God's activity in relation to humanity? Barth's early answer was cast in the mold of Schleiermacher's the-

ology of experience; so fascinated was he by the liberal theology that he even entertained briefly some notion of writing a philosophy of religion. His mature answer, of course, was decidedly different. From the days of the Romans commentary onward, the only "mode" of participating in the divine reality was a "mode" of God's own being, namely that mode which Christians call the Holy Spirit.

17. Cf. Karl Barth, "Extra nos—pro nobis—in nobis," in *Hören und Handeln: Festschrift für Ernst Wolf zum 60. Geburtstag*, ed. Helmut Gollwitzer and Hellmut Traub (Munich: Chr. Kaiser Verlag, 1962), 15–27.

18. See George Lindbeck, *The Nature of Doctrine*.

19. "Acknowledgement" (*Anerkennung*) involves (a) knowledge, (b) the relation of one person to another, (c) acceptance of control, (d) an encounter in contingent contemporaneity, (e) yielding to divine supremacy, (f) decision, (g) acquiescence before the enigma of God, (h) genuine human movement, and (i) responding to a "center" or "whence" outside the self (I/1, 205–8).

20. George Hunsinger, *How to Read Karl Barth*, 85, 286 n.1, and esp. ch. 7.

21. *Römerbrief*, 72 (ET, 91 [66]). Emphasis in the German original.

22. Karl Barth, *The Theology of Schleiermacher: Lectures at Göttingen, Winter Semester of 1923/24*, ed. Dietrich Ritschl, trans. Geoffrey W. Bromiley (Grand Rapids: Wm. B. Eerdmans Publishing Co., 1982).

23. Immanuel Kant, *Kritik der Praktischen Vernunft* (1788), ed. Benzion Kellermann, in *Immanuel Kants Werke*, ed. Ernst Cassirer, Band III (Berlin: Bruno Cassirer, 1923) (*KGS*, 3,4); ET: *Critique of Practical Reason*, trans. Lewis White Beck (Indianapolis: Bobbs-Merrill Co., 1956).

24. Hunsinger, *How to Read Karl Barth*, 154.

25. From the orthodox perspective, in fact, Barth's decision to place vocation at the center of the Christian life is somewhat strange. The orthodox would have placed it at the beginning of the Christian life rather than at the end. See William Stacy Johnson and John H. Leith, eds., *Reformed Reader: A Sourcebook in Christian Theology*, vol. 1, *Classical Beginnings, 1519–1799* (Louisville, Ky.: Westminster/John Knox Press, 1993), 112–13.

26. *Das christliche Leben*, 50; ET, 33.

27. The mention of the second moment pertaining to "possibilities" is inexplicably omitted from the English translation (ibid).

28. Albrecht Ritschl, *The Christian Doctrine of Justification and Reconciliation*, trans. H. R. Mackintosh and A. B. Macaulay (Edinburgh, 1900), 11.

CHAPTER 7:
AN OPEN-ENDED ETHICS OF OTHERNESS

1. Barth, *The Christian Life*, 14.

2. Emmanuel Levinas, *Otherwise than Being or Beyond Essence*, trans. A. Lingis (The Hague: Martinus Nijhoff, 1981). For comparisons of Barth and Levinas, see Johan F. Goud, *Emmanuel Levinas und Karl Barth: Ein religionsphilosophischer und ethischer Vergleich*; Steven G. Smith, *The Argument to the Other: Reason beyond Reason in the Thought of Karl Barth and Emmanuel Levinas*.

3. See John Macken, *The Autonomy Theme in the "Church Dogmatics": Karl Barth and His Critics* (Cambridge: Cambridge University Press, 1990).

4. Barth had lectured on the ethics of reconciliation during the 1959–60 academic year, leaving behind a brief section entitled "Baptism as the Foundation of the Christian Life" (which Barth himself subsequently published in 1967) as well as the remainder of his lectures on "The Christian Life" (posthumously published in 1976) (Barth, *Das christliche Leben*).

5. Barth actually addressed the ethics of redemption explicitly (as well as creation and reconciliation), both in a set of 1928–29 lectures delivered in Münster and in lectures on "The Holy Spirit and the Christian Life" delivered at Elberfeld in 1929 (Karl Barth, *Ethik I*, and *Ethik II* [ET: *Ethics*]; idem, *The Holy Spirit and the Christian Life*). When one considers these lectures together with the published and unpublished portions of the *CD*, the broad outline of a complete theological ethics begins to emerge. For a quite helpful recent synopsis of Barth's complete theological ethics, see Nigel Biggar, *The Hastening That Waits: Karl Barth's Ethics*, Oxford Studies in Theological Ethics (Oxford: Clarendon Press, 1993). A somewhat more dated treatment of Barth's ethics is Robert E. Willis, *The Ethics of Karl Barth* (Leiden: E. J. Brill, 1971). For a close reading of the posthumously published ethics of reconciliation, see the fine work by John Webster, *Barth's Ethics of Reconciliation* (Cambridge: Cambridge University Press, 1995).

6. *Das christliche Leben*, 50; ET, 34.

7. John Webster, *Barth's Ethics of Reconciliation*, 230.

8. See, e.g., William K. Frankena, *Ethics*, 2d ed., (Englewood Cliffs, N.J.: Prentice-Hall, 1973), 28–30.

9. Cf. Paul L. Lehmann, *Ethics in a Christian Context* (New York: Harper & Row, 1963).

10. *Römerbrief*, 477 [438]; ET, 453.

11. *Das christliche Leben*, 50; ET, 33. As noted earlier, the English translation neglects to translate the word *Möglichkeiten*.

12. See *Römerbrief*, 449 [412]; ET, 425–26.

13. See Walter Lowe, *Theology and Difference*, chs. 4—6.

14. *Römerbrief*, 463 [424]; ET, 439 (revised).

15. *Römerbrief*, 462–63 [424–26]; ET, 438–39 (revised).

16. *Römerbrief*, 449 [412]; ET, 426 (revised).

17. *Römerbrief*, 449 [412]; ET, 426 (revised).

18. Kant, *Critique of Practical Reason*, trans. Lewis White Beck (Indianapolis: Bobbs-Merrill Co., 1956), book II. See Lewis White Beck, *A Commentary on Immanuel Kant's Critique of Practical Reason* (Chicago: University of Chicago Press, 1960), part III; Roger J. Sullivan, *Immanuel Kant's Moral Theory* (Cambridge: Cambridge University Press, 1989), 223–29.

19. Barth's ethics have been interpreted by some as predominantly idealistic (e.g., essays in *Realisierung der Freiheit: Beiträge zur Kritik der Theologie Karl Barths*, ed. Trutz Rendtorff [Gütersloh: Mohr, 1975]; and John Macken, *The Autonomy Theme*) and by others as predominantly realistic (Ingolf U. Dalferth, "Theologischer Realismus und realistische Theologie bei Karl Barth," *Evangelische Theologie* 46 [1986]: 402–22; Paul D. Matheny, *Dogmatics and Ethics: The Theological Realism and Ethics of Karl Barth's Church Dogmatics* [Frankfurt am Main: Peter Lang, 1990]). Throughout this study, in contrast, I have pointed out the interplay between realistic and idealistic elements in Barth's theology.

20. Immanuel Kant, *Foundations of the Metaphysics of Morals, and What Is Enlightenment*, trans. Lewis White Beck (New York: Liberal Arts Press, 1959); idem,

Critique of Practical Reason. See generally, Roger J. Sullivan, *Immanuel Kant's Moral Theory* (Cambridge: Cambridge University Press, 1989), part III.

21. Immanuel Kant, "On a Supposed Right to Lie from Altruistic Motives," in *Immanuel Kant: Critique of Practical Reason and Other Writings in Moral Philosophy,* ed. Lewis White Beck (New York: Garland, 1976), 346–50.

22. H. Richard Niebuhr, *The Responsible Self: An Essay in Christian Moral Philosophy,* ed. Richard R. Niebuhr (New York: Harper & Row, 1963).

23. Lowe, *Theology and Difference,* 75–101, 102–26, 127–29.

24. See Karl Barth, *The Christian Life,* §78; idem, *Christengemeinde und Bürgergemeinde,* Theologische Studien 10 (Zollikon-Zurich: Evangelischer Verlag, 1946); idem, *Rechtfertigung und Recht,* Theologische Studien 1 (Zollikon-Zurich: Evangelischer Verlag, 1944) (ET: *Community, State and Church: Three Essays,* ed. Will Herberg [Gloucester, Mass.: Peter Smith, 1968]); idem, *Die Kirche und die politische Frage von heute* (Zollikon: Verlag der Evangelischen Buchhandlung, 1939) (ET: *The Church and the Political Problem of Our Day* [London: Hodder & Stoughton, 1939]). See also Robert E. Hood, *Contemporary Political Orders and Christ: Karl Barth's Christology and Political Praxis* (Pittsburgh: Pickwick Press, 1985).

25. See John Webster, *Barth's Ethics of Reconciliation,* 201–13.

26. See Arthur C. Cochrane, *The Church's Confession under Hitler* (Philadelphia: Westminster Press, 1962).

27. *The Christian Life,* §78.2.

28. Karl Barth, "The Christian Community and the Civil Community," in *Against the Stream: Shorter Post-War Writings 1946–52* (London: SCM Press, 1954), 25; cited in John Webster, *Barth's Ethics of Reconciliation,* 205 n.129.

29. *The Christian Life,* 212, 235.

30. *The Christian Life,* 211.

31. *The Christian Life,* 226.

32. John Webster is correct that it provides a test case for how one reads Barth's entire theological argument (J. B. Webster, *Barth's Ethics of Reconciliation,* 117).

33. Karl Barth, *Die kirchliche Lehre von der Taufe,* Theologische Studien 14 (Zollikon-Zurich: Evangelischer Verlag, 1953); ET: *The Teaching of the Church regarding Baptism,* trans. Ernest A. Payne (London: SCM Press, 1948). See Eberhard Jüngel, "Thesen zu Karl Barths Lehre von der Taufe: Ein Hinweis auf ihre Probleme," *Theologische Studien,* Heft 98 (Zurich: EVZ, 1968); Dieter Schellong, "Der Ort der Tauflehre in der Theologie Karl Barths," in *Warum Christen Ihre Kinder Nicht Mehr Taufen Lassen* (Frankfurt am Main, 1969), 108–42; A. Demura, "Zwingli in the Writings of Karl Barth—With Special Emphasis on the Doctrine of the Sacraments," in *Probing the Reformed Tradition,* ed. Elsie A. McKee and Brian G. Armstrong (Louisville, Ky.: Westminster/John Knox Press, 1989), 197–219.

34. Luther, *WA* 6, 497–573.

35. See also *The Christian Life,* 46.

36. The distinction between "sacramental continuity" and "attestation" is made by John Webster, *Barth's Ethics of Reconciliation,* 128. I have emphasized the persistence of a certain *symbolic* continuity in the later Barth and have modified Webster's terms accordingly.

37. *The Christian Life,* 46.

38. See §36.2 of *CD,* II/2, entitled "The Way of Theological Ethics."

39. *The Christian Life,* 185 (revised).

40. See Eberhard Jüngel, "Invocation of God as the ethical ground of Christian

action: Introductory remarks on the posthumous fragments of Karl Barth's ethics of the doctrine of reconciliation," in *Theological Essays*, trans. J. B. Webster (Edinburgh: T. & T. Clark, 1989), 154–72.

41. *Das christliche Leben*, §74.2, 55–73; ET, 36–46.

42. On addressing God in the vocative, see *The Christian Life*, §76.1.

43. *The Christian Life*, §77.

44. Ibid., §77.4.

45. *The Christian Life*, 178.

46. See *The Christian Life*, 176–204.

47. Ibid., 184.

48. *The Christian Life*, 153.

49. Nigel Biggar, *The Hastening That Waits*.

50. Cf. Trutz Rendtorff, *Grundelemente Methodologie und Konkretion einer ethischen Theologie*, vol. 1, Theologische Wissenschaft 13 (Stuttgart: 1980); ET: *Ethics*, trans. Keith Crim (Philadelphia: Fortress Press, 1988).

51. *Römerbrief*, 447 [410]; ET, 424.

52. Ibid., 469 [431]; ET, 445.

53. Ibid., 477 [438]; ET, 453.

54. Ibid., 501 [460]; ET, 476.

55. Ibid., 479 [440]; ET, 455.

CHAPTER 8:
EC-CENTRIC EXISTENCE AND THE CENTRALITY OF HOPE

1. See also *Das christliche Leben*, 151 (ET, 94).

2. John Macken is one of the few to take notice of it, and he mentions only the occurrence in *KD*, IV/3 and without any discussion of the connection with Barth's pervasive metaphor of the "center." John Macken, *The Autonomy Theme*, 197 n.184. It is also mentioned in passing by George Hunsinger, *How to Read Karl Barth*, 174, citing *CD*, IV/3, 548.

3. For a very fine discussion of this, see John Macken, *The Autonomy Theme in the Church Dogmatics: Karl Barth and His Critics*.

4. See Walter E. Wyman, Jr., *The Concept of Glaubenslehre: Ernst Troeltsch and the Theological Heritage of Schleiermacher*, AAR Academy Series 44 (Chico, Calif.: Scholars Press, 1983).

5. For a critique of Barth's treatment of love, see Gene Outka, *Agape: An Ethical Analysis*, Yale Publications in Religion 17 (New Haven and London: Yale University Press, 1972).

CONCLUSION

1. Jean François Lyotard. *The Postmodern Explained: Correspondence 1982–1985* (Minneapolis: University of Minnesota Press, 1992), 65.

2. See, e.g., David Klemm, "Towards a Rhetoric of Postmodern Theology through Barth and Heidegger," *Journal of the American Academy of Religion* 55

(1987): 443–69; Robert P. Scharlemann, "The No to Nothing and the Nothing to Know: Barth and Tillich and the Possibility of a Theological Science," *Journal of the American Academy of Religion* 55 (1987): 57–72; Stephen H. Webb, *Re-Figuring Theology: The Rhetoric of Karl Barth* (Albany: State University of New York Press, 1991). For a feminist contribution in this direction, see Serene Jones, "This God Which Is Not One: Irigaray and Barth on the Divine," in *Transfigurations: Theology and the French Feminists,* ed. C. W. Maggie Kim, Susan M. St. Ville, and Susan M. Simonaitis (Minneapolis: Fortress Press, 1993), 109–41. Studies are also beginning to appear that place Barth in conversation with such contemporary postmodern thinkers as Jacques Derrida and Emmanuel Levinas. E.g., Graham Ward, *Barth, Derrida, and the Language of Theology* (Cambridge: Cambridge University Press, 1995); Walter Lowe, *Theology and Difference: The Wound of Reason* (Bloomington and Indianapolis, Ind.: Indiana University Press, 1993); Johan F. Goud, *Emmanuel Levinas und Karl Barth: Ein religionsphilosophischer und ethischer Vergleich,* Abhandlungen zur Philosophie, Psychologie und Pädagogik, Band 234 (Bonn: Bouvier Verlag, 1992); Steven G. Smith, *The Argument to the Other: Reason beyond Reason in the Thought of Karl Barth and Emmanuel Levinas* (Chico, Calif.: Scholars Press, 1983). See also David F. Ford, "Hosting a Dialogue: Jüngel and Levinas on God, Self and Language," in *The Possibilities of Theology,* ed. John Webster, (Edinburgh: T. & T. Clark, 1994), 23–59.

    3. Francis Schüssler Fiorenza, *Foundational Theology: Jesus and the Church,* 285–89.

    4. I owe this illustration to Carl W. McCormack.

    5. Paul Ricoeur, "Hope and the Structure of Philosophical Systems," *Proceedings of the American Catholic Association* (1970), reprinted in *Refiguring the Sacred: Religion, Narrative, and Imagination,* trans. David Pellauer, ed. Mark I. Wallace (Minneapolis: Fortress Press, 1995), 211.

    6. Frei, *Types of Christian Theology,* 81.

    7. Ibid., 43. Cf. Ronald F. Thiemann, *Revelation and Theology: The Gospel as Narrated Promise,* esp. ch. 7.

INDEX